CW00730838

THANK YOU FOR CALLING THE LESBIAN LINE

ELIZABETH LOVATT

DIALOGUE BOOKS

First published in Great Britain in 2025 by Dialogue Books

3 5 7 9 10 8 6 4 2

A CIP catalogue record for this book is available from the British Library.

Hardback ISBN 978-0-349-70461-6

Typeset in Berling by M Rules
Printed and bound in Great Britain by
Clays Ltd, Elcograf S.p.A

Papers used by Dialogue Books are from well-managed forests and other responsible sources.

Dialogue Books
An imprint of
Dialogue
Carmelite House
50 Victoria Embankment
London EC4Y 0DZ

The authorised representative
in the EEA is
Hachette Ireland
8 Castlecourt Centre
Dublin 15, D15 XTP3, Ireland
(email: info@hbgi.ie)

www.dialoguebooks.co.uk

Dialogue, part of Little, Brown Book Group Limited, an Hachette UK company.

This one's for the lesbians.

Contents

Prologue 1
Enter the Logbook 3
Where Are All the Lesbians? 16
The Other Half of the Conversation 33
A Brief History of Lesbian Lines 45
Coming Out? 66
Gay, Lesbian, Woman? 95
Becky Rang 130
You Can't Choose Your Family (Except You Can) 159
Lesbian Lifelines 173
No More Lesbian Sheroes 191
White Fragility and the Failure to Listen 208
What Happens When a Lesbian Makes a Move 237
I Don't Want to Talk About Wanking in That Way 276
Stop Making Us Look Bad: Lesbian Break-Ups and Abuse 285
Trans Lesbians Exist: Get Over It 300
Gobs of Lesbians Online 326
What Are Lesbians Coming To? 371

Notes 385
Acknowledgements 401

A note on the text

The lesbian world is wide and ever-changing and lesbian experience is as varied as the lesbians who make it. I have listened to and read the words of many lesbians in the making of this book but it will never be enough. I can never capture the totality of lesbian experience. I see this as a good thing. We are too amorphous and expansive for that. If you do not recognise yourself in these pages I hope you can forgive me and I hope you can write your own story so that more of us might be heard and remembered.

Names and identifying details have been changed to protect the privacy of individuals. Some of the descriptions of volunteering at the Lesbian Line and the calls the volunteers receive are the work of my own imagination.All pronouns and identities used were correct at the time of going to print but may have changed since publication.

This book discusses topics such as homophobia, transphobia, family rejection, hate crimes, mental health, intimate partner violence and abuse which may make for difficult reading.

For support and advice you can call Switchboard on 0800 0119 100 (open every day 10am – 10pm) or visit their website switchboard.lgbt

Prologue

23.4.97 – log by Mary: *Had to put the phone down after twenty mins*

Sharon just wants to talk to a lesbian. Maybe it would help her figure all this out even though she hates talking on the phone. Everyone always tells her she's too quiet but she does her best to speak up. She waited weeks for her mother to be out on the right day, on the right evening. What if the line's busy? But it's not and the woman on the other end of the phone picks up nearly right away. She has a nice voice, clear and not at all quiet.

The woman says, Hello, you've reached the Lesbian Line, I'm Mary.

And then it's Sharon's turn to speak – the first lesbian she's ever spoken to! Sharon says hello and tells Mary her name. She pauses unsure what to say next.

Mary obviously doesn't believe in awkward silences and immediately asks if there's anything Sharon wants to talk about today.

It takes her a moment to find her voice but finally

Sharon blurts out, I'm starting to think I might be gay.

The clumsy wording makes her wince. She'd rehearsed it better in her head. She hopes she doesn't sound as naive as she feels.

But Mary doesn't laugh or ask her why. She says, that's great and does she want to talk about it some more?

And Sharon does, telling her all these feelings she's had and hasn't known what to do with them. What it might mean if . . . if she is a . . . She's not ready to say the word yet. Not ready to tell her mother certainly. Mary says there's no rush. Sharon has so many questions and thoughts and in the end they tumble out of her so fast she forgets she was ever even nervous. They chat for fifteen more minutes or so until Sharon tells her that she has to go soon. She's not sure how long her mum will be gone.

Mary says that she's welcome to call back anytime. Sharon hopes she will too. She can't wait to talk more.

Enter the Logbook

When I was twenty-eight years old I wrote a list of all the signs I might be gay. To even admit to myself that I was unsure of something so fundamental was terrifying. It felt overly dramatic for someone in their late twenties to be even asking such a question. And so, as I had in my teens, I started a diary. I titled it with my date of birth and password protected it on my own laptop, which already required a password to unlock. Like I was trying to hide it even from myself.

The objective of the list, despite its painfully self-aware joking-not-joking tone, was to document an impossibly detached survey of myself. It was intended to be an anchor of sorts because if I was gay, it meant I was a stranger to myself.

It read:

- tomboy growing up
- does not like wearing dresses
- likes plaid
- mainly female friends
- often jokingly called a lesbian (as if that's an insult)
- sitting with my legs open
- putting my arm across the back of chairs

- beer/shandy?
- sports?
- angry/scared/annoyed feeling when people joke/call me lesbian (happens less now)
- never *really* fancied a boy (therefore never loved a boy, but same goes for a girl)
- did I even fancy my first boyfriend ???
- random crushes/likes of girls outside of my friendship group (but never actual friends)
- can more easily imagine myself with a women for the rest of my life (whether platonic or not) than a guy
- get happy when I see gay women on TV
- smiling when female relationship/gay women are on TV and happy
- being bored when I see another hetero couple, find out someone is hetero, getting married/moving in etc.
- don't mind gay women proposing to each other stories (hetero ones give me eye rolls)
- seeking out gay women on TV/film/books
- surround myself with women
- I like to be around women and relate to them
- dislike male company
- penises look weird (do all women think this?)
- how awkward I am when boys try to flirt with me, or touch me
- thinking people are secretly gay = PROJECTING

The list is a mess of lesbian stereotypes and my own confused forays into queer books and TV, alongside a tentative prod at my past as a kind of test bed for my current confused state. I was so desperately looking for clues, for something concrete to cling on to, and I was at a loss as to where I should begin. The serious hurdle about trying to figure out who you are – or even just who you fancy – is that you only have yourself to go on. And how did I know if I could trust myself? These things were supposed to be innate, weren't they? Didn't most gay people know they were gay from childhood? I wanted definitive answers but all I had were a series of silly stereotypes and too many questions with no idea of how to find a solution.

If I was a different sort of person I could have asked someone for help. If I was a different sort of person, a braver one perhaps, I could have called a helpline set up for just this sort of situation. They still exist; you can even email or text them now. At the time my not-knowingness about whether I was gay honestly didn't feel important enough to tell anyone about. Not my best friend or my family and certainly not some stranger who might laugh at me, or worse, think I was wasting their time. What if I had made all this up in my head?

Had I been born ten years earlier and had this realisation ten years sooner, I might have been able to call a specific helpline set up for women who had questions about their sexuality. I could have called a lesbian line or a women's line, one of the many that used to exist, and asked them, objectively, list to hand, if I was in fact a lesbian. Maybe I would have found their number on a flyer at the library or a leaflet left in a pub. Maybe it would have been pinned to a noticeboard at uni, or maybe it would have waved at me from a banner as I mistakenly wandered into the path of a Pride march. Maybe, maybe, maybe.

And what would I have said, if I did call? What would I say right at the beginning of all this? Before I knew much about lesbians or all that history waiting for me to discover it? If I plucked up the courage to punch in those numbers and let the phone ring long enough for someone to pick up, if I could push the words out of my throat to speak, what would I have said? Likely there would be silence and perhaps my voice from somewhere small and deep inside asking someone unknown at the other end of the phone, 'Is this for real? I can't believe this is happening to me. I can't be a lesbian, can I? How do you know?'

And maybe the kind, bored, exasperated, young, experienced, terse, understanding, tired, new, old, caring volunteer would have taken a breath and said, 'Maybe, maybe not. It's more likely than you'd expect. Lesbians are everywhere. Maybe you should stick at it and find out?' Maybe, maybe, maybe.

29.7.93 – log by Rachel: *Wow! A brand new log book for all of us!!*

Rachel's worked on the phone line now for three years. She never thought answering the phone would be for her but her friend Dani practically bullied her into it. Dani has a way of using flattery as a weapon until Rachel couldn't find it in herself to refuse any longer. Besides, she likes London Friend, there aren't that many lesbian and gay places to hang out that aren't a pub and it was one of the first places she felt properly welcome when she moved to London. She went to the group for newly out lesbians and that was that, she never looked back. Sounds easy now but at the time she was terrified, terrified someone would think she didn't look enough like a lesbian, terrified someone might flirt with her, terrified she might flirt back. In the end she needn't have worried. She's made some really good mates here and it feels right to give a little something back. She does a regular Thursday evening shift twice a month and picks up other ones here and there when she has the time. Sometimes there's two of them on the phone even though at the moment they only have the one line plugged in, plus the answering machine. But it's handy to have someone else there either to switch out with after a difficult call, or to help you rifle through the drawer and Rolodex to find the address of a decent lesbian pub. The ones in London she mostly knows anyway but sometimes they get calls from the surrounding counties or even further afield. Usually when that happens she passes on the number for a more local line, especially if they're looking for a nearby group to go to.

Anyway, tonight it's just her in the little room downstairs with the phones. Only large enough for a desk, two chairs and the filing cabinet. They share it with the main London Friend number and the general mixed line which runs the rest of the week. Which is fine but does mean occasionally the gay men's stuff gets mixed in with the lesbian leaflets, or someone hasn't put the logbook back

> in the right place. Often, they end up sharing and the logs get jumbled up or put back in the wrong order. But not today, Rachel decides. She's been down to the stationery cupboard (which is really just a cupboard full of random crap in the back room) and nabbed a brand new notebook just for the lesbians. If anyone complains about a missing notebook she will deny knowing anything about it. It's not long after that the phone starts ringing and Rachel gets to work.

Three years after I start my diary, I am sat in the back room of Finsbury Library at a blue MDF desk that reminds me of school. Along one wall runs a shelf of thick brown books, in one corner sits a photocopier and a microfiche in the other – the archivist's reception desk and computers face out towards the door. Like many libraries it has the air of having one foot in the past and one foot in the not-quite-modern present. This is after all a council-owned space and so the equipment is perhaps five to ten years out of date in a way that is comforting rather than sad. I am here as a writer, part of a residency around Islington's Pride, an archive project based in Islington's Local History Centre and which catalogues and publishes the LGBTQ+ heritage of the borough of Islington.

Because I am here as a writer and not a normal member of the public (whatever that means) nothing in the archive is off-limits to me. It would seem that the word 'writer', in this instance, equals trust. It hangs heavily in the air, implicit as I walk through the entrance and tell the archivist at reception why I am here. Or so I think; he, to his credit, looks unimpressed. This is the most official I've ever felt and both my status as a writer and specifically as a *lesbian* writer feel fresh and uncertain. But I don't want the archive to know that. I've been a writer longer than I've been out. And before that I had no idea I was gay, which feels like an oversight on my part. Aren't writers, of all people, supposed to know themselves better?

Being so newly out does afford me a different advantage. I am filled with the eagerness of a kind of second youth alongside a burning need to know everything there is to know about being a lesbian. I am, as I have seen it described online, a baby dyke, in this respect. But I can't help feel excited at what I have to learn, like I'm on the precipice of another discovery. I've arrived at this archive full of questions: How could I not know I was gay for so long? What else is there I still don't know – not just about myself but other lesbians who came before me? I suspect there are even more questions I don't yet know to ask. That is, after all, the reason I am here: history, lesbian history, *my* history is what I have come to find, to research, to touch with my own hands. I want to put the archive to one of its intended uses as a place of holding and knowledge. A place of creation too – I just don't know where to start, or even if I should.

The first part I do know at least; I am signed in and reminded of the rules: no pens, no pictures without prior permission, no food, no hot liquids. The archive closes for one hour at lunch time. And most importantly: no putting things out of order. This rule will be related to me again over email the next day because unwittingly, despite being what I think is ever so careful, I do mix up some of the files. Already

I've broken the archive's trust in me. Not a great start. But for now I am left alone next to a trolley of brown boxes (and one incongruous orange plastic bag) the archivist has already put aside for me. Each box houses yet further manila folders carefully marked with a string of numbers separated by backslashes, written of course in pencil. I take out my laptop and notebook and wonder if Extra Strong Mints count as food.

A few hours later I am several pages of notes in on the various newspaper cuttings, annual reports and letters, minute meetings and flyers for long-gone events, magazines, newsletters and photo albums that make up part of Islington's Pride archive. I spend the morning poring over the lesbian magazines and newsletters. In *Diva*, the UK magazine for lesbian and bisexual women (one of the few still in print) I find a feature on *Diva*'s top thirty 'delectable women'. The list includes Jet from Gladiator, Jodie Foster and Moira Stuart. In case you can't guess from that cross-section of lesbian icons the magazine is from 1995. It's full of celebrities I recognise from my youth, but who at the time I either didn't know were lesbians or staples of lesbian crushes. There are other magazines here too: issues of *Shebang*, a '90s lesbian monthly magazine, and later issues of *Spare Rib*, the iconic UK second-wave feminist magazine that ran from 1972–93. In one box there was even *that* 1993 *Vanity Fair* cover of Cindy Crawford in a swimsuit holding a cut-throat razor to a besuited k.d. lang that until now I had only seen circulating on lesbian Twitter. If you don't know the one I'm talking about I'll wait while you google it.

I linger longer over the more home-grown newsletters. Most are printed on coloured paper and were available via mail order for those in the know. Many are from the '90s, like issues of *Lesbian London* ('Free, Also available on Tape'), o the *Lesbian Feminist Weekend Guide to London*. Some go back to the '80s, including the *London Lesbian Newsletter* (15p, but they do later write that regrettably they have to raise the price to 20p to help cover costs). I make notes as I go, not really sure what I'm looking for but unable to escape the feeling that I need to document it all somehow. Everything is so new to me.

After flicking through each one my final port of call is the classifieds. I pay special attention to them because the archivist had told me how often they are overlooked, and that even in the driest of meeting minutes there are stories to be found. Mostly they are straightforward lists of information for events and groups that leave me itching for something I lack: a sense of an active, in-person, lesbian community organised around a physical place and regular meet-ups.

The closest I had been to any kind of lesbian group or meet-up were queer club nights, a couple of Drag King shows and that one time I went to see England v Australia for a women's friendly football match (but maybe that's pushing it). Not so in the *London Lesbian Newsletter* times, there were listings galore: groups for young people, mothers, disabled people, newly out lesbians, film nights and discos and more, all followed by dates, times, addresses and contact details. And it was there that I keep seeing it: 'Lesbian Line', 'Women's Line', 'Friend's Women's Line', 'London Lesbian Line', followed by various phone numbers and opening hours.

The archivist at the desk reminds me that they are closing for lunch and as I am expelled back onto the London streets I can't stop thinking about the lesbian phone lines. Because in one of those boxes is something I am desperate to read

have pretended to myself, to the archivist, to
at I'm not interested in. I don't know why I
, I am scared to say what it is I want. Maybe I
know that once I reach it, the very last item at the bottom of a box marked 'London Friend: Miscellaneous', it will be all I can focus on. And it is.

Back in the archive the strip lights buzz overhead and bounce the too-bright light off the mottled, slightly grubby surface of the notebook in front of me. The notebook is A4 sized, hardback and bound in black shiny paper. It's bruised around the spine and corners where the cover is starting to peel away. I hold it gently in my hands and, despite everything I know it contains, it is surprisingly light. An ordinary-looking notebook that has seen better days. Except for one thing. The white sticker on the front is handwritten in thick green marker pen that reads *WOMEN'S LINE LOGBOOK*. Flanking the words on either side are overlapping ⚢ symbols. Someone else has added beneath in red scrawling biro: *Starts July '93, ends July '98* and yet another has amended it to *OLD*, squeezed in between the other words, this time in blue ink. The letters have been coloured in and outlined by various pens. In one corner there's the start of a check pattern. Before I even turn the cover it's clear that the logbook is the work of many different women.

This is the logbook of a community-run phone service who refer to themselves as the 'Women's Line' and then later the 'Lesbian Line'. It operated out of London Friend, one of the earliest LGBT charities in the UK, established in 1972 with a focus on befriending services, social groups and counselling.

In the mid 1980s the charity already had a well-established mixed phone line but lesbian volunteers and callers were scarce. They decided to set up a separate women-only line to encourage more women to come to the centre and to answer the specific needs of lesbians looking for advice, help, information or just a friendly ear. The line originally ran only once a week on a Thursday and for a long time shared its phone number with the daytime business number. This was far from ideal and resulted in the occasional call from gay men asking what groups were on that night. From September 1989 they had enough trained lesbian phone workers that they could run the service twice a week on Tuesdays and Thursdays from 7.30 p.m. to 10 p.m.

The volunteers taking calls acted as part information service and part phone counsellor. Inside the logbook's lined pages are short blocks of handwritten text, usually three or so entries per page, usually dated but not always, usually signed by the note-taker but not always. The calls cover a variety of questions and requests: about coming out; dealing with domestic and sexual abuse; rehousing or governmental aid; the availability of specific lesbian groups and advice on lesbian sex and motherhood. There are a lot of repeat callers, both pranksters and those in need of regular care.

The logbook, however, is more than just a way of tracking who's rung and what they needed. It is also a kind of diary for the phone workers (as they sometimes called themselves) and a way to talk to each other across their rotating shift patterns. Often, they leave each other notes about when they're next on shift or if a caller rang looking for a particular volunteer, as well as notes about going on holiday and issues to discuss at the monthly phone worker meetings. They record the bad calls, the abuse, the funny ones and the so-called 'wank' callers who ring to ask personal questions about the women's sex lives, posing as genuine lesbians. They get plenty of those.

I set to work reading the entries and immediately there is a sense of connection to the women who called the Lesbian Line. It's a logbook full of questions about how and who and why. The logbook feels more real in a way that the meeting minutes and flyers I was leafing through earlier do not. It's in the handwritten entries and the offhand casual notes made by the volunteers, in the voices of all the ordinary remarkable everyday women which crowd its pages. It's an oddity in a sea of official documents and news clippings, this logbook which overflows with thoughts and conversations from women in the '90s.

I was between the ages of five and ten when these calls were being taken. I presumed going into this archive I would find a history long since passed, yet here I am holding an object whose life easily overlaps with my own. Not that I knew it at the time. I wonder what I was doing when all this was going on. Just a kid in Leicester, going to school, hanging out with her friends, reading as much Jacqueline Wilson as she could get her hands on. My childhood was a normal one, as normal as any other working-class kid living in a mid-sized East Midlands city could be. Not much to report. I was completely unaware of the existence of anything even resembling a queer community where I lived. I knew no gay people growing up, saw hardly any in the books I read or the TV I watched.

If there was, they were usually gay men, camp and

effeminate and played for laughs. Certainly, no lesbians ... I knew of. Growing up I had no idea I might be gay, no idea one day I'd end up sat in front of a logbook full of the recorded calls of lesbians. The evidence laid out in front of me of lesbians living their real everyday lives – all these stories of joy, heartbreak, pain and hope unknown to me until now. Who would have guessed that one day I'd happily count myself among them?

Where Are All the Lesbians?

13.2.94 – log by Sam, Ros & Hannah: *She seems to be getting a bit less depressed but very slowly*
She wishes she had never heard of the Lesbian Line and never had to call them. But here she is at sixty-eight years old, with a dead husband and now her Joan gone as well. If she sounds callous about Carl she doesn't mean to be, they loved each other in their own way, in many respects it was a happy marriage. But losing Joan was different. She was her 'special friend', she tells Sam, who answered the phone that first time she called.

She doesn't remember much of that call, it was so soon after Joan had gone and she was at sixes and sevens about the whole thing. She doubts she made much sense. It was only two weeks after she'd died. She's trying but she can't motivate herself to do anything. Even crying feels like too much effort. She doesn't want to see anyone or speak to her other friends. Having to hide her grief from them is too hard and she doesn't want to lie about why she is suddenly so sad again just as she was starting to get over her husband's death. The woman on the phone asks gently if she would be interested in coming to one of their groups? They do have a Lesbian Bereavement group she might like to attend? But they're in London. She explains patiently that she lives in the countryside and without a car and only two buses a day, she can't really manage the journey. Besides I'm sure it's for proper, y'know ... not for people like me. They change the subject then and the woman on the phone lets her talk about Joan for as long as she likes and so she does. After all, she doesn't have anyone else to talk to.

It's a different woman next time she rings. Four weeks is a long time between calls but even so she doesn't feel like there's much new to say. Each day is the same. Empty and much too long. She dreads nighttime with a whole evening stretching ahead of her.

It's a funny feeling is grief, she tells the woman – Ros she said her name was – over the phone. In the day it's not so bad. I keep myself busy. Maybe too busy. The other day I caught myself thinking, I'll just give Joan a quick ring, I was halfway to the phone ready to call her like we used to before I remembered. We had this little code all worked out, you see. I'd give her three rings and hang up and then she'd call me back if it was safe to talk. Silly really but it made us feel better somehow. Hits you all over again then. Right out of nowhere. I was just standing there in the hall ready to give my three rings and realised there wouldn't be anyone there to pick up. Isn't that horrible to think about, a phone ringing in an empty house?

Ros tells her to call anytime she likes. Even though the line is only open two days a week the answer machine will pick up her message. Someone always answers eventually, Ros says.

She calls back a couple of weeks later, the day after the cremation. A different woman again, a Hannah this time. She's kind but practical – like a nurse with a child who won't take her medicine. She does listen, at least. She tells Hannah about the funeral. She was expecting it to be unbearable and it was but it's done now. She put on her best face and Joan's family thanked her for being such a good friend to her all these years, especially near the end. Hannah tells her that it just shows what great care and help she gave to Joan when she could.

Which she agrees is true, she did, she just has to come to terms with not everyone understanding what Joan meant to her. What they mean to each other. Hannah sets up a counselling session for her that can be done over the phone and she's relieved that for now she can continue just like this. Talking over the phone is easier. She isn't ready for anyone to see her that way just yet. She isn't sure she ever wants to talk about it again but she thanks Hannah for her time and says she'll call again and she's feeling a little better, even if she doesn't know how that could possibly be true.

There are other calls like this that I find in the logb… from older women. Stories of unknown and known desires. Women stuck in unhappy marriages. Women who have left their husbands and their children. Women who are afraid of what being a lesbian might mean. Women who have never spoken to another lesbian before or know other women feel the way they do. Women who think they've missed their chance. Often these calls are singular; they float like pockets of history throughout the logbook, unmoored from the busy lives of the phone workers and the lesbians who call often to update the line of the goings-on of the lesbian scene. These women feel disconnected from all that. There is no sense of shared history for them or community. Their feelings until now have mostly been kept hidden away from others, known only to themselves.

Lesbians have always existed; the words may change, but we're there if only you know where to look. Much lesbian history is so-called 'hidden history', both because it is often the realm of private relationships and because lesbians have been forcibly repressed and made to hide themselves. Historically, queerness and privacy, the right (or, as is often the case, the need) to remain secret, have gone hand in hand. For lesbians this was especially so, or rather they have been rendered less visible, not only because they were women but because lesbianism is so easily hidden within female friendship and encoded into subtext of 'the fairer sex'. It's there if you know where to look – if you're willing to conceive of desire that exists unrelated to men, but so often dismissed as 'the special friend', 'the roommate', 'gal pals'. From Sappho to Kristen Stewart, people have always found a way to rewrite lesbian desire as something more platonic, moralised away as a passing phase, or doomed to end in disaster. Often we are left to read between the lines.

Historically, when lesbian desire did raise its head above the parapet it was often censored or written off as hysteria. Take for instance *The Well of Loneliness*, Radclyffe Hall's early twentieth-century lesbian tale of the 'invert' Stephen Gordon, banned for its description of lesbian desire (despite there not even being any juicy bits). Or Sheridan Le Fanu's earlier gothic novel, *Carmilla*, where the titular character's vampiric lesbian desire quite literally drains her love, Laura, of life, until Carmilla is defeated and the heroine 'saved' from a similar fate. Lesbians could exist, could even experience love and lust, but ideally they would die at the end or be destined for a single lonely life full of regret. Thus proving that heterosexuality really was best.

That lesbianism in the UK has never been illegal is a backwards sort of privilege that was not afforded to gay men who were mercilessly prosecuted and imprisoned by the police. But with this strange legal void, effectively ignoring the reality of many women's expressions of sexuality, came an erasure of female desire. It was viewed as a desire not worth policing or, rather, dangerous even to acknowledge. It may be apocryphal that Queen Victoria chose not to outlaw lesbianism because she didn't believe it existed, but the sentiment still stands. What is recorded is that when, in 1921, the House of Commons tried to pass an amendment to the Criminal Law Amendment Bill to include prosecution for 'gross indecency' between women, the House of Lords ensured it was struck down. Famously the Earl of Desart opposed the amendments for fear of exposing genteel ladies to lesbianism: '[Y]ou are going to tell the whole world that there is such an offence, and bring it to the notice of women who have never heard of it, never thought of it, never dreamed of it.'[1] He was obviously afraid of giving the ladies any ideas. Total silence on the matter seemed to be the favoured governmental method of suppression of lesbian identity (regulated instead behind closed doors to pornography strictly for the male gaze). It was an effective one that ensured many gay women likely never explored their sexuality, or kept it secret for their whole lives, believing themselves to be alone in their desires. Yet of course it could not stop us all.

In the UK, while it was far from easy and often only the privilege of those with enough wealth and social status to defy convention (or at least those are often the records we have), some queers of yore could, and did, move through the world with a certain degree of freedom and openness about their sexuality. The rules too were different for men and women, cis (someone whose gender presentation matches the one they were assigned at birth) and trans people: a complex tangle of passing or hiding in plain sight, and power depending on class, wealth, proximity to whiteness and one's social position in society.

And that's before we've even considered that homosexuality and same-sex attraction are relatively new inventions, at least in the way we conceive of identity and labels today. Many people from the past whom now we might describe as lesbian, gay, bisexual or trans would not have defined themselves as such in terms of their sexuality or gender presentation. The historians Huw Lemmey and Ben Miller put it more succinctly in their book *Bad Gays*: 'nobody thought who they *fucked* had anything to do with who they *were*'.[2] The word 'homosexual' itself in English was first recorded in 1891 (referring usually to men), and in 1885 all sexual acts, 'gross indecency', between men was criminalised – before this only sodomy was deemed to be illegal. The French philosopher and historian Michel Foucault's influential book on the development of sexuality in Western society, *The History of Sexuality*, proposed that the creation of the category of the 'homosexual' as a pathologic 'perversion' was instrumental in shaping the way in which same-sex desire was thought of. He declared that: 'homosexuality was now a species', and that sexuality became not a societal phenomenon but a facet of our individual identities.[3] Now homosexuality was who you *were* not just who you *fucked*. For lesbians, this meant they were (mis)labelled as 'tribades', an older eighteenth-century medical definition, or 'inverts', as in their gender and sexuality were inverted to form 'manly' feelings for women. Both implied that lesbianism was against the 'natural order' and way of being a woman. Foucault argues that rather than solidifying a boundary around what types of sexuality were seen as perverse, by medicalising and bringing such categories into reality it forced them to fragment and disperse as a way of staying invisible (by virtue of having been made visible). Think of it like this: once being gay becomes part of your way of thinking about yourself, and it's known as a fault, then you will find ways to hide or encode that part of yourself to avoid punishment or 'correction'. But it is only through identifying it in the first place that it has to be hidden. Once out in the open, so to speak, the locus of sexuality shifted into a person's mode of being, and while for some this forced them into hiding, for others it was to be embraced.[4]

Certainly, some lesbians in the late nineteenth and early twentieth centuries did live their lives out in public, or as publicly as they could. But often not in the UK – Paris or Italy[5] was the place to be, as Diana Souhami's documents in her lively account of four prominent 'modern' sapphists, *No Modernism Without Lesbians*. Natalie Barney, a writer and socialite sought to make 'Paris the sapphic centre of the Western world. Unflinching, outspoken, unembarrassable, she did not hide behind euphemism ... Around her there formed a community of lesbians who could be who they were. Paris allowed such freedom.'[6] This freedom, though, was reserved mostly for the wealthy, upper-class women or their 'artistic' friends. Some formed 'lavender marriages' with gay men to cover their affairs, obtain their inheritance and to secure independent living for their lovers. They influenced or wrote many radical novels, plays and poetry of the time with covert and overt references to female desire, Sappho and their affairs. Later, in the 1920s, the club Le Monocle provided a place for lesbians to meet in Paris, an open secret to most, despite the police raids. In the UK the infamous Gateways opened in the 1930s, and while a mixed club until the '60s, was well known as a space that lesbians would be welcomed. There was a network for lesbians, if you knew where to look and had the means to access it. From there we have only grown in visibility, not just to each other but in heterosexual society in general, as we'll see later.

This historical lack of acknowledgement by the public and those in power of lesbian existence did not, however, prevent governmental, legal or societal discrimination for many. Many lesbians were still pushed to the margins, or given freedom only in select privileged circles or in the privacy of their own homes. The history of lesbian life is laced with this story of invisibility, always in tension with who is being forcibly hidden, who is hiding themselves and those unaware there might be another way to live. It's partly why it took me so long to realise it for myself. It's a conflict that persists even today, and runs throughout the calls in the logbook.

> **8.1.96 – log by Zeenat: *I wish I was as together as them when I was 13!***
> They make a pact to call together from Christine's house cos she has a phone upstairs that has speakerphone, and her mum is out on Tuesday nights for her painting classes. Unlike Charlotte's parents, Christine's dad is happy to let the girls play upstairs so long as they don't make too much noise when he's watching the snooker. Christine is the one who dials. The woman who answers the phone seems surprised that they are so young but she's nice and listens when Christine says they are both lesbians.
>
> She explains that they just need some advice cos their teachers are, like, a bit rubbish about stuff like this. It all happened when Christine told their other friend at school that she fancied her and did she fancy her back maybe? And then this girl did the grossest thing ever and went and basically told everyone at school that her and Charlotte were lesbians. And now everyone won't stop teasing them

about it. The boys keep telling the other girls not to go near them cos they'll perve on them and that.

Which is absolutely not true, Charlotte adds.

The woman on the phone asks if they've told a teacher about the bullying?

Yeah, Christine says, but actually that's why they're calling cos all the teacher said was if it got really bad at school they should report it to the police but then even more people would know and the police would probably tell their parents and they don't know what to do.

The woman on the phone scoffs when Christine mentions the police and says, that really wasn't very helpful. She asks if there's anyone else they could talk to at school instead?

Charlotte takes the lead then to say that there's these other two teachers at the school, the PE teacher and the history teacher. And maybe we could talk to them about it, she says, I know they live together and everyone at school says they are lesbians. But none of the other teachers ever mention it so I'm not sure. But they seem nice.

The woman on the phone agrees that it sounds like a good idea and to call back if the teachers can't help. The girls say thank you and hang up. Now to plan how they're going to talk to them. Charlotte does netball after school on Wednesdays so they can try the PE teacher then. Next time when one of them fancies someone else they'll be more careful about how they tell them. The woman on the phone told them there's a young person's Gay and Lesbian group not far from where they live and they can join as soon as they turn sixteen. It feels like a lifetime away right now but one day they'll get there.

I was born in 1988, the same year that Margaret Thatcher's Conservative government passed Section 28 as part of the Local Government Act. It decreed that:

> (1) A local authority shall not–
>
> (a) intentionally promote homosexuality or publish material with the intention of promoting homosexuality;
> (b) promote the teaching in any maintained school of the acceptability of homosexuality as a pretended family relationship.

Despite vocal opposition and protests from gay and lesbian activists, including public demonstrations (twenty thousand people took to the streets in Manchester), as well as a group of lesbians invading the BBC's Six O'Clock News and another abseiling into the House of Lords (my personal favourite), the Bill was passed.[7] It effectively prohibited any kind of education or positive representation of homosexuality in schools and prevented many teachers from being open about their sexuality at work. It was in many ways a reaction to increasing gay and lesbian liberation in mainstream life, justified through a moral panic that queer people might 'turn' children gay. Instead, of course, it only harmed LGBTQ+ people, reinforcing the falsity that their sexuality was something shameful to be kept hidden.

It's likely some of the volunteers from the logbook were involved in the protests surrounding Section 28. Certainly, volunteering for lesbian lines and protesting seem to have gone hand in hand. Which makes sense. Lesbians who were engaged in their community also cared about defending it and their rights. Reading about other lesbian lines, I've found plenty of evidence to attest to this. Such as Lorraine Birch, a co-founder of the Bradford Lesbian Line who campaigned against Section 28 in Yorkshire.[8] Or Paulina Palmer, who co-ran the Cambridge Lesbian Line while attending demonstrations to try to prevent it coming into law. She continued to run the phone service from her own home despite increased opposition after Section 28 was passed.[9] And of course it affected more than just the volunteers – many of the young women in the logbook who called the Lesbian Line grew up while Section 28 was in full sway.

I was eight in 1996 when those two teens called the Lesbian Line and like them my school was also bound by Section 28, not that I knew it at the time. I don't remember when I first heard the word 'lesbian', but I knew it was bad because we only used it on the playground when the teachers couldn't hear. It was the perfect insult, one you could throw at any girl who was annoying or different. 'Gay' was for boys and bad things, like saying 'that's so gay' if someone did something stupid or girly. 'Lesbian' was for a particular type of girl, someone dirty or gross. The best way I can explain it is that even though I liked Sporty Spice best I pretended I wanted to be Ginger Spice, because everyone knew picking

Sporty Spice meant you were a lesbian. And no one wanted to be a lesbian.

I was nothing like those two teenage girls who rang the Lesbian Line looking for advice, notably not about if they might be lesbians (that is never in doubt) but how to deal with the other kids and teachers around them who now treat them differently. I feel much closer to Zeenat, who took the call, when she wrote how surprised she was, and maybe a little jealous, that these teens knew who they were so young. My memories of my school years have none of this certainty.

The only maybe-lesbian I knew in 1996 was the pianist at our church. At least at the time I assumed she was but it was never a thought I fully articulated, I just knew she was different. No one ever mentioned it out loud but it was in the atmosphere, in the glances she was given and the way certain members of the congregation gave her a wide berth. It was in her short hair and perpetually single status that was never questioned. Objections were raised against her but never about *that*. I don't know how I knew but I did. When I was older my mum confirmed she also assumed the same, so perhaps I've just grafted that knowledge onto my younger self.

There's much I still don't know about her and her life. I know that our pianist was compassionate and softly spoken, that she had a brown mole on her upper lip and the kind of '90s bowl cut that is fashionable again now on teenage boys. I know that we always got on well and I was sad when she left. I do not know if she left because she wanted to or because she was made to feel unwelcome. I do not know if knowing for sure whether she was a lesbian when I was younger would have helped anyway. I'm not even 100 per cent sure now she was actually gay, but I don't think it matters. What matters is that as a young teen I had this unformed inkling she was gay and this was why people viewed her in a certain way. It made an impression on my younger self that I'm still only understanding now.

I have many memories like this, where the benefit of lesbian hindsight requires me to reassess previous feelings and actions. To realise when you are older that you are queer is a continual process of plunging through your past looking for clues like this. It turns you into a would-be archivist. Unlike many other queer people, I did not know as a child I was gay and it continues to be a source of doubt. I do not feel 'born this way'. Impossible to know if I liked a girl at school because I had a crush on her or because I wanted to be like her. Did I say I fancied Abz from 5ive because I really did, or because I knew that's what I was supposed to want? Perhaps straight children grow up this way too. We're primed from birth that a bouncing baby boy will be a 'lady killer', or that the girl and boy holding hands in the playground are a 'cute couple'. Offhand innocent jokes about marriage and flirting that make children blush but communicate an unspoken lesson. Of course, no one ever asks, 'When did you know you were straight?'

19.11.97 – log by Beryl: ***she always sounds a lot older than she is, but I'm pretty sure she is 14***

The call is a long one but Beryl feels she owes it to this young girl to let her speak. She's well-spoken, well-off sounding too – almost as if she's from another era. But then Beryl remembers what she was like as a teen: a bit too obsessed with Austen and the Brontës and keen to show off to adults that she was well-read for her age. It's *Jane Eyre* she's thinking of now, in fact, when the young girl tells her she's away at boarding school, run by nuns, no less. She's using her allotted family call time to ring the Lesbian Line instead.

Because, the thing is, Beryl, this wise-beyond-her-years teen says, I'm perfectly miserable here. She tells Beryl her parents are separated and that she hardly sees her father. Her mother is busy with a new man each week, if the girl is to be believed. The nuns, while not outwardly cruel, are devoid of warmth for the dozens of girls in their care. Much of what the girl says has the ring of truth behind what Beryl senses is some dramatic teenage license. Beryl knows from experience it is sometimes easier to tell your own story as if it is happening to someone else or borrow parts from other people's lives. Her words do sound rehearsed at times, but perhaps she was nervous about calling and so planned out what she would say in advance. That's not so unusual. The tears when they come certainly seem real. It's not Beryl's job to judge, but to listen.

She might be in love with the head girl, she sobs, she's awfully tall and awfully nice. (Beryl wonders if *Malory Towers* was also on this girl's reading list.) But being in love is making her miserable and she wants to know from Beryl if things will improve. Beryl assures her that they will, but likely

> not without some heartbreak in the process. Beryl hopes the promise of a little tragedy at this age might be reassuring as much as the promise of better things to come. You'll be all right, Beryl says, we all go through it. It won't be forever.

Not knowing what my younger self felt is difficult. We focus so much on this narrative of a fixed identity from birth and do not allow the unknown to dwell in us, especially in children. I've seen the acronym LGBTQQ+ used when talking about young people, the extra Q standing for 'questioning'. I like this very much. Growing up I didn't even know it was a question I could ask, but there is something optimistic to me in the present participle of 'questioning'. It conveys identity as a continuous process, one where the outcome is yet to be decided. Many people (queer and straight) have been that Q at some point in their lives. For me it was much later, but I wonder how different my childhood might have been had I known it was an option so much sooner. If like those girls who called the Lesbian Line, I knew the right questions to ask.

What little I knew of gay or lesbian lives in my primary school years was patched together from snippets of TV shows or films or other kids in the playground. And none of it was positive. Growing up the '90s you'd be forgiven for thinking gay people had only just been invented and every story was a sad one or there to be laughed at. Lesbianism, as far as I knew it, was a punchline, not a way to live.

When I was older, around fourteen, and I still didn't have a boyfriend that joke turned to me. The new gag around the dinner table became that maybe I was a lesbian. I don't remember who started the joke but everyone laughed while I went bright red and said *no I'm not*. I got used to friends and family and people at church asking if I had a boyfriend yet. When I finally found one a year later, I wrote in my diary that I felt 'normal'. It lasted about a year until I realised I spent most of my time making excuses *not* to see him. It was only a few months until the questions and jokes started again. Don't you have a boyfriend yet? Are you a *lesbian?* Section 28 was only repealed in England in 2003. I was fifteen and had never met an out gay person. I had lived through something I hadn't even been aware of, because how can you miss what you do not know is even there?

The Other Half of the Conversation

26.9.96 – log by Josie: *I hope she calls back – she was really upset and is in crisis*

She finds their number on a flyer in the library but doesn't dare take it home in case Bill sees it. Instead she memorises the number and the opening times. It's another week after that before she calls. Another week of repeating the number silently in her head each night to make sure she doesn't forget it. When she finally dials, a rare moment when Bill has fallen asleep in front of the television before 10 p.m., she's sure the number won't connect. Her hands shake the whole time. She can barely get the words out after the lady on the phone says hello. She doesn't say her name, only that she's married but is in love with a woman and has been for many years. She wants the lady on the phone to know right away that she isn't a lesbian, isn't one of those . . . she doesn't feel attracted to other women. Just Maggie. It's only ever been Maggie. She waits for a breathless moment, expecting the line go dead or for the lady to tell her the phone service is only for lesbians, but she doesn't.

The lady on the phone asks how she can help and so she tells her about Maggie. She's still in love with her, has been for many years, even after their relationship ended. A while ago now but not long enough that her chest doesn't hurt every time she thinks about her. In love for all these years and then it was over before it hardly had begun.

What do I do? she asks. I can't think, I can't focus. I'm terrified my husband is going to find out, he's downstairs right now, she whispers. But I can't go on like this, I've got nowhere to turn. I'm not myself any more.

If Bill could hear her he'd tell her to calm herself down, she's getting hysterical. She can hear it in the rise in her voice, the sobs that threaten to come out. She's never told anyone this before.

It's like my life has turned upside down, she says to the lady on the phone. Saying it aloud she sees how true that really is, everything feels different. Her head spins. She can't go back to how she was before with all this love and feeling stuffed down deep inside herself. But what about Bill? He could wake up any moment.

The lady on the phone is saying something about counselling, they have counselling slots and they could get her one, it's a bit of a wait but she can try . . . She doesn't hear the rest. Can only think about Bill and him waking up any second and what he would do if he found out. Thank goodness the children at least are grown, one less thing to worry about. But Bill, Bill would go spare, she'd be out the house in no time. He'd tell all her family. And the children, would they ever want to see her again? She'd end up . . . where? Sorry, she says, I think this was a mistake, puts the phone down and goes back downstairs.

Mainstream and official archives are one way the state has worked to erase such histories of LGBTQ+ people through the confines of official documentation and legal language within a government that did not recognise or allow queer lives to be lived openly. After all, I could not find a lesbian history by tracking births, marriages and deaths, which historically did not acknowledge queer relationships or lived gender identity (or not at least without subterfuge on their part). Western record keeping and the violence of colonialism has been instrumental in the erasure of much of queer history globally and in establishing anti-LGBTQ+ laws.[1] When we talk about hidden histories it's important to consider who held the power for that erasure. While I'm writing about a specific UK context there are many other cultures which did not always oppress or stigmatise LGBTQ+ lives until the influence of Western colonial law and religious beliefs. The legal legacy of a British rule that deemed homosexuality illegal can be found across Caribbean, African, Indian and Oceanian nations.[2]

It is into this landscape that the queer archive arrives, with a specific aim to actively collect, catalogue and display documents, leaflets, letters, diaries, writings, recordings, images and objects from LGBTQ+ organisations and individuals. Items that may once have only circulated within a closed group or were at risk of being lost are preserved and remembered. And while all archives to some extent work in this way, either through making official records available to the public or cataloguing and preserving private belongings, for the queer archive there is an intensification of visibility in their work and an added complexity to notions of public and private. It's found in both the items they present to the public (some of which may once have been deemed 'illegal') and by inhabiting a space exclusively for queer material that signifies it as 'other'. Often this is literal in the case of queer archives within larger institutions. Islington's Pride is one, which Islington Council denotes as a 'special collection' – evidence of its role as a deviation from the implied heterosexual norm of the mainstream archive. In asserting their difference, queer archives make themselves proudly known, working in direct opposition to the mainstream archive which once might have closed off such information from the public (often at the request of that person's family or donor). For queer people, visibility and acknowledgment go hand in hand with the risk of losing one's privacy or right to a life free of scrutiny. For LGBTQ+ people living our lives openly (a phrase which assumes we have something to hide otherwise) can be seen at best as 'activism' and at worse as dangerous. So often we aren't allowed to simply exist, we must have a reason to be who we are – we must give something up in order to be seen.

And so this divide between 'official' and 'personal', 'public' and 'private', 'queer' and 'mainstream', is never clear-cut. Queer archives like Islington's Pride straddle both public and private material, where alongside an individual's collected ephemera they also catalogue council meetings and news clippings relevant to LGBTQ+ history and Islington. In the archive I moved between folders of homophobic news headlines to those containing home-made zines that celebrated gay, lesbian, bisexual and transgender identities. Hardly surprising that even into the '80s and '90s the public records and news clippings in the Islington's Pride archive were more likely to show an open hostility to queer people than anything positive. In contrast the private material: the zines and the photographs, and the logbook too, of course, gave a much fuller picture of lesbian life. The queer archive lets us see ourselves in a way that a mainstream archive does not, cannot, without amendment or qualifying, without an instinct towards hiding or obfuscation. In the private material I found heartbreak, sadness and abuse, but also the mundane details of simply living, or the joyous celebration of sexual freedom: of fucking who you want, of being who you want, of falling in love or not at all. Expressions of feeling that were, for a time, only found in private.

Not all queer archives seek to make their collections public and put on display private feelings. The Black Trans Archive by artist Danielle Brathwaite-Shirley is both interactive video game and online digital archive – part of a series of genre-spanning work that takes both physical and digital form. The Black Trans Archive exemplifies the tension between public and private in the queer archive, between expressions of feeling and what might border on voyeurism. In this space she specifically centres the lives of Black trans people and addresses its visitors directly.[3] When you first encounter the piece you are presented with a moving image of stylised figures in an overgrown urban (cyber)space, text scrolling above and below inform you that 'THIS IS A PRO BLACK PRO TRANS SPACE. ALTHOUGH ANYONE CAN PLAY THIS GAME IS MADE TO CENTRE THOSE WHO IDENTIFY AS BLACK AND TRANS' and that 'THIS IS NOT A PASSIVE EXPERIENCE. THIS EXPERIENCE REQURIES YOU TO BRING YOUR OWN INDENTITY TO THE SPACE'. If you choose to continue you are asked to select how you identify from three options: Black and Trans, Trans, or Cis, and are encouraged to be honest in your answer. Depending on your identity the archive then decides what material you can view. On answering 'Cis', the user is presented with the archive's terms and conditions: to centre Black trans people and use your privilege to help them. It states 'THIS IS NOT A PLACE WHERE WE MAKE YOU FEEL BETTER!' This part of the archive confronts the cis viewer with such issues as performative allyship, trans tourism and erasure of Black trans lives from history. At no point does the archive attempt to make white cis viewers, like me, comfortable and nor should it. Brathwaite-Shirley describes the intention behind such a decision and its impact, especially within a shared in-person space:

> I realised people will always come and put their own things on top of these trans people's stories. Every person has to perform their own identity in entering the work . . . Maybe they haven't even thought about their identity, but, within this room, they're going to have to. That choice will then

> affect everything that they are allowed to see, how long they can be here, when they can leave, if they feel comfortable in the room. Once we implemented that, it was interesting to see the respect the space actually got and how people started thinking about their own experiences, the choices that they had made, and the people they have lost, without obscuring the trans people in the room.[4]

The Black Trans Archive keenly raises questions around what stories are privileged within an archive (even queer ones) and whom archives serve. It complicates the notion that archives should be equally accessible to all and forces its visitors to first reckon with their own positionality and reason for entering the archive. By questioning the process of making public the private marginalised identities for knowledge or representation, it ensures that those who access its knowledge are aware of their motivations for doing so and how their own actions can erase or uplift Black trans histories. It feels like a glimpse at the future of archives. Once I might have thought of archives as passive, dusty material waiting to be discovered, but by making an interactive work, Brathwaite-Shirley allows the archive to speak back to those who would use it. Asking as many questions of us as we do of them.

8.8.95 – log by Bea: *Ellen received the tape from GEMMA but was very disappointed with it*
Bea has rung round GEMMA, SPOD and KENRIC asking them all if they have any audio tapes of lesbian books they could send out for Ellen to listen to. There was no joy at SPOD, they have a newsletter

but it's typed out and no library of tapes that they could get hold of. They said not many of the publishers they work with do tapes of the books. Not unless the author records it themselves, there's not much of a market for it apparently. KENRIC said much the same. London Friend is similar, to be fair, the little library of gay and lesbian literature they've managed to scrape together is patchy at best but totally devoid of anything on tape that Ellen might be able to listen to. It feels like it shouldn't be too much to ask to have a couple of recordings of lesbian books but they seem impossible to find, at least official ones. Unless Ellen wants to listen to *Tales of the City* she doesn't get much choice. It's the sort of thing where you have to know someone to know someone to get hold of them. But they don't know anyone. And so it's Bea's job to ring Ellen and tell her the news. At least GEMMA has managed to find one, *Oranges Are Not the Only Fruit*, although Bea supposes it's a bit dated now. It's read by Charlotte Coleman, who was Jess in that BBC version. She suspects Ellen might have already heard it, everyone watched *Oranges Are Not the Only Fruit* when it first came out. Even her mum did, much to Bea's shock. She could try Silver Moon maybe and see if London Friend has a bit of spare budget from somewhere to buy Ellen a couple of new tapes if they have anything. Maybe Bea should start her own phone service. Lesbian dial-a-novel – that has a good ring to it . . .

To read the logbook is to eavesdrop on a conversation I was never meant to hear. I cannot ignore the obvious fact that the calls made by the women in the logs were confidential and most likely many would have been unaware that a record was even made. Early on in the logbook there's a note from one of the volunteers that has been pasted onto the page next to a letter from the support group GEMMA, for disabled lesbians. It reads:

> *Please try to retain a degree of anonymity for callers! – Dana*

The letter includes a caller's full name and someone, probably Dana, has neatly blocked out in blue biro her surname and written the note beside it. There are other instances in the logbook of text being erased or scrubbed out to protect a caller's identity. One entry from June 1996 is written in green ink and has been meticulously gone over with the same pen so that while the words themselves are obscured the shape of them remains. Someone took a lot of care to ensure the note couldn't be read easily but I can just make out '[name] rang' at the beginning and a question mark at the end. Even that feels like telling too much.

Many of these calls are intensely private as secrets and desires are spoken aloud, often for the first time. Others disclose histories of sexual abuse, illness and suicidal thoughts. Even the callers just looking for a chat did so thinking only the volunteers at the Lesbian Line would know about them. Certainly not that someone like me might write about them. It's important to examine why I so desperately wanted to read the logbook and write about it. Was it purely morbid curiosity of wanting to see what you knew was off limits to others? Did I want to claim 'discovery' of the logbook? Would doing so smother their voices with my own?

The narrative of 'discovery' is one that should be approached with caution. Hardly a great discovery to reach an item in the bottom of a box an archivist before you has carefully laid out, catalogued, numbered and recorded on a computer system. To suggest no one knows about the Lesbian Line ignores the long history and network of women (many still alive) who established and worked on them. Yet when I mention the phone lines to other lesbians my age, most don't know about them. This profoundly reveals how easily knowledge and lesbian history can be lost within a generation and speaks to the difficulties we have in connecting to our past and our community. This wasn't a history I was taught in school or that was passed down through my family; it wasn't on my TV or in my local museum. So despite knowing we have always been here, there persists this nagging feeling that lesbian stories still risk being forgotten.

There is a tendency whenever you are writing about a facet of your identity, particularly if it is one that is marginalised in some way, to overthink everything. Was wanting to write about lesbian history because I was a lesbian an unbearable cliché? Was it embarrassing? Even now I find myself afraid to say exactly what it is that I am so interested in: to my friends, to the archivist, to myself even. And it is that very reticence that urges me on. So let me say it now, what I am interested in is lesbians. There's no need to play it cool. I think lesbians are worthy of our attention. I want to tell their stories. I think they need to be heard, not just for me but others too. And to do that I need to share their stories, to lift them up above the noise of the world, at least for a moment.

And what of the callers' privacy? That is of the utmost importance. But I do not need to reveal their secrets to tell their stories. Even if I wanted to, I cannot share the real calls because they are already lost to time. All I have is the trace they left behind in the volunteers' call logs, and so to return a voice to them will require an intervention. Not with the true story, but *a story*. To write about the logbook will require an exchange of fact and fiction but also of my life and theirs, a layering of truths and could-be-truths. Something like that which Ali Smith in her own work of fact and fiction, *Artful*, describes as the machinations of imagination, 'the act of making it up, from the combination of what we've got and what we haven't, that makes the human, make the art, makes the transformation possible'.[5]

I need to work backwards through the gaps between myself and the volunteers who wrote the logs, the gaps between the volunteers and the callers, the gaps between the person speaking on the phone and the person they really were. A trace of a trace of a life partially unknown. To turn the calls from their already unknowable state to something fictional but hopefully still real. A leap of imagination is required but one that does not come from nowhere.

I am not treading new ground here. The pioneering academic Saidiya Hartman sublimely reimagines and retells the lives of enslaved people and other Black histories 'lost' in the archive. Including that of a lesbian chorus girl, Mabel Hampton. In *Wayward Lives, Beautiful Experiments* she describes what she calls the 'narrative written from nowhere' which writes against and beyond the limits of authority and power in the archive and instead tells the story from 'inside the circle'.[6] Deftly closing the gap between herself and history. There is the work too of the queer scholar Clare Hemmings, who, in her book *Considering Emma Goldman*, invents the lost archival letters of the political radical. She describes her archival work as 'the radical scholar's task [which] is at once archaeological (unearthing the hidden to change our view of the earth) and interventionist – retelling stories to allow for present living'.[7] This is what I aim to do: not recreate the calls to the Lesbian Line but *retell* them. To make them into something which happens now, as immediate as anything can be when written down, so that I might capture the intimate traces of their lives.[8] A projection into the past that might show a way forward.

The logbook speaks to me and I cannot help answering back. I cannot pretend I am doing this without a desire to understand something about myself. My own queerness, my own lesbian history. I want a way to connect myself to the lesbians who have gone before me. To do that I need to know how I arrived at the logbook in the first place – because finding it feels like both fate and coincidence. What I have is the logbook and myself and every unknown thing between. I'm trying to write the other half of the conversation.

A Brief History of Lesbian Lines

8.12.95 – log by April: ***If she calls, could you tell her when I'm next on.***

The difficult calls are hard but what's harder is when they don't call. April has been expecting Terri to call her back ever since she was last on shift at the start of the month but so far nothing. It was a long call and they covered a lot of ground. Although Terri never said it, April got the impression she was the first lesbian she'd ever spoken to. Or at least about all the things troubling her. Like always, April managed to tease out her life story. To be fair it didn't take much teasing, she could sense Terri has been bottling a lot up and was dying to talk to someone about it. In many ways it wasn't anything April hasn't heard before. A fairly standard childhood growing up in a small Northern town, marriage to an older man, no children at least, and then the marriage breaks down and Terri is left all alone for the first time. And for the first time she lets herself think about all those feelings growing up she learnt to ignore. April has heard many variations of this story but something about Terri has stuck with her even weeks after their chat. April supposes she sees something of herself in Terri, except she always knew she was gay and married a man anyway and thought that was how life was going to be. Thanks Christ it wasn't. It's been about three weeks and Terri still hasn't called back. April leaves a note in the log-book just in case. She doesn't want Terri to think she has forgotten about her, she did say she'd call again. She knows she can trust the other women to let her know if Terri tries to get hold of her. It's funny, they're not supposed to get so attached to the callers but April allows herself just this once a smidge of favouritism. She hopes she'll call – she'd like to continue their chat.

I am on a Zoom call with ten lesbians. They are not the lesbians from the logbook but they all at one point worked on a lesbian line. The women who fill the ten squares on my laptop are ex-volunteers from the London Lesbian Line and they won't stop talking all at once. For the most part I struggle to ask my list of questions, not because they are uncooperative but because it's impossible to keep them on track. The conversation zigzags across topics, conflicting memories and time periods in that good-naturedly and disordered way that occurs within a group of people who have known each other for decades. They are welcoming and a couple of the more in-charge types help to steer the conversation in the direction of my questioning. Checking occasionally that I am getting what I need and asking their own thoughtful questions to me in return. We talk for nearly two hours.

They asked that I keep the specifics of our conversation private, which I agreed to do – just as I have for the women and callers in the logbook. I tell them I am a writer, not a professional historian, and while the logs are the starting point for the calls I am not writing a history book. In turn they stress to me that they did not consider themselves professionals on the London Lesbian Line. They were not trained therapists or counsellors – in fact, they had no training at all apart from the experiences and knowledge they shared with each other. Writing in 1984, volunteers at the London Lesbian Line said, 'We at Lesbian Line do not see ourselves as "experts", but rather as a group of lesbians who, between us, have a range of ages, backgrounds and experiences that we would like to share with other women.'[1] They were lesbians talking to other lesbians. But despite their lack of formal training in that sense they were very clear that calls were confidential and that they were privileged often to be the keeper of a stranger's secrets.

They might be the first person to ever hear that caller name themselves as a lesbian.

They told me they saw themselves as part of a greater movement for change. They truly believed they would change the world. They certainly changed individual lives, of that there is no doubt. They described their time on the Lesbian Line as one full of excitement – of being young and free, living in London surrounded by lesbians and gay men. It was a different world. Every night there was a disco or a women's group or a protest planning meeting to attend. But they also spoke of the need to look out for one another. Of the men that hung around the venues waiting to hurl abuse and broken bottles. Of having to decide to leave alone early and inconspicuous or in a bigger group, more obviously dykes but perhaps safer in numbers. They spoke of never being able to hold their girlfriend's hands in public. It took courage to stand up to be counted – to be visibly a lesbian.

Listening to the women speak I am most struck by the feeling of camaraderie that perseveres so many years later. That is not to say they agree at all times. Far from it: there are differing opinions and remembrances contested during our conversation. But despite this the sense of them as a collective holds; these bonds formed in their youth during such a vibrant and important time in their lives is still present. They are loud and speak over one another – joking, teasing, frowning. They speak about the importance of the social side of the London Lesbian Line: for them it wasn't just about providing a service to help lesbians in need, but also to give them a good time. They didn't just work the phones but met in person; they had socials and discos to ensure lesbians weren't alone. The togetherness of being a lesbian was central to their lives and what the lesbian lines were about.

They wanted to show the positive side of being a lesbian, especially to those women who called where happiness as a lesbian was an unimaginable possibility. They described their service as 'one vital way of ensuring women have the chance of exploring choices rather than finding themselves forced into heterosexual roles'.[2] They spoke to many callers who were lonely or trapped in relationships with men, and believed themselves to be the only women in the world who loved other women. Being on the phones proved that wasn't true.

The history of lesbian lines in the UK is a tricky one to track: references to lesbian phone lines even in lesbian history books are few and far between. And so I throw myself into a haphazard kind of research with the fanatic enthusiasm of an amateur lesbian sleuth. There are many false starts and surprises along the way as more pieces of history fall into my lap, sometimes it seems quite by accident – perhaps best not to mention the number of leads I stumble across on social media . . . I am not the only one doing this work; most of the other people I bump into are scholars, PhD researchers who write posts about their findings, or older lesbians who throw out snippets of their lives in conversation that hint at the bigger picture. Alongside the archival objects I've already scoured they combine to form a network of branching paths to follow. I'm indebted to the hard work of queer scholarship and those who generously share their personal stories with me or give them over to oral archives. What I'm doing now, I hope, is another crumb along the way.

Before we arrive at the first lesbian line we need to look briefly at the history of gay phone lines which served both men and women, and whose histories and purpose overlap, and often outlived, the lesbian-only lines. One of the most well-known and longest running gay and lesbian phone lines in the UK is Switchboard, established in 1974, although at the time it was called London Gay Switchboard. As Lisa Power, Switchboard's second lesbian volunteer, notes, 'You didn't say gay and lesbian then.'[3] In 1986 volunteers voted to change its name to London Lesbian and Gay Switchboard.

Legend has it that *Gay News*, the first UK gay newspaper, founded in 1972, was receiving so many phone calls asking about gay pubs and social groups, as well as gays and lesbians desperately in need of someone to talk to, that the newspaper couldn't respond to them all. Two years later several gay groups met up in a pub and decided that there was an obvious need for a helpline for gays and lesbians living in London. And so Gay Switchboard was formed. It took its first call out of a back room above Housmans Bookshop in King's Cross. From the outset it received calls from women and quickly sought to recruit lesbians onto its staff.[4]

Other gay lines soon followed and not long after, women-only lines were established. One of the earliest came out of Manchester, named Lesbian Link. It was set up in June 1977 by a gay women's group, running initially every night from an old bicycle workshop in the back basement of Manchester's Gay Centre.[5] They set a pattern for many of the stories I've found of women and lesbian helplines: volunteer run, a back room or basement premises, discos for both fundraising and socials. Around the UK there are other examples of lesbian lines that I've been able to find: ones in Nottingham, Birmingham, Coventry, Bristol, Leeds and Glasgow, to name but a few. The Cambridge Lesbian Line was established in 1979 and began in the spare room of one of its five founding members (somehow without her own mother finding out).[6] In the same year the Leeds Lesbian Line was founded and initially took their calls in the basement of a building at the University of Leeds.[7] The establishment of phone lines around the country meant that many women living in rural parts of the UK as well as larger cities outside of London had someone local to talk to who knew the area and nearby communities. London also had the Black Lesbian and Gay Helpline, which opened in 1991 and ran out of the Black Lesbian and Gay Centre, originally based in Haringey. They provided specific support and information for Black lesbians and lesbians of colour, especially when there was no guarantee that someone who looked like them would be available on a lesbian-only phone line.

A common factor in the creation of lesbian lines was a reaction to what they saw as male-dominated phone lines which either didn't have enough lesbian volunteers or enough knowledge about lesbian-specific queries to cater for a growing and more public lesbian community. London Lesbian Line was no exception, and hot on the heels of Lesbian Link, they set up shop in September of 1977 as a breakaway group from London Gay Switchboard and Icebreakers, another mixed helpline, which along with London Friend's mixed helpline were the main three in London at that time. The first mention I find of any of the lesbian lines in a history book is from Lisa Power's short essay 'Voices in my ear', written in 1988. The essay details the founding of Switchboard and she mentions in passing the beginning of the London Lesbian Line. Chiefly to note the reason why many women left in the early years after Switchboard began:

> At around the same time [1977–8], after a number of bitter arguments, all the remaining women in the group left to join with women from Icebreakers to form Lesbian Line.

> It was at a time when many lesbians, angry at the lack of weight given to women's issues within the mixed movement and at the continuing sexism of many gay men chose to prioritise work with the women's movement. The decision of most lesbians with any political sensibility at that time to do this left many mixed gay organisations in a quandary ... in the early eighties a token lesbian was worth her weight in gold as a range of groups struggled to maintain a semblance of political balance.[8]

Lisa Power was one of the few lesbian volunteers from the early days who remained at Switchboard and was instrumental in educating many of the men on lesbian issues at the time. It's encouraging at least to find the first concrete piece of history I have on the beginnings of lesbian phone lines and from someone who was there when it happened. I'm not so surprised to learn the lesbian volunteers left Switchboard because they felt it was too male dominated. This was a common trend at this time as many lesbians sought to separate themselves from the gay (male) movement (and for some men entirely) to focus on women's issues such as women's health, domestic labour, equal pay, caring and parental responsibilities, intimate partner violence and misogyny. At the time this was a tense debate in lesbian circles: were gays and lesbians stronger together or better off focusing on their separate issues? Many women felt ignored and that the issues they raised were not taken seriously by male leaders in the movement. Opinion on lesbian separation was divided: some saw them as selfish and men-hating in the extreme, while others acknowledged the need for separate spaces. As ever it was more complicated and nuanced than history allows.

On a practical level the lesbian lines saw themselves as offering a service that was sorely needed. In an article in the GLC Women's Committee magazine from 1984 (a 'special lesbian issue'), the members of the London Lesbian Line state that 'their experience of working within these organisations [mixed lines] showed clearly that women would rather speak with another lesbian and that homosexual men often hold as many misconceptions about lesbians as the general public.'[9]

Power later went on to co-found Stonewall, and when I spoke to her she confirmed that some of the women at Switchboard decided to leave to set up a specific lesbian service, joining with other members of mixed gender services. Power joined Switchboard in 1979 and before this had usually worked within a mixed gay and lesbian milieu. But Power and other lesbian volunteers still had an upward battle to ensure women and lesbian issues were understood and catered for. Power is a lasting example of the important role Switchboard had in catering to the needs of women in the early days of the phone lines and in Switchboard's belief that the gay and lesbian community was better off together despite their early challenges.

Yet it's understandable that some women felt differently at the time and saw the lesbian lines as fulfilling an equally important role to support and focus on lesbians and women, even at the expense of dividing community resources and knowledge. As Power notes in 'Voices in my ear', going solo doesn't come without its difficulties or compromises:

> Even with no lesbian volunteers, some women continued to

> call [Switchboard]; women who'd never heard of Lesbian Line, women who couldn't call during the hours they were open, women who'd swallowed media distortions of separatist groups, women who preferred the service or needed information Switchboard had.[10]

Women still called Switchboard because many lesbian lines couldn't open as often, or afford multiple phone lines (and so were often engaged), not to mention the smaller pool of volunteers to call on to staff the phone. Switchboard had vastly more resources, training and volunteers and so could keep their phone lines open almost 24/7.

But the women who set up the first lesbian-only lines were determined to make it work and to find connection elsewhere. The London Lesbian Line in particular chose to actively align themselves with other women's organisations. Their first home was at the Camden's Women's Centre until it closed a few years later. They then relocated to the attic of a house on Gray's Inn Road in Bloomsbury, shared by various other women's and lesbian groups like National Abortion Campaign, Housing Action and Women's Aid. They all crammed themselves into a tall narrow Georgian house, just able to afford the rent between them. It was important to the London Lesbian Line that they were part of the wider women's movement, rather than an organisation for gay men or a mixed homosexual group whom they saw as unsupportive of their issues. In 1986, before the end of Greater London Council funding, they were given a contract to lease a space on Featherstone Street, near Old Street in Islington, and settled there until the line closed.

According to an interview by the Lesbian History Group with Helen Bishop, Pam Isherwood and Lynne Keys, three London Lesbian Line volunteers, there was much debate about what to call the phone line when it opened in the late '70s. Namely, whether it should be the Gay Women's Line or the Lesbian Line. The feeling was that there was a need to make lesbians more visible, even to each other, and to let women know that 'lesbian' was not a negative word. Sadly, the telephone directory didn't agree and it took some petitioning to get the Lesbian Line phone number included. Even then it was filed under 'W' for 'women's liberation' because the directory didn't want to include the word 'lesbian' in their listings.[11]

18.12.97 – log by Clare: *We should congratulate ourselves on the support we have given her.*

Even though Clare wasn't around when Carol first started calling she likes to think she's played a small part in her life. It's been weeks since Carol last called and when she finally does again it's only a short one. Carol wants to give Clare an update on what she's been up to, and to wish everyone on the line a Happy Christmas. Since moving to Somerset she's never been happier. She never thought she'd get bored of London but after twenty years there it really was time for a change. Carol says it's the best decision she's ever made because it's just far enough away from London and her mum to discourage travel between the two. Jealous, Clare says with a laugh. She missed her friends at first

> but as soon as she found the local gays she hasn't looked back. Every other day there's an activity or group trip planned and if not there's always someone around to drive her to her new local in exchange for a pint, a packet of crisps and the best gossip Carol can muster. Clare knows it's a good thing but she can't help feeling a twinge of sadness when after the thank-yous and the warm wishes Carol says she'll probably be too busy to call again in the future.

The London Lesbian Line was one of the first to establish itself in London, but others soon followed, including the Lesbian Line at London Friend, which, like Switchboard, already had a mixed line. The Women's Line began in the mid 1980s and rebranded around 1994/95 to the Lesbian Line. As one phone worker notes in the logbook: 'I meant the Lesbian Line here under its new catchy name', but was also referred to as Lesbians at London Friend or the Women Only helpline across the various leaflets and annual reports.

Unlike many of the other lesbian lines which were operated out of people's homes or university basements, the London Friend Lesbian Line had its own premises as part of the wider London Friend organisation. They were initially based at 274 Upper Street in Islington, a stone's throw from Islington Town Hall, until they were forced to move in 1987, eventually securing a lease in an empty shop with a basement room on 86 Caledonian Road near King's Cross. In the 'special Lesbian edition' of the GLC Women's Committee magazine, there's a half-page spread dedicated to the 'Lesbians at London

Friend'. In it, a phone worker, Jo Smith, describes how on a Thursday evening (before they ran two nights a week) they 'monopolise London Friend's Islington headquarters' to offer not only the phone line service but also a social group that meets in person. She stresses the benefit of being part of a wider community group:

> As very few advice giving services have premises like this we think we're providing a service that isn't otherwise available. Both on the phone and at the group we're meeting a lot of women just coming out, or lacking contact, or new to London – and a large part of our function is providing a starting point.[12]

In some ways the London Friend Lesbian Line, open only two nights a week at its peak, feels like the little sister to the larger, more established London Lesbian Line, which eventually was open five evenings and two afternoons a week. However, as part of London Friend, they had a wider remit of services to which they could directly send callers. Alongside the phone line they also offered individual face-to-face counselling services, or invitations to the various groups that ran there such as Changes for newly out or questioning lesbians, and Lesbians at Friend on Sundays. LAFS, as is was known, was a more chilled affair for those who didn't like the scene or needed more support. They would start off in the London Friend coffee bar before moving on to a discussion group or video showing.

I spoke to Annette O'Connor about her time volunteering for Changes in the early '90s. She worked with many women over the years, often newly out as a lesbian and sometimes referred to the group from the phone line. She volunteered there for four years and found it a deeply rewarding time. For her, being at London Friend was about helping women of all ages find friendship and connection as newly out lesbians: 'We were trying to get them to think about becoming friends and creating their own groups so that they felt like they had someone to phone', she explained – especially if they were going through a tough time with their own families. Annette told me often she would say to the women, 'Tell them [a friend from Changes] at seven o'clock tonight, I'm going be telling my mum, or whoever, and have them on the speed dial, be able to phone them up and say, "Oh, my God, that was bloody awful", or "She already knew!"' Much like the phone lines, Annette's role varied from person to person, from a sharer of information to being living evidence that you could be out and proud: 'I felt like I was giving back to my own community, and reassuring my own community that they could be okay.' She was a listening ear and source of advice for those worried to come out to friends or family, and answered questions about dating and safe sex. While there wasn't a limit on how many times someone could attend the group, ultimately the goal of Changes was that the women would no longer need them. Once they were confident lesbians, the hope was that they would not need to see them again.

Other groups over the years included the London Bisexual Group, ONYX for Black lesbians and lesbians of colour, and Shakti (South Asian Lesbian/Gay Network), which had a women's group, as well as running pub quizzes and 'Friendly Discos' for both gay men and lesbians. Unlike London Lesbian

Line, which was firmly separated from gay male causes, the Women's Line aimed for a middle ground between providing a service directly and exclusively for women while operating within the wider gay and lesbian community. They benefited from being part of a larger gay organisation: able to share premises and funding while maintaining services exclusively for lesbians. Separate but together.

The annual report from 1985 in the early days of the London Friend Lesbian Line show that they received 178 calls in a year, with only an average of fifteen a month, compared to an average of around 291 to the general line. In contrast, by 1984 the London Lesbian Line had five hundred calls a *week*.[13] The percentage of lesbian or gay identified callers to the London Friend Lesbian Line, however, was higher at 71 per cent, opposed to 59 per cent to the general line, but their data doesn't split out lesbian and gay men so it's impossible to say how many women preferred to call the general line over the women-only one. In 1988 the total number of calls had risen to 4,342 across both lines – an enormous increase in just three years. By 1988, for the first time, there were also regular lesbian counsellors on the mixed line, not just the Women's Line. It wasn't until 1990, however, that the London Friend committee would achieve equity of gay and lesbian members, with eight of each represented. The report states that it hoped the move would continue the trend of an increase in lesbians coming to London Friend.

Unlike, say, Switchboard – or even the London Lesbian Line – I haven't been able to find any pictures of the lesbians who volunteered on the line at London Friend or what the room they took calls in looked like. I do have some clues, at least. I've seen a photograph of London Gay Switchboard when it operated out of the room above Housmans Bookshop. In this black and white picture three phone workers sit in a line, two men and a woman. The woman is closest to the camera. It's Lisa Power, phone in hand, blunt fringe covering her face. The men each clutch a receiver to their ear, the cord spiralling down to rotary phones sat on the desk that stretches along the length of the wall. They each have a notebook or a diary open in front of them, and stuck to the wall are notices and maps, too grainy to read properly. There's a coat hanging on the back of the wall. The room is extremely cramped.

I imagine the London Friend lesbians in a similar room to this but on an even smaller scale. They only had one phone, not three. I imagine a desk, the rotary phone, the clunky answering machine next to it. The logbook and biros open in front of them. I imagine those kinds of uncomfortable wooden chairs that charitable organisations always seem to have – salvaged from a council office or municipal building. I imagine no windows, maybe a basement, like so many other lines. They have a rota on the wall, a filing cabinet behind them and shelving with folders. There must have been some storage for all that information they had to impart. I imagine boxes of flyers sitting around at their feet – the pastel pinks of the annual reports waiting to be distributed. I imagine this space to be organised but messy – there are too many people using it for it to be neat. I imagine boxes that get dumped there when they run out of room and old Blu Tack stains on the walls. For certain, I know there was the logbook, its shiny hardback cover slowly scuffing through the years of being put away and taken our again twice a week, pressed open to the relevant page so that each phone worker could add their reports or occasional doodles. The one place to deposit the torrent of emotion and information that tumbled towards them through the telephone wire during every shift.

On another visit to the archive, I spend more care rooting through the brown archival boxes and I finally get a glimpse at some of the people who worked at London Friend. There's a stack of photographs: some are extremely '90s, volunteers posing with a giant teddy bear decked out in London Friend stickers; the fashions for the lesbians are oversized sweatshirts tucked into jeans, for the gay men tie-dye T-shirts and tartan vest tops. No sign of a phone in these but they do have an impressive library of books behind them. It's not too long before I find another picture that sparks my interest. There are three men, one, David (helpfully everyone is wearing name tags) sports an impressive Freddie Mecury-esque handlebar moustache and leans on a tabletop, a phone pressed to his ear. The cord curls away out of frame next to the other man. This is Malcolm Macourt, which I know because he's holding a copy of his book *How Can We Help You?*, published in 1989 about counselling for gay men and lesbians. On the cover a man also holds a phone to his ear.

Above them the last man leans in. He looks familiar, even before his name badge gives him away. It's Michael Cashman, the actor and now politician, who in 1987 was one half of the first gay kiss in a British soap in *EastEnders*. What I'm most drawn to, however, is the background because although this is a picture of gay men, I'm sure this is the phone room the London Friend Lesbian Line would have shared. On the walls are a map of London, a poster advertising Changes and, pinned onto a noticeboard, various newspaper clippings. The only two I can make out are one about living with HIV and another on David Hockney.

I move on from the photograph to the stack of annual reports and London Friend newsletters from the '80s and '90s. In the February 1989 issue I find a reference to Malcolm Macourt's book and his forthcoming visit to London Friend. But there's another paragraph that catches my eye: a reference to an appearance of three lesbians in the 18 January issue of *Just Seventeen* magazine and to a photograph taken in the phone room with the women. It notes that the feature has brought in dozens more letters and calls from isolated young lesbians who have been referred to Changes or will be connected up with other Friend groups close by. Moments later I am searching eBay. It doesn't take long to find what I think is the right issue, but there's no mention of any lesbians on the cover. There's only a picture of male and female models close up wearing leather jackets, the promise of an interview with Andy Bell from Erasure and a poster for Fine Young Cannibals and Marc Almond. Original price, 50p. Miraculously, however, there is another seller and this one has taken the time to upload some spreads of the interior. I scan the contents page and find a reference to 'Chat Back: On Homosexuality', but no still no Lesbian Line. I scroll through some more images, and I kid you not, make an involuntary gasp when I see it. It's a terrible scan with a big light streak across it, but still it's enough of a glimpse to convince me to purchase. In a few days the magazine is in my hands open to a full-page spread featuring a black and white picture of three lesbians from London Friend; they are sitting on unconformable-looking wooden foldable chairs (I got that detail right, at least) and behind them are two noticeboards strewn with flyers. If I squint I can make out a sign for LAFS and there, hidden right in the corner, is a telephone. The three women sit posed as if in conversation, two smiling at the other. They are all young, white and in their early twenties – one rests her arm nonchalantly on the back of her chair. There are polo tops tucked into wide blue jeans and big slouchy jumpers, one plain, one with a heavy knit pattern. The two on the left sport short hair, earrings and fashionably baggy tops. It's unclear if the women being interviewed volunteer for London Friend or are users of its services, since the focus is on their experiences as young lesbians.

The article covers questions such as: 'When did you first realise you were gay?', 'Did any friends or family turn against you when they found out?' and 'Do you think AIDS has made people more anti-gay?' Despite the negative assumptions in the questions the article is actually full of positive lesbian representation, giving space for the women to share their stories and show the differences in their experience of coming out. They even touch on the derogatory stereotypes of lesbians that they want to combat: 'Lesbians tend to be invisible or portrayed as the Greenham Common-type radical . . . You should let them know you are a lesbian and *proud* to be a lesbian.'[14] There is a hint here of the media portrayal of the '90s lesbian that is to come, that of the more mainstream, assimilated lesbian who wishes to distance herself from the radical feminist stereotypes of the '70s. Yet this does not mean they are not political. All the women condemn Section 28 and explain the negative impact it has had on them and other young people. They point to services like phone lines which are there to help:

> [T]hen you're speaking to a lesbian or gay man, and they have more experience and knowledge to share with you . . . If there really is a dilemma then at least you know the helpline is always there. Mulling it over with someone who is anonymous can be the first step towards accepting yourself.[15]

As the readership of *Just Seventeen* was mainly teens, it makes sense that the article focuses on coming out and acceptance from family and school friends. There is a small box at the end of the article featuring numbers for London Friend, the Lesbian and Gay Youth Movement and Lesbian and Gay Switchboard as well as a list of book recommendations.

Looking again at the smiling faces of the women pictured I can't help but think of the young people who would have seen this article and felt a twinge of recognition and hope. I can imagine seeing this before I was out and wondering how I'd ever get to be like them. I'd envy the ease with which they took up that space, the casual arm on the chair, how comfortable they look in their own skin. They really do look like they get on. It reminds me of what Jo Smith said when speaking about London Friend's volunteers: 'Nobody is pressured to do anything they're not happy with. Maybe this is why we're all good friends (as the saying goes) and as well as late nights and frustration, we have a lot of laughs and fun together. We think it's worth it and so, we hope, do visitors to the group and callers on the phone.'[16] This echoes what Annette told me about volunteering at Changes: it was bloody hard work, but so worth it.

The lesbian and women's lines of the '70s, '80s and '90s all had broadly the same goals in common: to provide a space where women could ask questions, seek advice and simply talk to another lesbian. Many arranged meetings between callers and ran socials as a way to create safe spaces for women to meet up and form a community. All the lines experienced harassment in the form of prank calls, or men ringing thinking they were some kind of sex-chat line or brothel. But despite this the volunteers continued and the calls from women poured in.

At a time when discrimination against lesbians came from the government, the street, the workplace and one's own family, these phone lines were one of the few places to which questioning women and lesbians could turn for information and support. And for many, they provided a space in which women could speak truthfully and privately without the fear of being rejected for who they were. The role played by such lines in improving the lives of lesbian, bisexual and gay women across the country shouldn't be underestimated. As one volunteer at the London Lesbian Line noted, '[It was] the idea that you could change someone's life in twenty minutes, it allowed you to make direct contact with one woman and turn her life around, just by saying to her, it's perfectly all right to be a lesbian, you are completely normal, you can be happy, there will be a future for you.'[17]

Coming Out?

18.9.94 – log by Nise: *not sure if they're lesbian or not*

She calls mostly for advice. She thinks she's a lesbian but doesn't know how to meet other women. She's never tried anything like this before. But sometimes she finds herself thinking about the other women she works with at the hospital and if any of them might be like her? One of them is a bit like that, y'know the sort. A bit . . . more manly than the others. Never wears make-up. Is that okay to say? If she's a lesbian does that mean she has to stop wearing make-up too? Oh she knows that's a silly question, don't answer that. It's just nerves. If they could just give her the name of a lesbian bar or a place to go to maybe that would help? All the pubs she used to go to with Steve were full of loud men and sticky floors. Surely a ladies only pub would be a lot nicer? She just needs a place to start and then maybe she'd know what to do next about all this. A push in the right direction.

In my late twenties, I met the woman who would become the object of my first gay crush at a networking event in a city that was not my own. I recognised in her all the things that I was not: she was funny, confident and, most importantly, sure in her sexuality. In the workshop we were asked to pair up with someone we didn't know. I can still hear the woman leading the session challenging us in a gentle Leeds accent that rather than stick with a friend to 'approach someone who catches your eye, someone you like the look of'. My eyes went straight to her. The woman with the short black hair and bright blue jumper, I'd noticed the way she made the woman sat next to her laugh so easily. She had an easy cool-girl charm. Not like me, who never thinks before I speak. And that's how I ended up calling over to her and the person she was with to suggest we pair up. They both agreed. And then in a classic moment of cowardice I suggested that she go with my colleague, over some lame joke about them both wearing the same shade of blue, and off they went. Crisis averted.

For the rest of the day I found ways to talk to her. We chatted easily, finding plenty of books and humour in common. Later, she made a casual joke to me about a girl she was dating that left me feeling oddly deflated but also like we were somehow in this together, this difficulty of loving women. That moment made my head spin. Did she sense some queerness in me, even after knowing me for such a brief amount of time? At this point I still thought of myself as straight. But the conspiratorial way she had shared this joke with me made me feel seen. We lived in the same city and caught the train home together afterwards, joking and talking the whole way. I didn't think it was a crush, not then, I only knew that

I liked her – a lot. I wanted to be her friend, I thought, or at least someone she thought of favourably. Looking back now I can pinpoint this as the age-old clichéd lesbian dilemma: do I want to be *like* her or do I just *want* her?

We crossed paths back in London, moving in similar circles but not directly. Now there was a constant running monologue throughout my day, wondering if this was a crush, and what that might mean if it was. I didn't know what to think. This was what made me start a diary and put everything into words. Of course it was a girl. That was the real reason for my list. The diary opens with a set of statements:

Here are some things I know:

- I am 28 years old
- I have no idea what my sexuality is
- I am questioning what that could be/mean

The first entry after my list is a long rambling mess of questions: Could I be gay? Was I gay? Did I just want attention because I thought being straight made me boring? I almost couldn't believe something like this was happening to me. I am always the sensible, sure one. I don't 'do' drama and this all felt so dramatic. I wrote about her in my diary and worried that in doing so I was conjuring up feelings that weren't really there. That by writing about her I was keeping whatever it was going, and turning her into something she was not. A fictional crush seemed like the perfect way for a writer to try and sort out her feelings. I have always preferred the safe space of the written page over action, and this crush – distant and improbable seeming – was the perfect platform to explore such feelings.

While I questioned whether I wasn't quite as straight as I had assumed, I clung to every story I heard about women who came out later in life. Those women who had been married or single and suddenly their lives had seemingly shifted. Minor celebs like Mary Portas, and Sue Perkins's (then) girlfriend Anna Clare Richardson, or Lauren Morelli, the writer from *Orange Is the New Black* who fell in love with Samira Wiley on set and left her marriage to be with her. Women who, it seemed to me, woke up one day and had fallen in love with a woman. I read every blog post and interview with them I could find. I rewatched comedian Tig Notaro's documentary about her cancer survival, searching for a clue in Stephanie Allynne's eyes as she told the story of how their relationship went from friends to lovers. How did they know? I was twenty-eight and had never been in love and now it was possible I had been looking for it in all the wrong places.

It's said that coming out when you're older is like going through a second adolescence and certainly that was my experience. Going through teenage-like intense crushes when you are twenty-eight is a ridiculous, slightly wonderful tumult of emotion. At least I know this is not a new feeling, nor am I the first or last to experience this. Unrequited or lost love punctuates the logbook. I may not know what it is like to be trapped in a marriage when you love someone else, but I do know what it is like to have feelings for a woman that you have to hide from everyone, including yourself. Most of us know what it's like to want someone you can't have.

Crushes in general are ideal for this. In my opinion a crush, whether on fictional characters, celebrities (who basically hold the same status as a fictional person) or even real people should be unattainable or unreciprocated. The distance is what makes the desire. A crush lives in the mind of the crushee not the crushed. Teen movie romance might try to convince us that mutual crushes are cute, but my experience in real life is that it's far more likely to be one sided. If my crush had turned into something real I know it would never have lasted. Which is also why I told no one about my IRL crush; speaking it out loud would have destroyed the fragile awakening that was happening.

Likewise, I doubt I would have called the Lesbian Line if it had still been in service. I didn't know about Switchboard back then. I think talking to someone about it over the phone, rather than typing *how do you know you are gay* into the anonymising internet, would have been too scary a prospect. Online felt a safer, more hidden space than the reality of a telephone call or conversation with a 'real' lesbian. I was afraid, I think, afraid of making that seismic shift to my world. Up until this point I had thought I had finally settled into who I was as a person: I had a good career, a solid group of friends, I had hobbies. Aside from my chronic singledom everything felt like it was on track. Being gay would upend all of that. What would it mean for my work, my family, my friends if I came out? It all felt risky and like too much effort.

Despite sensing that nearly everyone would be supportive there is always a fear of rejection. And an even bigger fear of getting it wrong, both by society's standards of what is expected of young women, and getting it wrong internally – of claiming an identity that wasn't my own. It's sad to think that for me, my first inkling that I might be gay brought with it not the joy of discovery (that did come later) but fear and sadness. How brave those women were who rang the lesbian lines, no matter how many times it took and how often they hung up. To speak a question out loud and face a truth you don't want to look at takes great courage or great desperation. How much I hated being called brave when it was my turn to speak.

In the end my emotions gave me the proof I had been looking for. In early September that same year I was at Tate Modern with a friend when I saw my crush and her girlfriend across the gallery. My stomach dropped. My heart pounded. My temperature rose. There was a sort of rushing sound in my ears – I swear I lost my vision for a moment. A distant part of me thought, *Oh that's what this is like.* My friend was still talking to me about a Picasso we were looking at, but I could barely nod along. When I glanced back my crush was leaning in to whisper into her girlfriend's ear, a gesture so intimate I immediately looked away. They were so clearly together. I had never seen her girlfriend before: a trendy-looking butch in shorts and a T-shirt, a little older than me, hair buzzcut short. Heartbreakingly cool. I thought about going over to say hello; I wanted to, or wanted her to notice me. But the idea of awkward small talk and introductions was too awful to contemplate for long. I was shaking as we moved along to the next painting, the urge to turn around and look at them again so strong that I couldn't focus on anything in front of me. The rest of the exhibition was a blur of trying not to think about her, wondering if we'd bump into each other again and feeling guilty for not listening to what my friend was saying. It was equal parts exhilarating and embarrassing. I felt like a teenager, but there was something in the way my heart had jumped at the sight of her that I knew was more significant than just a fleeting feeling. What had for so long felt like it only lived in the vague blank spots in my brain was translated into an embodied experience I couldn't ignore. No longer the realm of fiction but empirical fact before me. I needed some sort of proof and here it was. A small moment, really, but here was that seismic shift I had been so afraid of.

Just under a year later, on 17 September 2017, I added a comment to the opening statements in my diary, addressing my former self. It simply said, 'You're really fucking gay dude'.

> **20.9.97 – log by Polly: *worried about how she feels and didn't mean to upset her mum by being a lesbian***
>
> I find often the younger ones just want someone to listen to them. The girl on the phone is only sixteen and already she sounds so tired. Why do we teach girls at such a young age to put other people's feelings before their own? She was so worried her mum would be upset at her because she knows she's a lesbian that she is too scared to come to Changes or any of the groups I suggested that might help. I wish I could send her some newsletters or book or something in the post to show her that everything is going to be okay and there's a whole world of lesbians out there living happy lives. And some of us even get on okay with our mums! I told her that

> everything would be okay and she wasn't wrong to have those feelings. She laughed and said she couldn't help it, could she! It was nice to hear her laugh after the call started off on such a downbeat note. I told her she would need that sense of humour, it'll serve her well for the next few years at the very least to get through it all. I really hope she calls back. I remember when I was her age and I didn't have anyone to talk to either. It wasn't easy but I made it.

I knew I was a lesbian a year or so before I told my family. Telling them felt like the final step to acknowledging that this new, gay self was here to stay, and so, of course, I hesitated. I felt like there was still so much to learn about myself and what being a lesbian meant that I wasn't ready to share it with any straight people, let alone my own family. Not because I thought they would be horrified or disown me, but because telling them would make it real in a way I wasn't yet prepared for. And so I hid what was maybe the biggest realisation of my life so far from them for as long as I needed to. I avoided what felt like my mum's endless questions about my weekends and evenings – suddenly seeming so invasive, where before I would have happily told her every mundane detail. I drew myself away and avoided talking to my parents because I didn't want to lie to them. Wanting distance from the painful silence between doing 'nothing much' and going on a date with a girl for the first time, the untrue silence between 'I'm fine' and lying awake at night trying to figure out my newfound feelings.

I don't regret it, nor do I think it was wrong to hide that part of my life from them for a time. It was difficult but necessary while I came to terms with who I was and this new way of seeing myself. I was caught somewhere between protectiveness and a sense of distorted embarrassment about what I was going through. Before I came out to my parents I wrote in my diary about how worried I was that I would be a disappointment to them. I wrote of my fear that coming out would 'make me not the perfect daughter. I worry that they won't be proud of me any more? or think me normal, not understand me, think me a bit strange?'

I have always positioned myself as the 'good' daughter: the daughter that doesn't cause any trouble or act out. My mum likes to tell a joke about how other parents will complain to her how difficult their daughter was as a teenager and she will shrug and laugh and say aside from a few moods she never had any problems with me. I was the daughter that did well at school, volunteered at church groups, didn't drink or smoke – I did what was asked of me. My parents were never pushy, but they were proud I went to university and moved away to London, that I had a job in the arts. All the things perhaps my mum might have done if she had the opportunity and funds. I was afraid that coming out to them would disappoint them because I would become a person they didn't know. That they would have to answer awkward questions or correct people when they asked if I had a boyfriend or a husband. I felt like being gay would be a difficulty for them. With distance I can see this as a consequence of my own internalised homophobia as I struggled to accept myself. It's unfair that I projected all this onto them – that I would be a problem they didn't need.

Yet at the same time I was more and more certain it was something I needed to tell them.

Sara Ahmed writes in *Living a Feminist Life* that being a lesbian is to 'stray away from the path you are supposed to follow if you are to reach the right destination'.[1] The path you are supposed to follow, of course, is a heterosexual one: marriage, children, a good home, a good job. It's a story that traps all sorts of people: women who don't want children; people who want to live outside of a capitalist, individualistic system; men who are expected to be the providers; and children who have to grow up to want the same. The list goes on. For many it's a path that we don't even know we're on or think to question.

I was walking multiple paths: mostly out to my queer friends, trying to hide my newly lesbian status to the few dates I'd been on, ambiguously out online but not to my family and work colleagues. One foot still on that expected path but unable to see a way to that right destination that Ahmed speaks of. The author Jenn Shapland also talks of paths when she writes of her own coming out as a lesbian after years of denying it, even while in same-sex relationships: 'To open my self, my life to queerness was to eradicate the carefully hewn path that had lain before me since I knew anything ... Queerness required me to throw legible futures out the window.'[2] Shapland identifies that to be queer, but especially to be a lesbian, requires seeing a different future outside of heteropatriarchy. And with a dearth of happy lesbians from history, a leap of imagination is required to get there. I like this idea that lesbianism is tied to imagination and throwing off the seeable future to embrace the unknown. A creative necessity born out of a constraint that makes us seek out a future that others can't even envision.

It also requires acknowledging that you may have been looking for this future in the wrong places for quite some time. As the nature writer and gardener Alys Fowler does in her memoir *Hidden Nature*, which sensitively charts her journeying back and forth across Birmingham's canals alongside her own realisation she is gay and falling in love with a woman, despite being married to a man she also loves. Again, the image of a pathway surfaces when she describes coming out later in life: 'admitting halfway through that I'd been on the wrong track was a mighty strange thing. Though I believe wholly that negative capability is essential . . . it is an extremely uncomfortable place at times.'[3] Throughout her memoir she struggles with this lack of understanding of herself: how could she not know? (How could *I* not know?) It is only by embracing negative capability – that unknown and uncertainty within the self that Keats so valued – that she could forge a new future. But as Fowler says, this is a difficult place to be. Part of coming out, especially when older and having lived a 'straight' life for so long, is to learn to dwell in this uncertain and shifting self. To embrace the self at the crossroads. All those illegible futures.

Before I 'fully' came out I felt like a huge imposter, not gay enough to be queer, not straight enough to be 'normal'. My diary at the time is wrapped up in this binary language, that being gay was to be difficult and different and that being straight was the good, right way to be. A lifetime of heteropatriarchy: straightness written into every story I saw around me, in the narratives I inherited from friends and family, at church, in TV, books, films. Everything told me that relationships were structured around men and women. The few that weren't framed it as either something to be kept secret or something which would involve hardship and sadness.

It's an old story but not that old. One that Adrienne Rich argued effects not just lesbians but all women. She described it as 'compulsive heterosexuality' which acts as an 'enforcement of heterosexuality for women as a means of assuring male right of physical, economic, and emotional access', and ensures the erasure of lesbian experience from history, society and media.[4] Rich proposes instead an understanding of lesbian experience as a 'lesbian continuum', which might encompass both heterosexual, friendly relationships between women, alongside sexual and romantic relationships. A way to extend lesbian understanding of life both historically and contemporaneously with women's intimate experiences and lived solidarity under patriarchy. Rich argues that compulsive heterosexuality dangerously reinforces and romanticises heterosexual relationships as the inevitable, even when such relationships are harmful. Simultaneously rendering lesbianism as either 'deviant' or 'abhorrent' or else 'invisible',[5] where the only representation of lesbian desire is seen as erotic or perverse.

It's a trend you can chart from lesbian pulp fiction novels that often, when written by heterosexual men, ensured the lesbians died at the end lest the reader think the author was in favour of such things, to today's 'bury your gays' trope identified in modern media, where gay and lesbian characters are more likely to be killed off in service to the (often straight) storyline. All seeking to reinforce the assumed narrative that heterosexuality is the norm. During the period of the logbook lesbians were more 'mainstream' than ever, but for every indie film like *Go Fish, The Watermelon Woman* and *Show Me Love* which featured more complex, nuanced portrayals of lesbians, there were films like *Chasing Amy* and *Basic Instinct* in which queer women were either a challenge to turn straight or a murderous bisexual psychopath. As Rich concludes, compulsory heterosexuality not only affects lesbians or confines women who desire women to the 'closet', but also stymies and limits all women in 'the lie that keeps numberless women psychologically trapped, trying to fit mind, spirit and sexuality into a prescribed script because they cannot look beyond the parameters of the acceptable'.[6] Rather than pathologize lesbianism, Rich repositions heterosexuality as an systematic structure governed and created by male-enforced laws (both legal and cultural), religion and economics that bears examination as a 'political institution' to deconstruct. She believes that doing so should be central to feminist politics if it wishes to progress towards true equality.

To exist within a heterosexual world is to always be in tension with one's own status as 'out'. A lot of emphasis is put on coming-out stories but often it's a story that privileges a 'straight' way of thinking. As many LGBTQ+ people know, coming out is a continual process across a lifetime: to family, friends, co-workers, waitresses who ask if you're waiting for your boyfriend, hotel receptionists who check you really did mean to book a double room, doctors who want to know how you're 100 per cent certain you're not pregnant. Coming out is only necessary within a heteropatriarchal society which assumes everyone is straight and puts the onus of disclosure onto a queer person. As the actress Jen Richards explains in the documentary *Disclosure*, about trans representation in the media: the act of disclosure, especially when portrayed as something which leaves a person feeling betrayed or lied to, 'reinforces their assumption that there is a secret that is hidden and that I have a responsibility to tell others. And *that* presupposes that the other person might have some kind of issue or problem with what's to be disclosed. And that their feelings matter more than mine.'[7] We don't owe straight people anything and acts of disclosure have for too long not been on our own terms.

Yet coming out can also be a tool for demanding equality. During the 1970s and the fight for gay liberation, coming out publicly was used as an important political act of visibility and solidarity in defiance of overwhelming discrimination. Gay Liberation Front's manifesto, written in 1971, ends with the bold statement 'GAY IS GOOD! ALL POWER TO OPPRESSED PEOPLE! COME OUT – JOIN GAY LIBERATION FRONT'. It demonstrates the central role coming out played in demands for equal rights, by making themselves visible in a way that wasn't reliant on the respectability politics used in the homophile movement of the 1950s and '60s. For GLF, coming out was a positive way to reclaim what society had forced them to keep secret or sidelined through fear of oppression and abuse. As Rebecca Jennings writes in *A Lesbian History of Britain*, 'For GLF, personal and collective visibility represented both a political statement about the validity of lesbian and gay identity and a means of reaching out to other gay people and to the wider community.'[8] They did this through street theatre and 'zaps' (short and fast interventions) like gay-ins and kiss-ins, or protests that drew media attention. They transformed the deeply personal act of coming out into a political, public statement.

I should stress, of course, that queer people have existed throughout history and have always found each other and community away from the straight gaze. It is only entering into an oppressive society that forces queer people to hide themselves. Nor is coming out an equal position for all people within the LGBTQ+ community. For Black queers, queers of colour, working-class queers, those who are neurodivergent, disabled, or who are gender non-conforming, intersex or trans, or sit across these intersections, disclosure and coming out can be met with disbelief, dismissal, or very real danger. Notions of 'out' or 'not out' offer a binary Western way of thinking and for many queer people, globally and in the UK, this language is not useful in how their sexuality is rendered to themselves and in their relationships for a myriad of reasons.[9]

Historically in Europe and North America, the few lesbians and gay men that have lived more publicly have been upper-class, white and cis, those that, as a result of their wealth or privilege, wider society has seen as more 'tolerable' or 'respectable'. For GLF this was not enough. They wanted to give back the power to all gay people (using their language) to come out on their own terms and with full equality. In coming out and sharing their personal stories, the queer community made themselves more visible than ever as part of the public, someone's friend, parent and co-worker, and they demanded to be treated fairly.

*

As the '80s came about there were more lesbian and gay social groups and activism collectives than ever in the UK. However, many lesbians still struggled to find them or connect to a community, especially if they were based outside of larger cities such as London, Birmingham, Manchester or Liverpool. A case in point is the story of Cheryl Slack, who's oral history is held in the archives at the British Library as part of the Hall-Carpenter Oral History Project. Cheryl speaks of the London Lesbian Line in a recording from 1985 when she was twenty-one. She sounds young, hesitant, as she takes sporadic drags on a cigarette. She talks about her early life growing up in Merseyside, running away to Manchester and becoming homeless for a short while. She ends up in London and finds work in a café in Earl's Court.

It's all right for a bit but as soon as the manager finds out she dates women the homophobic comments start. Eventually she is forced to leave. She's blasé about it, aside from the odd comment: 'it was awful, really awful'. It's said quickly in an accent that has lost all trace of her Merseyside roots and sounds more Estuary in some of its nasal vowels. It's an accent borne out of her move from countryside to city, from North to South. A voice that, like mine, is not quite her own any more, absorbed by the city. She speaks fast, so fast that I have to go back and listen to her clips over and over again to transcribe them properly. I don't need to, but I want to capture all her 'ums' and 'ahs', all her stutters and repeated words.

Cheryl rang the phone line in search of a women's group to join, fed up of her flat share and having just lost her job. The woman she spoke to on the phone offered to meet Cheryl and take her out. They went to the West London Women's Centre and ended up dating for a few weeks. Later Cheryl goes along to the London Lesbian Line's fifth birthday disco in 1982. She's exhilarated by seeing so many women together, saying:

> I walked into this town hall and it was packed full of women and y'know some were on their own and some were kissing in the corners and some were doing this, that and the other ... it was quite frightening, y'know, and quite relieving as well to think that there were this many. There was this many women who would come to a women-only disco.[10]

On the recording she repeats 'y'know, it's like *amazing*, y'know'. Her 'y'know's increase in frequency as she describes what she saw there, as if she needs to convince her interviewer that it was real, *Do you know?* she asks. It's addressed to no one, really, yet I can't help silently answering back. I do know. Those 'y'know's hit me one after the other. Tiny shots of recognition.

Cheryl's sense of astonishment comes through on the recording even thirty-odd years later. I replay this section the most, listening to how her speech slows down, taking its time over the *amazings*, pausing for emphasis. I imagine Cheryl leaning forward into the microphone and taking a drag of her cigarette as she tells of the importance of this moment, tripping over her words:

> I was glad I went. I, certainly, it opened up my eyes to a lot, it made me feel easier about, um, not exactly coming

> out, to terms, with the fact that you're not, I'm not on my own, for all that time thinking, feeling so isolated, with that feeling of oh my god I'm so weird, I'm so queer, there's nobody else like me, I'm lost, I'm just going to die because, I can't handle the reaction to not being heterosexual, or not having a boyfriend.

Listening to Cheryl speak, she is far away and close at the same time. Things change and some things stay just the same. I understand her wonder at stumbling upon a queer world by chance through an advert for the London Lesbian Line in *Spare Rib* magazine. It's only a small part of Cheryl's recording but it's one of the few times she speaks about herself and her sexuality explicitly. She ends by saying, 'It all seemed to change for me, it became something so much easier to relax into what I think I knew all along, that I was queer and I could be proud of it.' She ends with a laugh, one I know well, a laugh at the naivety of her former self, a laugh tinged with sadness, an incredulousness that she ever thought she was alone when there were so many others. A laugh that acknowledges the role chance had to play in where she is today. At her own ambivalence towards coming out, that it's never a straightforward line. That calling the Lesbian Line was only one small moment in her life and that it was completely life changing.

While the '90s heralded a more mainstream acceptance of lesbians coming out, for many it was still a risky business, even for public figures. When the broadcaster and comedian Sandi Toksvig came out in 1994 she was dropped as a performer by the charity Save the Children for their 75th anniversary event.[11] In response the protest group Lesbian Avengers leafleted the venue and the charity eventually apologised, explaining they had cancelled her appearance due to fears that reports of Toksvig and her wife being parents to three children might 'distract from the events of the day'.[12]

It would seem that Toksvig could be a champion of any children but her own. Despite such rhetoric, most of the lesbians I spoke to who were around during this time generally agreed that things were getting easier for women coming out and living a more public lesbian life. A trend which has thankfully continued.

So while I grew up during the '90s under the influence of Section 28 and, to my eyes, a lack of positive lesbian role models, because of the activism of early movements like the GLF, CHE (Campaign for Sexual Equality) and then later ACT UP, Lesbian Strength Marches and groups like the London Lesbian Avengers, there was a greater acceptance of LGBTQ+ people already on the cards. And as a cis white lesbian living in a large city, I have the luxury of being more ambivalent about my status as 'out'; for me acceptance is not guaranteed but broadly expected. It's a sorry state of affairs, however, if this low bar of tolerance is seen as the baseline. For some, acceptance is not something to be aimed for anyway – why would you chase approval from someone who has no business having an opinion on your life? Likewise the generation below me, depending on where they live and the people around them, may never even have to come 'out' at all, as more and more young people identify as LGBTQ+, sexual difference is nothing notable.[13] This is not to say that coming out isn't still an important, difficult or meaningful process,[14] nor that young people do not strongly identify with these labels, but rather because of the successes and hard work of other queer people we are afforded the privilege of caring less about it, or even skipping over it entirely and getting straight to the good part of being gay: living our lives.

Mallory, the protagonist of Eley Williams's novel *The Liar's Dictionary*, sums this feeling up well when she ponders why she is not 'out' to the world: 'It's not interesting. It *is* interesting. It shouldn't define me. It definitely should.'[15] Mallory is an intern at Swanby's dictionary, which, despite its long and illustrious history, remains incomplete. She is someone deeply concerned with the meaning of words and the potential they hold to be many things at once, saying, 'I wish I had an easy way to remember how to spell *mnemonic*. I wish I could remember how to use "surely" and "definitely" when it comes to finding words for myself.'[16] She exposes here the uneasy tension between exact definitions and changeable natures. Earlier in the novel Mallory lists words like 'butch', 'dyke', 'gay' and 'queer', which she looked up in the dictionary as a school child, listing their standard 'straight' definitions that she found there:

> *butch* (v. transitive), to slaughter (an animal),
> to kill for market. Also: to cut, to hack
>
> *dyke* (n.), senses relating to a ditch or
> hollowed-out section[17]

Mallory comments that 'I didn't realise that a dictionary might be like reading a map or looking in a mirror.'[18] Queerness as a pathway or a map should be a familiar metaphor by now. But alongside this is the image of the dictionary as mirror: not because it reflects what Mallory is, but because it reveals that words, like people, hold multiple meanings contingent on both context and subtext. To be queer is to move between text and subtext where words hold such double meanings. It's what allowed Kenneth Williams to speak in Polari – a kind of gay dialect which borrows from a host of Romance languages like Italian and Romani as well as thieves' cant and theatre slang – on national radio without publicly being outed.[19] He could exist in parallel, textual spheres: obviously, deliciously out and campy to those in the know, amusingly affected and effeminate to those who saw him as overly theatrical and didn't question his sexuality, or perhaps enjoyed his comedy too much to examine it closely. There are a thousand ways that a queer person can read another in straight spaces like this.

I like Mallory's ambivalence to being out. It captures something which I feel to be true, that being gay is both a deeply central part of my existence and also something so ordinary that it should hardly register. The paradox is that to me, being gay is the most natural thing in the world, that at home with my wife we do not conceive of ourselves as politically 'out' lesbian bodies, we are just us, making dinner in the evening and deciding what to watch on TV. Without the straight gaze the concept of 'out' ceases to hold any meaning.

The same is true is all-queer spaces. No longer seen as 'other', the detail and texture specific to each person is allowed to emerge. In an all-lesbian space you are lifted out of the homogeneity of a shared label and the nuances of your self unfold. There's a sense of this freedom too in the logbook; there's no need for them to discuss their sexuality or explain themselves. They are there to do the work and because they are all on the same page (literally) with who they are. They have a shorthand with each other. Some things do not need to be said, they just *are*.

When I spoke to other volunteers working on lesbian and gay phone lines they told me they would sometimes share their coming-out story but only if it felt like it would be useful to the person they were talking to. Not if the person was hostile or abusive – they did not need to prove anything to those kind of callers. Our stories about how we discover ourselves can be some of the most precious stories we hold and we may choose to share them carefully. They can be difficult and complicated, but just as easily can be boring or of little note. Either way it should be up to us whom we tell them to.

It should be a private, personal and individual decision to be out and who to be out to, if we care for the label at all. Being out is to exist in this dialogue of (not) interesting and (not) definite, and asks us to question where exactly we are coming 'out' from? Why is it being asked of us and who is doing the asking? It feels like such a binary state when for most queer people 'outness' is a spectrum of behaviours, ways of being and circumstances. Likewise, the binary of 'out' or 'not out' belongs to a heterosexual definition of the parameters. If we are 'out' then where is the 'in'? In the closet? And if it is in a closet, well, then who put us there? Or rather who built the closet around us?

10.1.96 – log by Bronwyn: *admitted she'd rang many times before. She has a girlfriend now.* Her name is Sandy she tells Bronwyn and just like her name she has sandy-coloured hair which she thinks is the funniest thing ever. Don't you think that's the funniest thing ever? She doesn't even wait for Bronwyn to agree but ploughs on, You should see her eyes – they're like a blue-green, not like ice-blue, nicer than that. And the way she walks, it's so cute – sort of with her toes pointed out in these little quick steps so even though Sandy is taller than me I have to slow my steps down so we can walk side-by-side. I can't stop thinking about her – isn't that silly?

Bronwyn tells her it isn't that silly. Plenty of women feel that way. Is this your first girlfriend? This question prompts another ten minutes' worth of accolades about Sandy. Bronwyn recalls the first few times she called – quiet as a mouse and barely able to say even hello. Half of those early calls were hang-ups, the other half were her calling back to apologise for hanging up. She would ask one question per phone call. How do you know you're a lesbian? When did you first tell someone you were gay? Do you think I should tell my parents? What does a crush feel like? Do you think two women can be happy together? On and on like that it went for weeks. She always listened patiently to the replies and thanked them for their time. She often rang when Bronwyn was on shift, something about their schedules must have aligned. Bronwyn wonders now she has a girlfriend if the calls might become less frequent. In her experience they often do.

In the end, I came out to my mum by accident, although I had been thinking about it for weeks. In July 2017, ahead of an old school friend's hen party, I'd travelled back home to Leicester, where we were due the next day to drive for an overnight stay in a cottage in the Peak District. Although unplanned, I had conveniently given myself an escape route should I need it; perhaps some subconscious survival instinct kicked in. My mum and I were sat in the garden idly chatting not long after she'd picked me up from the train station. I always love to sit out in my parents' garden, especially fresh off a hot, cramped train from London. It felt like a luxury to have a quiet strip of green space that I didn't have to share with strangers. We sat on the patio, outside the house I grew up in, chatting about nothing much until my mum asked why I was no longer tweeting – most likely after she caught me staring at my phone mid-conversation. And because when I am surprised I am a bad liar, I floundered for an excuse before telling her the truth. The truth was I had blocked her from following me weeks ago because I didn't want her seeing any of my posts, which were sounding a little more *gay* than usual. I wanted to protect the lesbian identity I was still exploring online. I suspected (rightly, she later confirmed) that the only reason my mum had started following me on Twitter anyway was because she had felt (again, rightly) that I was pulling away from her. Usually, she abhorred any social media. I think she followed only me and Julian Clary.

She asked why I had blocked her – was there something I didn't want her to see?

Perhaps she sensed that I needed to tell her but couldn't find a way to bring it up.

And so, after I long pause, heart in my mouth, I told her I was gay.

I'm gay, I said.

Hardly original but perfectly functional.

My mum smiled at me and told me she loved me, that she knew. I think that's what she said first, those two words, 'I know', in a voice halfway between serious, laughter and surprise. She asked if I had a girlfriend (no). If I'd always known (no). She asked half joking if I wanted to be man (no, with a quick segue about the difference between gender and sexuality). She asked if I was going to cut off my long hair (no, but silently I added a 'not yet anyway').

These questions were to be expected and are common stereotypes: that being a lesbian meant I was wanting to be a man or look like one, at least. The ingrained assumptions that being a woman meant femininity and desiring men, and so desiring women meant a rejection of that femininity as understood by our prevailing social mores, codes of dress and gesture. My mum's fear that I would cut off my hair was a fear that I would lose my femininity. Not because I had never cut my hair short before, but because after coming out to my mum it took on a new significance. There is a refusal to see butchness as beautiful, to understanding that masculinity and femininity are not confined by binary ideas of gender. To be a lesbian is to unhook the barbs of aesthetics from such perceptions. Why limit what beauty there is in the world? I was only just beginning to learn this for myself and certainly no way I could articulate all that to my mum yet.

And in that moment none of that mattered, because I had come out to my mum and she was still proud of me.

23.2.98 & 5.3.98 – log by unknown volunteer: *She just called back! – her name is Vanessa*

Vanessa has already rung once but she wants to make sure, wants to double double-check that Clare's going to get her message. It's Vanessa, she says, when the woman picks up, Vanessa from Coventry, she blurts out just in case there are other Vanessas. Her heart is beating fast and because she's over-excited it all comes out in a rush: please can you tell Clare, a big thank you from me!?

She waits until the woman on the phone writes it down, her leg jigging about the whole time.

You got it? Vanessa asks.

The woman says she does, Clare will see it when she's next on shift.

Vanessa's eager to get off the phone even though she doesn't need to rush. No more begging off her best-friend to use her mobile credit, now she can use the home phone. She doesn't need to hide from her mum any more. It all went really well. Really well. Better than she could have dreamed. Big thanks, yeah, Vanessa repeats one last time before ringing off and carrying on with the rest of her big, happy life.

Coming out to my mum was a small shifting of my world. A (not) interesting moment. The world rearranged around us and I jumped from one path to the other. Or rather I began to join up my disparate paths. The world continued as it was and I bounded off for the hen-do weekend, grateful when my mum suggested that she tell my dad while I was away. Not because I was scared of his reaction but because I didn't want to have to be the one to go through the initial emotional turmoil of disclosure, the surprise, those early awkward questions.

I got home from the hen do full of a newly found confidence: I had casually come out to my friends while away, telling them I'd been on a few dates with some women, thankful that my best friend was there and another queer friend. They had accepted it easily. I could do this. I knew my mum had told my dad, but I was avoiding talking to him about it until my mum all but pushed me into the computer room where he always sits. We talked. It was fine. He was mostly concerned that I might get messed around by other women, based on his friend-down-the-pub's lesbian daughter who was a serial monogamist, and by my dad's standards (who met my mum at eighteen) had been through a fair few women. I reminded my dad that she was also now married with three dogs, a son and a set of twins on the way.

My dad, like me, does not enjoy awkward conversations and would rather talk around than directly at an issue. If he can find a way to worry about something he will. I think his fears about the dating lives of lesbians was more about my heart getting broken than anything else. He worried too about me being different, about this meaning I didn't want children, marriage. That life might be more difficult for me. His first instinct was to protect me. My brother was more excited, I think, to tell his lesbian friends that his sister was one of them too. I think they all felt smug that those jokes around the dinner table were right after all.[20]

Unlike some of the women in the logbook I didn't have to give up my family when I found my queer one, and my coming out was met only by love, acceptance and the odd awkward question and ill-placed joke. For that I feel lucky and grateful. But even my sense of 'luck' and 'gratitude' is tinged with sadness because those feelings are a symptom of relief, relief from knowing it doesn't always work out so well. Sadness for myself, that my first instinct had been fear. Once word spread to my wider family and friends that 'Elizabeth was out', I received messages letting me know how 'brave' I was. I hated being called brave. To be called brave in the context of coming out by a straight person is to acknowledge that outing entails danger and risk: that you might be disowned, that you might be harmed, that you might be making life harder for yourself. All of this may be true, but the bravery is only there because straight society has forced us to be brave. It's hardly felt like a victory at times. Often it was a chore.

So, what's my coming-out story? Was it when I realised I was gay? My first crush on a woman? Telling my best friend? Telling my parents? Is it still being told? Was there never much to tell anyway? In retrospect it feels so insignificant yet at the time it consumed my daily thoughts. That it really wasn't a big deal in the end is a story in itself, one I'm intensely privileged to have when so many don't. There are lesbians in the logbook who could not come out to their families or partners for fear of what might happen, or if they did were thrown out, abused and cut off from their family. My coming out shouldn't matter. It really, really *should*. The ordinariness to my story is testament to all the lesbians who came before me and made my path an easier one. Perhaps I should have written this story more concisely: I'm a lesbian. I'm loved. I had found my right destination.

Gay, Lesbian, Woman?

18.12.95 – log by Ellen: ***she reassured me that she wasn't bi – I said it didn't matter to me if she was***
It's happened too many times to me now to be a coincidence – do you think it could be how I dress? I ask the woman at the Lesbian Line. I rang the Lesbian Line on purpose, I tell her, to make my point. Not the mixed line, not the gay switchboard, the Lesbian Line cos I'm fed up with everyone saying I'm not a real lesbian, that I must be bisexual. I'm not even bi. I don't care if you don't care, I don't care either, but it's other people saying it that gets on my nerves. Yeah I've slept with guys but you show me a lesbian that hasn't slept with a man once or twice, gay or straight, and I'll show you a liar. It shouldn't matter anyway.

I'm fed up with it, I'm sick of it, every lesbian on the scene just assumes I'm bisexual as soon as I mention my kids or an ex-boyfriend and suddenly they want nothing to do with me. I haven't so much as touched a man in years. Doesn't make a bit of difference to some of these lesbians. Some of them will even say they don't have a dad, that they never even so much as looked at a man let alone kissed one. It's always the ones that protest too much, I find ... anyway I'm just fed up of the whole scene. The lot of them.

It's the same bars, the same women, the same exes and arguments and the same sodding songs.

Honestly, it needs some life injecting into it. And the way these lesbians suddenly decide that so-and-so is out just because of something they said or a funny look they gave to one of their girlfriends, it's disgusting. It's downright depressing. Lesbians are supposed to be better than this, aren't we? If we're the ones shoving each other down then what hope do we have for everyone else out there who already looks at us like we're the bottom of the barrel? Maybe it's for the best they all think I'm bi – just because I wear lipstick and nice shoes but still don't look girly enough for their little femme/butch games.

So outdated anyway. I think I'm just bored of it all. Maybe I should move or find someone new? What do you think? Do you go out much? Do you want to get a drink sometime – what did you say your name was? Oh. Wait, not that Ellen that went out with ... Oh actually, sorry, I have to go. Bye!

Perhaps it's prudent to explain why I refer to the London Friend Lesbian Line as the Lesbian Line and not the Women's Line as it more often called itself. I've not been able to find any official record of the phone line changing its name – it's only in the offhand remarks from phone workers in the logs. In one they have crossed out *Women's Line* and written *LESBIAN LINE!!* in all caps above it – a sign perhaps that the name was new to them or a sticking point for some. The majority of the women-led helplines were called Lesbian Line so maybe it was to show solidarity with others around the country. Perhaps it felt important for the women to be able to proudly declare that they were lesbians. Perhaps it was for efficiency, so they wouldn't be confused with a line for heterosexual women. It's possible the name change to Lesbian Line was, like the London Lesbian Line, a way to make a clear public statement of who they were, or simply that the word 'lesbian' became more fashionable and accepted by the mid '90s and better articulated the service they were providing.

While the Lesbian Line was open to any women who wished to call, regardless of their sexuality, its name does imply a certain singularity, and to 'queer' ears today it might even sound passé, old-fashioned or exclusionary. Bisexual people are notably absent from any of the early phone line names, for instance, both the single-sex lines or mixed lines, and chimes with a long history of bisexual identity which is often forgotten or erased.[1] When the first lesbian lines were conceived of in the 1970s 'lesbian' held a broader meaning, and could include people that, then and today, might identify as bisexual, pansexual, gay, queer, transmasculine or non-binary. Words, like people, change their meaning over time and vary in their use between individuals or situations.

Lesbian as an identity is one that has and continues to contain multiple definitions which are shaped by those who use it today. Labels are useful until they are not and any definition I can give comes with caveats. I don't even know if it needs defining; don't we all know what a lesbian is, especially if we are one ourselves? Surely, it's less a question of what *is* a lesbian, but what do lesbians *do*? Broadly, a definition might be as follows: a lesbian is a woman who loves other women. But should that be 'love' or 'desire' or 'has sex with'? And does that only reduce us to who we are attracted to, that we must always exist in a state of desiring or in relation to another? And what of non-binary lesbians or lesbians who date non-binary or genderqueer people? I'm not interested in definitions of lesbians or womanhood that reduce us to a binary understanding of gender and sex – that ignores the history of gender non-conforming, trans and intersex people who have found their home in the word 'lesbian'.

Are you a lesbian because you say you are? Is being a lesbian defined by how you dress or speak or carry yourself? Is lesbian found in a set of certain behaviours? Or how others acknowledge you? I lean towards a definition which the lesbian scholar Liz Gibbs described in the '90s, as 'one of identity and community rather than simply sexual acts'.[2] I'd actually rather not reduce being a lesbian to whom I choose to have sex with – that seems like a rather empty definition to me. Once you start to prod at any definition of 'lesbian' it shows itself to be a leaky one. That is, of course, precisely why I like it and why it continues to be contested, fought over, discarded and reclaimed.

We can look at the etymology of the words used to describe women who love other women (don't worry, 'gender', you're next). There was 'tribade' from the eighteenth century, based on a laughably sexist misunderstanding of biology: that an enlarged clitoris was either a consequence or prediction of a woman's desire to have sex with another woman, and was seen as a medical definition. We can trace the rise of 'Sapphic' in the nineteenth century – from the poet Sappho, whose poetic fragments lovingly address women as well as men, and whose place of origin, the island of Lesbos, gives us the root for 'lesbian'. There was 'invert' too in the late nineteenth century, favoured by the writer Radclyffe Hall and the artist Gluck – a term which manages to be almost both homophobic and radical at once (depending on who was using it) as acknowledging a reversing of the 'natural' order of things and an adoption of 'masculine' desire as understood at the time. It was eventually overtaken by the use of 'lesbian' in the late twentieth century and was favoured in the English-speaking world predominately by white middle-class women in the UK and across North America.

As the term rose in popularity as well as in medical and public usage, so did a need for lesbians to identify themselves to each other without exposing themselves publicly. As such, many burgeoning lesbian organisations did not refer to themselves directly as 'lesbians'. Groups like the Daughters of Bilitis, founded in the US in 1955 and named after another poet from Lesbos (although actually the fanciful creation of Pierre Louÿs), provided a useful cover for lesbians who wished to meet in secret. 'If anyone asked us,' one of the founders noted, 'we could always say we belong to a poetry club.'[3] The UK's oldest social group for lesbians, KENRIC, was founded in 1965, its name taken from the boroughs of Kensington and Richmond where it was first formed. As well as *Arena Three* magazine, which ran from 1964–71 – originally subscription only – its subtle name allowed for an element of subterfuge if posted to a family household. One of its editors, Jackie Forster, would go on to found *Sappho* magazine, first published in 1972 and continued the tradition of lesbian 'sapphics'. But in contrast to *Arena Three* its first issues carried the very clear tag line: 'gay women read SAPPHO', as lesbians finally went more public and 'gay woman' and 'lesbian' became much more commonly used. Over in the US in 1970, the Lavender Menace was formed, a radical feminist lesbian group who took their name from Betty Friedan's infamous description of lesbians within the feminist movement, whom she saw as causing division. In fact it references a much longer history of lavender as both a coded colour and a word for homosexuality in the UK and the US.

Throughout these changing descriptions, from 'invert' to 'sapphic' to 'gay woman' and 'lesbian', a picture emerges of the ways throughout history lesbians have defined themselves for themselves, to both include and encode their identity to others. The move towards magazines and other media which plainly state their intentions as being made 'by lesbians for lesbians' show how confidence in lesbian identity was formed and fought for during the rise of the gay rights movement and wider public (read: straight) awareness of lesbian lives.

If the '70s show a push towards an understanding and 'acceptance' of lesbians, then the '80s and '90s saw an explosion in the visibility of lesbians in counterculture and radical spaces. By this point, 'lesbian' and 'gay woman' had become the commonly used terms for women who loved other women, but of course these were far from the only words in popular use, and as long as there have been 'lesbians' there have also been 'dykes', 'butches', 'studs' and 'femmes' with their own specific meanings and cultural history. Punk and alternative scenes, sadomasochists (SM) and later the riot grrrl countercultures all saw a new wave of self-identified dykes, butches, studs, rebel chicks and lezzers come to the fore, out and proud and taking no prisoners.

In the US Alison Bechdel's comic strip *Dykes to Watch Out For* ran from 1983–2008 and in the UK, Kate Charlesworth's *Auntie Studs* featured the everywoman dyke throughout the '80s and '90s in various gay and lesbian newspapers and comic collections such as *Dyke's Delight* (1993–4). Meanwhile, artists such as Jill Posener, Del LaGrace Volcano, Mumtaz Karimjee, Ingrid Pollard, Pam Isherwood, Pratibha Parmar and Tessa Boffin captured lesbian and dyke life in photography, film and performance.[4] Lesbians were no longer the realm of polite members-only clubs behind closed doors; they now wrote their names on banners and T-shirts. The dyke and lesbian strength marches, the HIV/AIDS epidemic (which also affected lesbians, as well as the many lesbians who supported gay men as they dealt with misinformation and neglect from the government and healthcare workers), alongside the protests around Section 28 and actions to increase lesbian visibility by the London Lesbian Avengers, all ensured lesbians were part of the public consciousness[5] and front page news.[6]

In the 1990s this culminated in the creation of 'lesbian chic' and 'lipstick lesbians', as lesbians entered popular culture like never before. No longer were lesbians easily spotted across the room, now 'the majority look exactly the same as heterosexual women'[7] – unless lesbians were part of a specific subculture, there wasn't much to tell them apart, something which enraged both radical lesbian feminists and homophobes alike. Of note is how once the mainstream heterosexual public came to recognise the word 'lesbian', they then attempted to take ownership of it. This is evident in the way the mainstream press used the term 'lipstick lesbian' as a kind of patronising shorthand to show that lesbians were sexy now and more feminine, no longer the stereotypical Doc Martens-shoed radical feminist of Greenham Common. Alongside this 'lesbian chic' aimed to present lesbians as 'just like straight women' – playing into fears of more masculine lesbians while patronising more feminine ones. Within the lesbian community there was much debate about this assimilation into the mainstream and accusations that this new generation of lesbians were not politically engaged enough, caring more about looks than activism. For others it was about subverting expectations of what a lesbian should look like and being true to themselves.[8] We see again and again how definitions of what a lesbian is and does (and looks like) have always been contested.

Lesbians were now suddenly fashionable; they were on TV and in the news, no longer afraid to say the word or show lesbian love. Instead, mainstream media found new ways to fetishize and water down lesbian experience to appeal to a heterosexual audience. As one writer put it: 'With the sudden craze for "lesbian chic", we have become hot property. Dykes grace the pages of the Sunday supplements and every respective soap opera has its lesbian character, kiss and controversy.'[9] You can feel the sense of pushback from lesbians as they try to retain ownership of their language and identity now that they are suddenly so 'popular'.

In 1994 *Diva* magazine began, adding to the roster of other

UK feminist and lesbian magazines like *Bad Attitude, Quim* and *Spare Rib*. Now there were multiple magazines which presented an array of different interests and facets of lesbian life. Unlike some of these earlier more radical feminist magazines, *Diva* and other mags like *Shebang* aimed to have a pop culture and celebrity focus, alongside political interviews and articles. *Diva*'s tag line was 'the lesbian lifestyle magazine', and so an interview with Sarah Schulman rubbed shoulders with Valentine's Day fashion tips, or activist Joan Nestle shared cover copy with *Diva*'s Top 30 Delectable Women. A new kind of public lesbian identity was emerging, one which could be political but also cared about fashion and popular culture – one who didn't take themselves too seriously.

Lesbians gained new heights for representation on television too with numerous gay women appearing in British soaps for the first time and a slew of programming from Channel 4 such as *Out on Tuesday*. But there was still much progress to be made; Channel 4 tended only to feature lesbian issues during set seasons and there was still a sense of hesitancy, as one lesbian TV historian notes:

> [There was a] continuing paranoia/homophobia/resistance (whatever you call it it's all the same) of major networks . . . We've come a way in the last decade but we're still light years away from the time when a TV executive will say, in all seriousness, 'I'm thinking of doing a homosexual soap opera. You know, *The Dykes*.'[10]

The '90s saw a tussle for definitions of lesbians and dykes, and a reckoning with what it might mean for lesbians to be given more of a voice in popular culture and mainstream media. On the one hand, more people than ever had access to what it meant to be a lesbian and to see lesbians represented in TV, film, art and mainstream news. By now 'lesbian', 'gay woman' and 'dyke' become the terminology most commonly used by both those in and outside of the community, with queer theory mostly the realm of academic circles – although 'queer' was growing in use as an identifier or descriptor.[11] So while it was still certainly shocking to some ears to hear the word 'lesbian' on the telly, it was getting exposure like never before. *Brookside* famously aired the first pre-watershed lesbian kiss in 1994. Yet much of the mainstream coverage was still subject to the control of straight producers or editors, and for many lesbian filmmakers and viewers there was a feeling that there was much progress still to be made for positive and lesbian-led media.

It was during this time that some of the stereotypes around lesbians that we know today solidified into culture – particularly within white lesbian vernacular in the UK, which was heavily influenced by the US. It was created and reinforced by both lesbians and non-lesbians. One typical article in *Diva* magazine, for example, is titled, 'Where do dykes go on their second date? Honeymoon of course!' – a nod to the stereotype that lesbians are quicker than most straight couples to declare themselves in love, move in together and settle down. Stereotypes about lesbians when from outside the community (perhaps obviously) focus on the negative: we're masculine, ugly, wife-stealing, prick-teasing predators who are too loud, too feminist, too proud, with no fashion sense, who are trying to indoctrinate young girls into our devious way of life. If lesbians do exist, then we should be there for the pleasure and spectacle of men. These stereotypes seed unhelpful definitions and often lead to danger.[12]

Every lesbian I know has encountered these outdated and unwarranted stereotypes but I'm more interested in the way lesbians create definitions for ourselves and the joyful way they actually create community and common ground with each other. One way this is done is through stereotypes that we make and reappropriate for ourselves. It's a language of shared cultural touchstones that only we are allowed to joke about. I present here a non-exhaustive list for your consideration:

- Moving in together after the first few dates (U-Hauling in the US)
- Dates that last for three days
- Getting a cat baby
- Getting a dog baby
- Sitting with your legs open
- Tool belts
- Being good at DIY in general
- Sensible footwear (e.g. Birkenstocks, hiking boots, Clarks shoes)
- Staying friends with your ex
- Dating your ex's ex
- Your exes dating each other
- Cutting your hair short after you come out
- Mullets, undercuts etc.
- 'Terrible' haircuts in general
- Being sporty

- Being outdoorsy
- Wearing baseball caps
- Denim
- Thumb rings
- Carabiners
- Not dressing for the male gaze
- Short masc/tall femme
- Matching on dating apps but being too scared to message first
- Fancying your straight friend
- Thinking your friend invited you to hang out but actually it's a date
- Not realising someone is flirting with you
- Being unable to make the first move
- Multiple orgasms
- Having short nails
- Strap-ons

It's an incomplete and ever-changing list based on my specific identity as a white Western woman – for other lesbians they will not resonate at all; some of them share stereotypes with bi, queer and trans people. Part of being a lesbian (or any queer person) is being able to play with these stereotypes, either to ham them up as an in-joke to others, or to tease straight people with them. There's a power play in excluding a group first who would exclude you. *We don't need you,* our in-jokes say, we have our own thing. It's a common joke online to reply 'are the straights okay?' to some outlandishly heterosexual thing like a gender reveal party or an article about why they hate their marriage. 'Are the straights okay?', like most jokes, flips the expected narrative. Gay people were once (and still are by some) seen as medically and socially deviant, very much 'not okay', and so this mock concern for 'the hets' inverts the assumed norm, implying that gayness or queerness is a superior way of being. Which of course it is (see, I just did it there).

Being a lesbian should be fun. I think these stereotypes we make for ourselves are a way to embrace this humour and create shared recognition of similar but different experiences. The internet has helped to amplify these stereotypes and ways of expressing lesbian identity so that what were once specific cultural codes become more globalised ways of signalling one's queerness. We'll look at this more later, but social media in particular has been instrumental at spreading micro-lesbian stereotypes, such as making earrings out of household objects or cutting a slit in your eyebrow. But we also risk erasing localised and global majority vernacular and idiolects if the default markers of lesbianism are seen as those created only by cis white lesbians. Likewise, the increased visibility of such lesbian identifiers, especially as fashion trends, means that they are more easily subsumed into other mainstream straight culture and lose their unique lesbian context. Just look at the price of Birkenstocks now.

As we moved into the era of Web 2.0 in the 2000s we finally see the first serialised lesbian-centred TV shows with *The L Word* in the US and the UK's *Lip Service*, and for many these became important cultural touchstones for lesbian identity. And while both titles gesture towards the word 'lesbian', neither of them outright say it. *The L Word* in particular played on this notion that it was still a taboo word. In 2001 *Buffy the Vampire Slayer* was a notable entry in mainstream telly when Willow, one of the main characters, kissed another woman with little fanfare. I don't think you can claim there's been a tidal wave of lesbian content since then, but there's certainly been a steady flow of more lesbians being represented in TV, film, music and magazines outside of lesbian-centric spaces. Lesbian Visibility Week in the UK was relaunched in 2020 by *Diva* publisher Linda Riley, and aims to spotlight lesbians and the specific issues that affect our community. It also highlights key lesbian public figures across entertainment, activism and sport. The waxing and waning obsession with lesbians in mainstream media continues even now: according to *Wired*, lesbians finally went 'viral' in 2019,[13] in case you had missed the memo. Every other year or so the media will declare we are a hot new 'trend' in fashion, film and music while we continue to simply be ourselves. Online, words such as 'sapphic' and 'wlw' (women loving women) have grown in popularity as 'softer'-sounding labels, especially for books, film and music. They also have the additional benefit of bypassing some social media's censorship of words like 'lesbian', 'queer' and 'dyke', and in including bi and pansexual women in their definitions.

So, while 'lesbian' as a word has gained much wider acceptance and usage over the years, what does that tell you about how I understand and use the word 'lesbian'? And how might that effect how you understand the word 'lesbian', and how *that* understanding hinges on a hundred other usages and understanding of lesbians. If it's a word you use to describe yourself, or someone you love. Of how many times you've heard it spoken in a whisper, or in shame, or as an insult?

How it's said on TV or in the news. How it's said by someone you know, or said by a stranger. Of some unspoken, hidden understanding of a word you didn't even know you held close to you until you had to think about it. There's much more to being a lesbian that just the word, although the word remains important.

These definitions, stereotypes and labels can point to a shared language of lesbianism that spans gender, race, class and age to some extent or another, but as we have seen it should be acknowledged they have the power to exclude also. Especially when lesbian in-jokes and language often encompass an unspoken and assumed whiteness. Queerness is often about 'in-groups' and 'out-groups', who's part of the clique and who's not. It's a tricky line to tread. Close groups create important bonds and friendships but they can and do exclude others.

For Black lesbians and lesbians of colour[14] this was (and is) an ongoing question, where often a lesbian group or club comes with an implicit 'white' prefix and thus a careful consideration of whether they will be welcome in that space or be the only person who looks like them at that event. Several Black volunteers at various lesbian lines noted that they wouldn't be sure if by volunteering they would find themselves the only Black lesbian on staff, or be required to answer only calls about race.

It should be noted that well into the '90s, 'Black' as a descriptor was still used in a political sense as a broader inclusive term. As the London Black Lesbian and Gay Centre stated, it included descendants and inhabitants from 'Africa, Asia, the

Pacific nations, Latin America and the original inhabitants of Australasia, North America and the islands of the Atlantic and Indian Ocean'. In *Lesbians Talk: Making Black Waves*, an anthology of essays and interviews with Black lesbians edited by Valerie Mason-John and Ann Khambatta, the authors spend a chapter discussing different labels within the Black lesbian community used in the '80s and '90s and the variety of attitudes to them. This speaks to the variety of individual definitions within Black and lesbian of colour spaces, and like all the labels and definitions I've discussed so far there is no one-size-fits-all approach, nor is there universal agreement on the nuances of each label.

For instance, Mason-John and Khambatta explain, of the Black lesbians they interviewed in the '90s, some much preferred the word 'dyke' over 'lesbian'. For Black dykes in particular this word has specific resonance, derived from the American word 'bulldike'. The origins of 'dyke' are not fully known, but one of the first cited uses appears around the 1930s in American blues songs. That 'dyke' came to be associated too with butch or more masculine presenting people, Mason-John and Khambatta posit, is because of the racist association white people have made between Black women and masculinity, noting that 'during American and British slavery, women of African descent were forced to do traditional male jobs and were rarely perceived as feminine by White people'.[15] For Black dykes, calling themselves such is a powerful reclamation of this history and gives them agency over their definition. Likewise, in the UK and the US 'stud' has historically been understood as a term used by butch Black lesbians for similar reasons.

For others they interviewed the word 'lesbian' was an

important part of a shared identity. As Femi Otitoju (another former Switchboard volunteer) notes in *Lesbians Talk: Making Black Waves*, 'lesbian' works for her as she first came out through the women's liberation movement (historically a white middle-class movement, unlike activist groups such as OWAAD, the Organisation of Women of African and Asian Descent): '"Lesbian" identifies me, because it is part of the European culture within which I was brought up, and which allowed me to find an identity.'[16] For Femi, calling herself a lesbian is a way to signal the culture and community she experienced at an important point in her life. As we've seen over and over, labels are incredibly personal to the individual.

All this is to acknowledge that language is not neutral. Western terms such as 'lesbian' and 'gay' risk erasing specific local terminology and identities and it should not be assumed that such labels can directly map onto global majority identities or culture.[17] For instance, because of the English, and originally Greek, origin of the words 'sapphic' and 'lesbian', some Black women in the '90s saw these as terms that did not apply to their experiences, unable to be detached from their white European beginnings. For some Black women 'Zami' was a preferred descriptor during this time and is still in use today. Mason-John and Khambatta identify 'Zami' as significant within Black communities during the '80s and '90s, especially for lesbians from, or descended from, African-Caribbean nations. Originally a Caribbean word from the island of Carriacou (perhaps derived from the French word for a female friend, *amie*), Audre Lorde made it popular in her hugely influential 1982 'biomythography', *Zami: A New Spelling of My Name*. She uses the word to describe women who love, and have sex with, other women.

This term soon gained popularity in the UK and inspired two Black lesbian conferences: Zami I and Zami II, with the first held in London in 1985 and then Birmingham in 1989. It was also the inspiration behind Zamimass, which began in the late 1980s as an alternative Christmas celebration for the Black lesbian community. Eventually it became a monthly event for Black lesbians to meet one another, host art events and organise collective action.[18] We can see the legacy of such events in UK, for example Black Pride, co-founded in 2005 by 'Lady Phyll' Phyllis Opoku-Gyimah and other Black lesbians – now the world's largest celebration of LGBTQI+ people of African, Asian, Caribbean, Latin American and Middle Eastern descent.

For some, 'Zami' was and is a useful term that allows for some fluidity of meaning, or that connects them with home. And its relative obscurity to both straight society and white lesbians meant it could be deployed in situations where outing yourself could be harmful but you wanted to signal to another that you were alike. Mason-John and Khambatta also note that 'Zami' had other connotations to some Black lesbians as a stereotype of women 'who walk around with African prints on, and say if you don't wear ethnic clothes you're not Black enough'.[19] This comment reveals the complex negotiations Black lesbians and lesbians of colour have to navigate between race and sexuality – a perception (from both white and non-white lesbians) that they have to perform their Blackness and their sexuality in a certain way to be accepted.

Rani Kawale, in her study of the performance of emotion work by lesbians and bisexual women in London, notes that for South Asian lesbians navigating their identities across white and non-white spaces had an emotional toll:

> [T]hey managed their identities to pass as 'British' or sufficiently westernised in most places and, if they visited them, as sufficiently 'South Asian' in South Asian spaces . . . it became apparent from the research that they experienced the emotional space of the scene as racialised subjects warranting the performance of emotion work in racially sexualised spaces within it.[20]

White lesbians, however, according to Kawale's research, never saw themselves or the all-white spaces they created as racialised, or the spaces they created as exclusionary. The implicit 'white' in front of the word 'lesbian' for them was never a problem and so they couldn't see it as such.

This is just one example of how digging into the word 'lesbian' reveals that as a catch-all term it will never be sufficient. The word 'lesbian' is never a neutral one and when it is deployed we must be aware of what silences and erasures we also create around it. Yet it is a word which still has great importance and relevance to many of us. The variety of responses and usages across lesbian culture, and the nuances of labels between Black lesbians, lesbians of colour, white lesbians, cis, intersex and trans lesbians show just how context dependent and personal labels are, and that unity over a defined meaning is never possible. This calls for an expansion in our meaning and understanding of the reality of lesbian lives today and should not be used to exclude or restrict others from that label.

Throughout history and today, there is no shortage of options for words to describe how you as a person move through the world: 'sapphic', 'dyke', 'butch', 'Zami', 'lezzer', 'invert', 'stud', 'gay', 'lesbian' or 'queer', and so many more.

You may use exclusively one or shift between them depending on context and company. They can be a single identity or a group term. Or like 'queer', they can also gesture towards ambiguity, a no-label label that shifts and changes. And then there are those who do not label themselves at all or aren't interested in making a label the sole defining feature of their personhood (of course no person is just one thing or just one word). That we have so many words available to us and the freedom not to choose any of them should also be celebrated. All words have a history, all words must wrestle with personal and collective definitions.

Speaking to Diana James about her time at Switchboard, and her experiences as its first intersex and trans lesbian volunteer, helped me to understand how the language we use about ourselves changes over time, and how deeply personal it can be. During our conversation she referred to herself as both a lesbian and a dyke. 'Dyke' being a word that was most often thrown at her as an insult in the street, along with stones, bottles and fists, as she described it to me. But she also spoke of how in recent years she had been made to feel unwelcome as a trans and intersex person in some lesbian and feminist circles. Because of this she had felt little solidarity or appeal in the word 'lesbian', despite being part of the lesbian and feminist movements for most of her life. However, when I caught up with Diana again a few years later she told me that her attitude towards the lesbian community had shifted again, and she felt many of the new lesbian events and spaces were now very explicit in their trans inclusivity. Diana asserted (and I agree) that the vast majority of lesbian and queer cis women welcome the inclusion of trans women in such spaces, but that before many didn't know how to speak up, or why it was so important to be loud in their support of trans lesbians. She now feels much more positively about the lesbian community which she felt had lost its cohesion, telling me that 'I have now more confidence in the power of dykes and lesbians to organise, I have no hesitation in going to events and feeling totally included.'

That someone could be made to feel unwelcome in a community that they long supported and were part of is a stark reminder that those who share our identity have the capacity also to cause harm, perhaps even more so as it comes from a place where we expect safety. I understand the need for separate lesbian spaces away from heterosexual society – I'm part of them myself – but when those spaces do not include all lesbians, what then? When we think about groups that form around shared identities to promote solidarity we must face the opposing question of whom we are keeping out, both explicitly and implicitly. When we say a group is for lesbians what exactly do we mean and who are we talking about?

Such inclusion is demonstrated not just in words but actions: in the creation and protection of such spaces for all lesbians to be welcomed. Yet the words we use remain important. During that conversation with Diana she had referred to me as a dyke, and although it's not a word I often claim for myself, I felt deeply honoured that she had bestowed on me the same label she used for herself. The same word she had fought so hard to use and reclaim. It was a moving, tangible example of how language can gesture towards a wider community.

Like many reclaimed words, 'dyke' has a certain spiky

taboo inherent in its use. Femi Otitoju said of it that '"dyke" for me is about being strong and difficult. I use it among men' – I can almost hear her laughing after that statement, it's intentionally joyful, provocative and funny – said for the benefit of other dykes.[21] Because one of the great benefits of being a dyke is that you get to forget what other people think about you, especially straight men. You get to speak dyke on dyke. Even now there is a shock value that remains, incantation-like, in its deployment. It's a word that dykes like me can say, but which in a straight mouth is at best misplaced, and at worst abusive. But being called a dyke by another dyke is an act of love. It offered me a reminder that as much as words and definitions can splinter us, they also form bridges across vastly different life experiences. Such connections offer an opportunity for understanding for others and ourselves.

Labels can and do serve a purpose, but we can also decide when that purpose no longer serves us. There is nothing wrong about finding those new words. We should be free to use as many or as little as it takes to find out who we are and how we want others to see us. The Lesbian Line worked as a name in the end for London Friend, not because it was perfect, but because it was fit for purpose. It helped people find the words and the other people they needed. Its aims – to be visibly, proudly, there for other lesbians – were, I believe, honest ones, despite their flaws.

For me, while I might slide between 'gay', 'queer', 'lesbian' and now sometimes 'dyke', it's 'lesbian' I always return to and reach for when talking about myself. It is the word which cleaves itself closest to me. Because for me that was the word I had to fight the hardest to say, not least against my own association with lesbians as someone, or something, who is wrong or bad. A description which still risks erasure or misunderstanding. That still, when I hear it said by a non-lezzer, makes me hold my breath for how I will be talked about. A word which is so often preceded by a hitch in the throat or said in a whisper in the mouths of others. Growing up it was most likely to be said under the breath as a joke – on telly, in the playground, around the dinner table. All this I had to work against to understand that 'lesbian' is not a dirty word. Taboo words hold power and I'm not willing to give it up to those that would force it back into a narrow definition of womanhood, femininity, biology or sex. The history of lesbians, the good and the bad, is what makes it important to me and worth continuing to define. Because definitions should free us, not hold us back.

26.1.98 – log by Gabby: *I do have some friends who have masculine sounding voices*

Gabby's been on the phone lines long enough now to get a good sense of how a call might go but this one throws her for a moment. The voice on the other end of the line is soft-spoken but has a masculine twinge to it – just something about it is a little off. But the caller's been talking for a while now and Gabby doesn't want to challenge her on it. She's usually pretty good at spotting the men who ring up for entirely different reasons and this call doesn't feel like that. Usually, abusive calls take a turn pretty quickly into personal questions about what lesbians get up to in bed and she isn't shy about putting the phone down on them when they get abusive. But this call isn't like that and so Gabby gives her the benefit of the doubt. The caller started by asking if this was the Lesbian Line and wanted information on Changes as she'd only just come out. She mentioned she'd watched a couple of 'blue movies' with lesbians in and that was what had made her think more and more she might be one. It's the only time the question of sex comes up. Gabby gives her the information she asks for because who is she to refuse her just because her voice is deeper than some of the women who call. She leaves a note asking the other phone workers if she did the right thing by not saying anything?

It's not just the definition of 'lesbian' that changes over time in the logbook, but womanhood too. Or rather the way the women address each other. Many have their own idiosyncratic forms of address. When I first read the logbook I wrote them all down like a detective sorting clues:

- *Dear Gals*
- *Dear Girls*
- *Dear Grryls*
- *Dear Wimmin*
- *Dear girlzzz*

Impossible to know, of course, if they were using such language ironically or sincerely. The use of 'woman' or 'girl' has a long history in feminist and linguistic theory. Often feminists fought against the use of 'girl', seeing it as patronising and infantile – what we might associate now with that strange breed of man who still insists on calling women 'fillies' or 'females' – a red flag if ever there was one. 'Grryls' and 'girlzzz' invokes this history and subverts it with its alternate guerrilla spelling. An influence, no doubt, of the riot grrrl movement underway at the time and which remains fashionable today.[22] The first formal writing programme I ever did, way back in 2014, invoked a similar aesthetic, was titled 'Write Like a Grrrl' (and run by *For Books' Sake*, a feminist and queer organisation that brings affordable writing classes to women and non-binary people across the UK, India and Russia).

Similarly, 'wimmin' has a radical feminist history, alongside 'womxn' and 'womyn', coined by the writing of Black feminists as a way to reclaim 'women' from patriarchal Western language. Pulling 'woman' away from its root of 'man' (the 'x' literally crossing out 'man'/'men') and as a way to signal a more inclusive definition of both womanhood, femininity and gender. Many people and activists still use these various spellings as a way to signpost inclusivity and reference the feminist principle they were built upon. Yet for others language and understanding has evolved, changing 'womyn' into a word which conjures the figure of white hippies and 'womyn's festivals', such as the Michigan Womyn's Music Festival in the US which notoriously excluded trans women. In popular culture these alternate spellings of 'women' now hold an ambiguous place – unclear if it's a genuine move towards inclusion, a satire of passé language, or as a subtle indication of transphobic thinking.[23] It has the potential to erase the marginalised genders it is (sometimes) setting out to include, such as non-binary or gender queer people, by not naming them specifically and making it unclear if they are welcome. Another reading might even argue that such a term harms trans women by not including them within the definition of 'woman' with a standard spelling. Of course, nothing is clear-cut; some trans women prefer 'womxn' as a way to explicitly show they are welcome and acknowledge the differences in their experience of womanhood compared to cis women. Whereas some cis women are uncomfortable with being included in the category of 'woman' without qualification as it comes with decades of assumptions and boundaries for how femininity and gender should be performed.

You see how quickly a question like 'why did they call it the Lesbian Line?' tangles itself in knots of definitions and unintended meanings. As far as I can tell from the logbook, the volunteers use their various spellings of 'women' and 'girls' affectionally to address the group and as a kind of shorthand to show that this is a logbook full of women, sure, but they're doing womanhood a little differently. Often its intended use is one for humour and solidarity.

To me one of the greatest gifts of being queer is that I am prompted to consider gender and my relationship to it. I say prompted because gender and sexuality are different, of course, but to be queer is to breach the lines of gender drawn arbitrarily in the sand by a heteropatriarchal society and so I think we all benefit from a moment of consideration when it comes to our assigned gender at birth. For many this consideration may take only moments: a simple confirmation that yes, their experience of their gender and the one society sees them as does align and that is that. For others, they might want to deconstruct this assumption a little further. I'm a woman who loves other women in a society which expects women to love men. What would it mean to define womanhood outside of these narrow parameters? What makes me a woman in that case? Feminism historically has also questioned these lines of womanhood and what it means to be a woman, as Sara Ahmed notes in *Living a Feminist Life*: 'to be engaged in the creation of a world for women is to transform what it means to be women'.[24] Lola Olufemi also echoes this statement, writing in *Feminism, Interrupted*:

> 'Woman' is a strategic coalition, an umbrella under which we gather in order to make political demands ... In a liberated future, it might not exist at all. It has no divine meaning absent of its function as a strategy; that does not mean we cannot feel, reckon with and grapple with our own private experiences of womanhood. For some, gender is an unshakeable truth and for others, it is always on the move. But a binary understanding of gender helps no one.[25]

They are both building on the work of Monique Wittig, who famously in 1992 (just before the beginning of the logbook) declared that 'lesbians are not women' since womanhood could only be understood within a heterosexual system.[26] And later Leslie Feinberg's *Transgender Warriors* when zie wrote, 'I think that if we define "woman" as a fixed entity, we will draw borders that would need to be policed. No matter what definition is used, many women who should be inside will be excluded.' Feinberg was presciently arguing for greater solidarity between trans people and women, seeing their shared struggles and political aims as key in creating safe space for all without invalidating the lived reality and oppressions for many women.[27] Likewise for Sara Ahmed, creating a world for women is to 'deviate from the category "women" when we move towards women';[28] i.e., to make a world for women without the prior heteropatriarchal hang-ups of womanhood, it makes sense we have to redo womanhood.

But as Feinberg warns, we must be careful as we work to remake what womanhood might look like, that we do not create further policing. I know butch women, for instance, who have to fight to be read as women because people assume different pronouns for them based on their outwardly masculine dress or short hair. When we allow womanhood to be so narrowly defined and controlled by patriarchal assumptions of what a woman looks like (feminine, thin, cis, able-bodied, white: designed for the male gaze), then it harms all women who do not fit this mould. I don't think we need to scrap everything about womanhood, but to widen its scope, to reimagine womanhood for those who wish to claim it. To point us towards liberation and happiness. We can continue to fight for issues which effect a larger proportion of women (issues surrounding sexual violence, access to healthcare and childcare and workers' rights, to name just a few) while still acknowledging where the boundaries of what it means to be a woman cease to become useful or where these fights overlap with trans, non-binary and intersex political struggles.

*

I find myself these days thinking of my gender more as a habit than an identity. A woman in name but perhaps not in practice? What does it mean to be a woman? What does it matter? Like being a lesbian it both matters hugely and not at all. For me, part of my queerness is being able to hold these two states together at once. For others it is being able to define themselves as a woman who loves other women. These two states do not need to contradict each other.

My body is often one of these sites of conflicting emotion. There are times when I want my body to convey who I am and there is always a gap between this and how others will read it. I think this is true for all of us, whatever it is we are trying to say with them: a body is a conversation – with yourself and with others. For disabled, racialised, trans and older women this is often an uneven conversation with a greater emphasis on how their body is read by others than on their own autonomy. Poet Joelle Taylor articulates this beautifully in her poem C+*nto,* which explores the body and its relation to butchness; in 'the body as backroom' she writes: 'not one of my friends was allowed to live in her body unaccompanied. always a lodger pacing the box room always a landlord collecting rent'.[29]

This complicated relationship to our bodies as queer women finds some overlap too in the work of trans writers. When the essayist Daniel M. Lavery wrote about wearing a chest binder (a tight-fitting garment worn under clothes to give the appearance of a flat chest) for the first time, he deftly captures this feeling, and one that resonated with me, of experiencing a body that at times can be unknowable even to yourself. He writes:

> There are things about living in a body in the world that feel inaccessible without quite being impossible; inaccessible in the sense that the gap between fantasy and reality is always present regardless of how one looks, inaccessible in that one often fears the extent, scope, and reach of one's own desires, inaccessible in the sense that learning more about what one may want does not necessarily translate into being any closer to getting it, or even asking for it, or that there will be anyone to ask it of, inaccessible in the sense that what one wants is not always consistent, recognisable, or even legible, to oneself, much less anyone else.[30]

I like Lavery's insistence that the body can do multiple things at once, that what you desire your body to communicate, whether that is in relation to gender or some other aspect of your understanding of how your body and your personhood might coalescence into a sense of self might not quite come off how you like, but that this only *feels* inaccessible and therefore not completely impossible. I think trans and cis people alike can relate to this feeling. Our bodies can do so much. And God loves a trier, right?

The writer and zine maker Darcy Leigh's prose poem/zine *boi tits* further extrapolates on this idea of a body that can be both wanted and sexy, and uncomfortable and embarrassing. In their prose poem they list the different ways 'boi tits' are both used by their owner and perceived by others. It's a sharp, funny poem ('boi tits are never "the girls", except when they are, because ownership, domination, men')[31] that explores the reality of having breasts as someone reconstructing how femininity and masculinity reside within their body. It teases the reader with the idea that there is any right answer to be found: 'boi tits are touched by cis lesbians and not touched by trans queers and neither are correct but both are lucky to have had the chance to get it wrong with boi tits'[32] or later:

> *boi tits are a thrill to reveal when sir'd*
> *boi tits are a secret to be kept when sir'd*[33]

The playfulness and defiance that Leigh embodies in the many different aspects of 'boi tits' is a reminder that gender dysphoria and gender nonconformity, while challenging, can sometimes be celebrated also. Or at least pushed back on. There's a profound truth in saying there's no right way to do this and you're going to get it wrong and other people will read you wrong and sometimes that will hurt and sometimes that will put the power in your hands. At least that's how I felt when I first read *boi tits*.

I'm just one dyke among many who feels apathetic about her boobs but I don't think getting rid of them would make me less of a woman unless I wanted it to (stop me if this is obvious) or that my ability to get pregnant is the sole defining feature of being a woman. Or that lesbians who want big breasts and babies and make-up and any other stereotypically feminine thing are less of a lesbian. Just as loving another woman doesn't make me a man.

Recently I went to a meeting for butches in which we got to talk about what being butch means to us. Everyone had a different way of defining it and a different way of expressing it. Some of the butches there identified as women (cis and trans), others were transmasculine or non-binary. But what united us was our sense of butchness. We were discovering and expressing aspects of masculinity and femininity in ways which made us feel most ourselves. I'm hardly on the vanguard here and I'm sure many people would look at me and simply see someone who dresses like a baggy teenage boy. I barely dip my toe into gender nonconformity with my barber-clippered hair and trousers-only dress code, yet it's enough sometimes to throw people off. Being a little butch makes me biased, but I would argue we're onto something here when it comes to finding ways to move through the world unconcerned with the gaze of cis straight men.

Other people do it differently – and more femme lesbians still have to work to combat the assumptions people make about them from both the queer community and straight society. When it comes to how I think about my own gender I owe much of it to the writing, lives and fashions of trans and cis thinkers alike. For me being butch is not about what clothes I choose to wear, or how I style my hair, or sitting with my legs open, hairy ankles poking out of my rolled up trousers. It's about being comfortable and feeling at home in myself. The rest follows from that. I cut my hair and stopped wearing dresses when I came out not because I was a lesbian now, but because it finally gave me the confidence to stop caring about how others thought I should look. It's not about rejecting femininity, although there is a rejection of how society would paint a very thin portrait of it, but about untangling notions of masculine and feminine from a gendered body and from the expectations of others.

This is the future that Jack Halberstam sees for butches and his concept of 'female masculinity', which he first defined back in 1998. In the new preface to the twentieth anniversary edition of *Female Masculinity,* Halberstam writes:

> Female masculinity is a term that describes simultaneously an evolving role; the shifting surface of girlhood and womanhood; a porous limit of gender variance; an alternative edge to manhood, and a historical trajectory that extends back beyond modern sexual and gender definitions . . . Female masculinity continues to apply pressure to hegemonic forms and even as it represents a seemingly old-fashioned form of queer identification, it may also hold the seeds of future genders.[34]

What Halberstam lays out here is that there *are* other possibilities for how we might choose to live; to redefine how we present ourselves and how others see us outside of traditional, limiting definitions of what a man or a woman is. And that female masculinity – in particular the ways that lesbians, trans men and butches throughout history have presented themselves – is a demonstration of how we might all live with a freer sense of gender, unmoored from the expectations of others and wider societal institutions.

When I look at our current climate of the over-policing of people's bodies, gender expression and the attempts to take away a person's agency over their own body, these hopes for the future feel more urgent than ever. We are living through a time when abortion rights are no longer secure, where gender-affirming care is being removed for young people, where NHS gender clinic referral times are creating a two-tiered system for those who cannot pay for private treatment, where gendered violence against women and trans people is either ignored or 'solved' with an increase in policing. Where we can no longer assume that teachers and educational institutions will protect trans children,[35] despite the evidence that acknowledging a child's gender identity is vital to their well-being and that such provisions are protected under the Equality Act.[36] Where the press seek to manufacture a cultural war between cis women and trans people, despite many of our oppressions coming from the same source.[37]

I know many women – straight, gay, trans and cis – who feel the pressure placed upon them to be feminine, to be a mother, to be thin, to be caring, to be young, to be quiet, to be in a relationship, as one which is unbearable. This is hardly a new idea. If it sounds like feminism to you, then . . . bingo! Womanhood is too broad a category for us all to ever agree on a single definition or a single way of 'doing' it. Nor should we – that's the patriarchy's game. It's a category I have to share with a small minority of women who think that they are being radical and 'feminist' by saying that gender is only about biology, who want to reduce women to their body parts and what they can or can't do. Who would seek to deny the existence of trans women and anyone doing gender differently to the way they want.[38] I disagree with this definition of womanhood (as do most people in the UK) but they remain a vocal minority who seek to limit what a woman can be. It's naive to think that the people trying to tell trans women they aren't women will stop there. As Travis Alabanza points out, when we define womanhood from a heteropatriarchal, ableist, colonial mindset, we harm all those who fall outside of this definition:

> What society views as a successful woman (and in extension femininity) itself is often based around proximity to whiteness, weight, ability and conformity to gender. The upholding of the gender binary and punishment of those outside of it, will not just harm non-binary people but everyone, relying as it does on conditional acceptance.[39]

A trans person's existence doesn't undermine, conflict with or harm my femininity, my masculinity, my personhood. Far from it.

Being a woman is complicated. And it's complicated for anyone who sits within the leaky boundary of 'woman'. So, get over it. It doesn't really matter, is what I'm saying; you do you. But actually, it matters a whole lot because sometimes gender is just between yourself and your mates and sometimes gender is something you have to reckon with strangers, with institutions and with the government. It matters that I'm a woman who loves other women in a world that still sees that as something strange. As lesbians we should recognise the truth and the solidarity to be gained by expanding the bounds of womanhood, not to erase what it means to be a man or a woman but to make is easier for people to be themselves. I want to talk about masculine and feminine qualities in a way that isn't defined by being a boy or a girl. We've tried that and it's only got us this far. Make it easier for people to have children or not have children, is what I'm saying. Make it easier for people to have access to housing and healthcare, is what I'm saying, to fair wages and secure employment. Make it easier for people to be who they want to be. Make it easier for us to live.

Becky Rang

VERY IMPORTANT –
IF BECI PHONES PLEASE TELL HER GABBY HAS MIȘLAID HER NUMBER AND WOULD SHE PHONE HER AT HOME – THANKS!

Dani, 7.6.95

Becky's calls punctuate the logbook and she is one of the few consistent repeat callers throughout the years. Becky is a lesbian of unknown age with an undisclosed disability, she sometimes uses a wheelchair when out and about and has regular carers who visit her at home, and she has to contend with other health issues during the period of her calls. Mostly she calls the Lesbian Line for a chat, despite having a number of friends she sees regularly, otherwise she calls to complain about her health, her living situation or the local council's inaptitude to provide her with the transport equipment she needs. At times she calls weekly but there are gaps of several months where it's unclear if she didn't call or no one recorded them. Becky's calls are often missing key context and can contain several different moods within a single log. Her calls taken together are a quite literal example of what the academic Ann Cvetkovich describes as an 'archive of feelings' – queer histories which are '[s]ubject to the idiosyncracies of the psyche and the logic of the unconscious, emotional experience and the memory of it demand and produce an unusual archive, one that frequently resists the coherence of narrative or that is fragmented and ostensibly arbitrary.'[1] This could equally describe Becky herself, prone as we all are to the inconsistencies of emotion, feeling and memory that make us human. In many ways it could just as well be speaking about the logbook as a whole, with its multiplicity of voices that bicker, celebrate and commiserate together to parse the feelings of the callers they record. This is true particularly when the phone workers are writing about themselves, but even more so for Becky, who is shaped not by herself but the words the phone workers use to describe her.

She is variously written about as:

29.10.94 *not in a good state*
22.11.94 *still in a bad way*
24.1.95 *sounded humorous and strong*
12.4.95 *really fed up*
16.4.95 *surprisingly cheerful under circumstances*
30.7.95 *Amazingly enough she didn't sound depressed though*
14.8.95 *bearing up*
18.8.95 *sounded good and although pissed off about things was v. humorous*
27.8.95 *sounded extremely pissed off understandably*

31.8.95	***sounded ok. Cheerful, chatty***
11.9.95	***despite all this, she seems to be coping as ever, determined as ever***
28.9.95	***swayed a bit in moods***
6.10.95	***finished positive***
13.10.95	***fed up***
?.12.95	***feeling pissed off and frustrated***
11.12.95	***feeling a lack of control in life***
8.1.96	***quite cheerful***
30.1.96	***v. depressed & can't get motivated & seemed a little more positive, or am I just hoping?***
8.2.96	***still won't accept it or give up***
2.9.96	***irritable and tired***
10.12.96	***positive***
28.2.97	***same old feisty Becky!***
24.3.97	***Calmer by end of call & chatty***

It's a kind of portrait in miniature, a collage of her shifting moods. She remains, as all of us do, in some sense unknowable. While Becky's calls are as close to a full picture of a person as I can get in the logs, that is still far from who she was as a 'real' person. This is evident even down to the spelling of her name, which the phone workers are unable to agree on. She is variously *Becky, Beci* or *Bekki* throughout her time calling the Lesbian Line. I suppose no one thought to ask.

The phone workers are keen to see her as a fighter, and for every *pissed off and frustrated* there are notes attesting to Becky's resilience and tenacity in spite of her mental and physical health difficulties. But I'm cautious of this narrative, knowing that abled-bodied people are quick to assign heroic fantasies onto disabled bodies. The logbook shows that there is no stable position for Becky and no one 'battle' that she must 'overcome'. Nor, of course, do the call logs tell the whole story. There are large chunks of time in the logs where I have no way of knowing how she was doing. The Becky in the logbook leads a complex, busy life and the calls record her successes and failures, the joys and the struggles. Hers is not a life that can be summed up in a few sentences. As no life should be.

29.10.93 – 24.3.97 – logged by various phone workers: *Becky rang again tonight*

29.10.93

It's been a while since Becky had to call the women at the line and when she does it's only because once again her social services counselling has fallen through and she needs someone to talk to. And since the council never pick up anyway why not call the Lesbian Line. There's a possibility the counselling might come back, but it means another round of assessments and waiting and Becky doesn't know if she has it in her right now for all the rigmarole it takes.

So, Becky tells Dani who's on the phones tonight, it might mean I'll be ringing more often. Becky likes Dani, she always has time to chat. Dani said maybe they could be a bit more long-term on the Lesbian Line for her as an exception if they can't get her a slot with the proper phone counsellors. She's careful not to get her hopes up for that sort of thing, but at least she knows the girls won't mind if she calls a little more. They'll muddle through together.

14.9.94

They get into a good routine. Becky calls at least once a month, sometimes twice. She's not too fussed whom she speaks to, but she has a few favourites. Sam or Clare are always happy to chat. They let her talk for an hour or more sometimes if it's a quiet night. Some of the other volunteers try to hurry her along, but Becky likes to take her time. She likes asking them questions as much as talking herself. It makes her feel less like a bother and more like they're having a proper chat. That and she's always been curious about other people (nosey, her mum used to say), but she likes to know what the women have been up to, what clubs are trendy now and any morsels of gossip she can tease out of them. She keeps them updated on the comings and goings at the flat (noisy, the carers are always late), what books she's got out of the library (never enough about lesbians), how things are going with the social services (slow, always so slow). Still no counselling of course, but she manages to get out to a few GEMMA meetings and some of the lesbian nights at London Friend. Life ticks along for Becky just fine for now.

6.10.94 – 18.11.24

Such a stupid way for it to happen, how many times has she got herself from her wheelchair to her bed without any issues? It was her leg that was the problem, it caught on the bottom of the bed, hooked onto it somehow and when she tried to jerk it free it tipped her straight out. She hit the ground pretty hard, enough that she's still feeling it in her lower back and shoulder when she rings the line a week later. No, she hasn't told her carers, it was early in the morning when it happened and she managed to drag herself back to her chair. They'd only fuss and then tell her she should have waited until they got there and she doesn't need telling off by two blokes young enough to be her nephews, thank you very much. Not that it stops her back from hurting, or her shoulder. Damn it's sore. Add to it that the new antidepressants she's on are making her feel sluggish and sick a lot of the time. It's Sam on the phone so Becky admits for once she's in a bit of a bad way at the moment. At least Sam understands and listens patiently, she knows all the ins and outs, which saves Becky from laboriously going over her whole medical history again. Sam lets her get her complaints out without saying stupid things like 'look on the bright side' or 'it'll be all right in the end'. None of that nonsense. Sam's far too practical. Instead she asks about her medication and if she's spoken to the doctor about them if they're causing so much trouble? If it was anyone but Sam saying that she'd probably tell them to piss off and of course she's thought of that, but Becky knows she means well and keeps quiet.

I'm just so tired and irritable all the time, Becky tells her. Maybe that's why I fell out my chair in the first place. The pills make me feel foggy but then at night I can't sleep, even more so now my back's playing up.

She's not afraid to tell Sam she's pretty fed up about the whole thing.

24.1.95

Over two months she's been waiting for her operation and they've only gone and cancelled it at the last minute. Maybe Becky ought to know better by now but she'd really psyched herself up for it. Got up early (not that she'd slept well) and packed her bags and booked the taxi. Her stomach was a knot of nerves and no breakfast allowed neither. And then the phone rang to tell her not to bother coming in as it wasn't going ahead. Some flimsy excuse about bed space and emergencies. Well, wasn't she an emergency? She's been on the waiting list for months. No way would she let the rude receptionist put the phone down on her without getting put through to the proper consultant to give him a bit of what-for. She wasn't going to be treated like this, not after months of waiting.

Actually, she tells Gabby on the phone line (she must be new, sweet thing, though), she's feeling quite invigorated by it all. You should have heard the doctor when I refused to be fobbed off without a new date, like a little lamb by the end of it, Becky says with a laugh. Some of these doctors get so used to people doing exactly what they say and never speaking their mind they're shocked when they do. She's been around the block a few times and then some to know that doctors aren't the be-all-and-end-all. Half the time Becky knows more than they do.

She's booked in for surgery early next week and if all goes well she won't be in for too long. Anyway, enough of that, Becky says, suddenly wanting to talk about anyone but herself. So tell me about you, Gabby, Becky says, how do you like working on the phone line?

4.2.95 – 21.3.95

Nothing much changes and a few months go by. Becky calls the line now and then but she tries not to take up too much of their time. Not when she doesn't have much to say. The operation is delayed by a month and then delayed again, and again. She tells the girls that fixing her back has become an 'if' rather than a 'when'. No 'if' about getting pissed off, though, that's already there. Still, she keeps herself busy, by the end of the calls she usually feels a little better.

12.4.95

Well that was one way to get her operation moved up. She calls the line after she's been in hospital almost two weeks and still they haven't told her much of anything. The pain finally became unbearable, big spasms that left her gasping. One of her carers came and saw the state she was in and rang for an ambulance.

By luck, it's Gabby who picks up the phone again tonight and Becky only talks for fifteen minutes or so, she doesn't want to keep her long and she's feeling rather tired. The doctors make her tired. All this waiting is making her tired. No one, it seems, can tell her what's actually wrong or how long she might have to be here for. All this time waiting to get sorted and now all she wants is be home. And the ward! How anyone gets any sleep in hospital is beyond her, all the comings and goings. There's a Mrs Anderson three beds down who screeches in the night at the first pinch of pain. Not to mention the nurses doing their rounds every hour checking for who knows what in who knows where. And not a single good-looking nurse among them either! Not even the men – at this point she's getting desperate.

Gabby doesn't have much to say (bless her) but she's a good listener, she ums and ahhs in all the right places and knows when to ask how she's *really* feeling. Gabby must have heard it in her voice. She tells Becky about the other Lesbian Line, apparently the other London one is now open five nights a week so she could try them if she still needs someone to talk to when their line is closed. Becky isn't sure if it's a tactic to get her to call less or if Gabby is genuinely trying to help, so she just says thank you and gets off the phone as soon as she can without sounding rude.

16.4.95

A week later and she's finally home. The pain is still there, sharp stabbing pokers up her back, but what's new? she jokes to Cora on the phone. She's not her favourite volunteer truth be told, she can't help feeling like Cora is waiting for her to say something more interesting or hang up the phone. The useless doctors still don't know what's causing the ongoing pain but she's not going to let it get her down. Note even Cora will stop her – she's got so many new updates to share. It all started with an absolute disaster of a call to the other Lesbian Line that Gabby suggested. Well, she's never doing that again! What a waste of time, honestly the woman on the phone sounded like she was near death or dying! And no one wants to go on about their troubles to someone you're worried is going to croak at any second. Becky was barely on the phone for ten minutes talking to her, sure at any moment she'd hear a gasp and a thud and that would be that. Quite the poor old dyke. And here Becky was thinking that the London Lesbian Line was where all the hip young women went. Far from it! She won't be calling them again, she tells Cora quite firmly, even if they are open five nights a week.

Cora asks her about her van and Becky is impressed she remembered. She's still waiting on the council, of course, they'd promised it months ago. The bastards. She's rung them nearly every week and every week they say it's coming and they just have to check the MOT and her accessibility needs, blah, blah, blah. She's used to the council flimflam now. She can spot the pencil pushers from the ones who actually have half an idea what they are talking about. It's not going to stop her going to Pride, Becky tells Cora, either way she'll get herself there. If the council actually pulls their finger out and gets the van to her next month it'll be plain sailing, but she won't hold her breath.

15.6.95

Pride is round the corner and still no van, Becky tells a sympathetic April on the phone. But whatever happens she's going. She's already made up her mind. It's been too dull and painful a year not to go and have her bit of fun. There's supposed to be disabled access along the route if only she can find it beforehand. Becky's sure if her van doesn't come through the volunteers at the line will figure something out for her, right, April. She doesn't phrase it as a question exactly and she knows April's too polite to turn her down, saying that she'll call if she gets stuck. Becky rings off with a sense of triumph under her belt. Pride '95, here she comes.

One of the first things I find on the 1995 London Lesbian and Gay Pride is a YouTube compilation of the concert held at Victoria Park in Hackney. It's a reel of '90s hits from D:Ream singing 'Things Can Only Get Better' only a year after it was a number-one hit, followed by Erasure's 'A Little Respect'. There's Chaka Khan belting out 'Ain't Nobody' and Dead or Alive grooving to 'You Spin Me Round', Pete Burns glorious with a black fringe, heavy lip liner and fishnets commanding the stage. There's a set from Paul O'Grady, or rather Lily Savage, dragged up and familiar to me from *Blankety Blank*. The crowd is jammed in together, mostly white gay men bouncing to the beat. Rainbow flags pop up now and then. The few comments below the clip predictably assert the '90s Prides were the best ones and marvel at what is without doubt a stunning line-up. I'm not sure where Becky would be in the crowd – or even if they had wheelchair access for outdoor concerts like this in 1995. Perhaps she wouldn't have stuck around for it anyway, maybe the march was what she was really there for. The logo that year is made of overlapping rainbow ribbons which form the shape of a heart.

I keep looking out for Becky until, scrolling Instagram one day I come across an image that snaps me out of my internet-numbed brain. It's a picture of a woman in a motorised wheelchair with a breathing tube at a Pride march proudly displaying a sign secured behind her back, on which there is a pink triangle with a stick figure of a wheelchair user drawn over the top. Above this written in black paint is the phrase 'Trached Dykes Eat Pussy Without Comin' up For Air!'[2] This could be Becky! It's probably not Becky, but what if this was Becky . . . The look of glee on the woman's face feels very Becky-like. There's no source but how many references to 'Trached Dykes Eat Pussy Without Comin' up For Air!' can there be on the internet and so off I go to look for her.

It takes some working backwards to find the source of the image on @h_e_r_s_t_o_r_y's feed (since deleted) and further googling lands me on a Tumblr page that references a possible source. It confirms what I knew would be the case: this is not Becky. The time period is right but not the location. This is in fact an image of Connie Panzarino, who is, as Alison Kafer described her in *Feminist, Queer, Crip*:

> [A] long time disability activist and out lesbian, [she] would attach this sign ['Trached Dykes Eat Pussy Without Comin' up For Air'] to her wheelchair during Pride marches in Boston in the early 1990s. Shockingly explicit, her sign refuses to case technology as cold, distancing or disembodied/disembodying presenting it instead as a source and site of embodied pleasure.[3]

Kafer goes on to describe this sign as a kind of 'blasphemous humour borne of community', which works to recentre pleasure and value in the disabled body. I think Becky would have appreciated the radical humour in Connie's sign. So often able-bodied people forget that disabled people are perfectly capable of leading full lives, including sex and relationships, and from reading between the lines in the logs Becky went on dates and met plenty of women. Her logs show the reality and the difficulties disabled people faced (and continue to face) to participate in gay and lesbian events, but signs like Connie's remind us that the joy, fun and messiness of queer love and sex is as much a reality for disabled lesbians as it is for anyone. Yet it also comes with other considerations and hurdles, usually because accommodations have not been made, or by limited perceptions of what life with a disability is like. This is obvious but is easily forgotten. I can't help but wonder what Becky at Pride looked like and what her own sign might have said. Did she see herself as a disabled lesbian activist or was she just there trying to have a good time and catch up with her friends? Whatever the reason for her going to Pride was I'm glad she was there.

30.7.95

It's over a month later when Becky calls the line again. She's on the phone constantly during that time just not to the Lesbian Line. She calls her GP to see if there's any news from the hospital. She calls the council about her van which is now over ten weeks late and counting. She calls the housing association about the leak in her flat. Nothing gets done. She hardly talks to anyone else. Susan who used to pick her up and take her to her groups can't any more. The days are starting to blend into one another. It's like she's dropped off the face of the earth. Out of sight, out of mind.

On bad days when the pain is unbearable and

she feels especially alone she wants to phone up her supposed friends who haven't been round in ages and give them a rollicking. She keeps herself busy, at least, the library continues its drop-off service and one of her new carers brings her pretty decent gossip. When she does call the line again, it's Cora who answers. Becky wishes she could chat to someone who didn't only talk to her because she's disabled. It would be nice to talk about other things for a change. It's been too long since she spoke to one of her actual friends. Cora gives her the usual spiel about the line and she can talk about anything, they're here to listen etc. etc. And Becky honestly appreciates the effort and it does cheer her up, but she does wonder if she didn't have to would Cora really want to listen to her prattle on?

14.8.95

Ah now here's something she can get her teeth into. She's on a call with Nise, updating her on the van (still no joy) and the horrible rash that she picked up last week that has her sweating like mad, when Nise mentions another one of their callers and asks Becky if she might be up for helping. They're trying to find audio tapes to send to her as she's blind and wondered if Becky, keen reader and listener to audio tapes that she is, knew of anyone who might help? She jumps at the chance to be useful and reels off a list of tapes she's managed to check out from the library: a few feminist ones and even one or two about lesbians. She also remembers that at the beginning of each tape for the *Pink Paper* they say a man's name and phone number that you can contact for more information. She doesn't have the number to hand but promises Nise she'll relisten to a tape and then call back with his number to pass on.

She quite enjoys their chat after that, almost forgetting the growing list of grievances that made her call in the first place. She tells Nise about a new book she'd just started called *Curious Wine* about a woman who thinks she's straight but falls in love with another woman who's staying in the same holiday home as her. Apparently, it came out years ago in the US but it's only just made it over here, Becky remembers hearing about it at the time and so it was a bit of luck to see it pop up in her library. Nise has read it too. Sam had bought a copy from Silver Moon and it had gone round the Lesbian Line volunteers like wildfire. Anything that juicy always did. They discuss the author for a while, American, she is, but Becky won't hold that against her. Nise wonders aloud if she is a lesbian and Becky replies that she has to be to write sex like that. Nise snorts down the phone. It feels good to make Nise laugh. She rings off with a promise to call back soon with the man's number from the *Pink Paper*.

18.8.95

Becky calls again next week with the number for a visually impaired gay group she read about and asks Gabby to let her know if there's anything else she can do to help. She quite enjoyed herself ringing round on someone else's behalf for once. If it's one thing that Becky is good at, it's talking on the phone.

27.8.95

Becky tells herself she won't get angry but by the end she's almost yelling at poor Zeenat. It was the van that got her going, still nothing from the council but somehow that got her onto her friend who's going through a bad break-up which Becky could have told her from the start was going to end in tears. Her friend calls up to earbash her about how utterly heartbroken she is and how she'll be alone forever. Becky wants to tell her, well, welcome to my world. She's not been out for weeks and there's not exactly a line of women knocking down her door right now.

It was lucky that Becky got her off the phone when she did because the consultant rang after to say that he might be able to bring forward some of the treatment she's been waiting for on her back. It's still not right and she's in almost constant pain. Now if she could only get that damn dog next door to stop barking she could get some rest. Becky's always been more of a cat person, far more independent. Zeenat's a good sport and says she'd be extremely pissed off too about the dogs and the van and all that. Becky knew she always liked Zeenat, she likes a woman that isn't afraid to swear.

3.9.95

The van is finally ready but of course now it's here there's already something wrong with it. Becky's had to send it back to the council so they can put in a new steering unit. She has a good chat with Joseline, updating her on the neighbours who for now at least are quieter, and the latest library book she's listening to. She's out and about again which is good, Susan's car is back and up and running so she doesn't mind driving her places while the van gets sorted. Even had a nice chat with a woman at bar the other night after LAFS, we'll see how it goes . . . She's starting an anger management course as well, someone at GEMMA suggested it and Becky hopes it'll help her cope with her carers better and who knows, maybe one day she'll be able to help teach it. Although Becky doesn't mind telling Joseline that if her carers weren't so careless then she wouldn't have to get so angry at them. One of the new ones wrenched her leg trying to help her put on her shoes and she could have screamed. But that's life, Becky tells Joseline, not much I can do but get on with it.

29.12.95

Becky hates the nothingness between Christmas and New Year. She calls the Lesbian Line to find out what is on at the next LAFS but Zeenat doesn't have any information. She tells Becky she'll leave a note in the LAFS pigeonhole to ask them and that the other volunteers can keep an eye out so they can let her know next time she calls. More waiting then.

13.1.96

It's not until January that she manages to summon the energy to call the Lesbian Line again. Because it's Sam who picks up the phone she confides in her that she's been taking sleeping pills to get through the day. They feel blank and empty. The pills make her groggy and unable to sleep at night. Becky knows without Sam saying anything that she needs to stop taking them. Christmas means most of her groups shut down and so she's easily forgotten. Not that she could have gone to any of them because the van repair still hasn't come through and of course the garages were all shut over the bank holidays. She's got a lingering cough from the nasty flu she picked up after New Year's Eve. Must have been from one of the carers as she's hardly been out and when she has, she's made sure to wrap up warm. They're not supposed to come to work if they're sick, so they don't spread it round. But then they don't get proper sick pay so she can't blame them, really. Becky doesn't often wish her life were different but on days like these she feels quite badly the lack of control. She wishes she could just pop to the shops whenever she wants without it having to be a twelve-step operation. Or at least not have to have her life be organised around her schedule of medication and visits by the carers and calls to the council. Now that her friend is over her heartbreak she's stopped calling and Becky hasn't spoken to anyone properly since. Sam tells her they are here to support her as much as she needs.

19.1.96

The van has a flat battery now which Becky has decided she finds funny rather than annoying. Maybe the anger management course really did help? They gave her some ridiculous breathing exercises to do and to pause and 'imagine a happier future' which Becky did try. Anyway, Becky tells April, that's not why I've rung. She's after the details of a gay mental health group that she's heard about and wants to try but she's not sure if they have an accessible entrance. April doesn't have their number to hand but says she'll make a note in case someone else knows about it.

8.2.96

Well, 'imagining a happier future' was a complete waste of time. She almost didn't call and had actually put it off several times. Why bother? She can't bring herself to care about anything. She didn't go to the gay mental health group in the end, they offered to pick her up but when she thought about having to go through the whole introducing yourself again and talking about herself she found she couldn't be bothered. Anyway, she's been having these spasms in her hands lately and even holding the phone is a struggle. She's in so much pain most days she can't think straight. It's a bad joke and Sam's laugh down the phone is probably just her being kind. She can't get into any of her books and her antidepressants seemed to have stopped working, or she's got used to them or something. Knowing her luck it won't be long until she ends up like a fucking vegetable, at which point it's all over. Sam stays on the phone with her for over an hour letting her get it all out and then suggests perhaps they can see about her going back to LAFS? Set a few goals, is how the ever-practical Sam puts it. I'm sure the girls would love to see you, Sam adds. Becky doesn't have it in her to argue with Sam today and so she agrees. By the end of the call she's even telling Sam that she's possibly thinking about a humanistic counsellor (she never trusted those Freudian types) and maybe that would be good for her. She needs a change of perspective. Saying it out loud makes Becky believe it could be true.

18.3.96

Becky gets hold of Heather just before her shifts ends so she doesn't want to keep her long. She keeps it short but lets her know she's off the sleeping pills now. They weren't doing her any good and she was worried about getting addicted. Of course, now she's off them and having a bad time with withdrawal symptoms – still no sleep!

2.9.96

It's a long while before Becky calls back, but Heather is still there and she has more time to chat tonight. For which Becky is glad as she's had a rough time of it. Her thyroid's not right and she thinks it's making her tired and irritable. She's fully off the sleeping pills, at least. But her latest carer is a right arse ache. Every time Becky mentions LAFS or GEMMA he frowns and says he can't understand why she needs to go to any of her gay groups (as he calls them). In the end she just yelled the word 'LESBIAN' and hoped it would shut him up. She asks Heather's advice about putting an ad in the *Pink Paper* or in one of the local papers to meet someone. Not a girlfriend, Becky says, although she wouldn't mind that, but just someone new to chat with and go to things together.

10.12.96

Somehow, it's almost Christmas again. Time flies and Becky's been so busy but Heather is still there, ready to take her call and listen to her. Becky tells her about an old friend she bumped into last week at a bar. She'd moved out of London so she hadn't seen her in forever. They'd got on so well, like no time had passed – they've made plans to see each other again, Becky might even go down to Margate to visit her. It's not so far and it would be nice to see the sea. She even offered to put her up for the night and save Becky the drive back home. Knowing her, the van would break down anyway so it might be a good idea, don't you think, Heather, to stay over . . . ?

28.2.97

It's well into 1997 before Becky calls again. She was in hospital for a while and then she lost track of time, she tells Sam she's sorry she's been so out of touch. Maybe Sam didn't care, but Becky's missed them all. The hand spasms got worse over Christmas and she was having trouble again with her stomach. Her doctor was worried about her losing too much weight and so off she went to hospital for another round of check-ups and endless blood tests and scans. She's lost the feeling in one of her hands, and Sam murmurs her sympathy. And so Becky says, at least it's not her favourite one, because sometimes a joke is easier than the truth.

The main thing is that she's home now and she's got loads to sort out. She's already rung the council about adapting her bathroom finally so it's a proper wet room, and to see about getting the van up to scratch so she can drive it with one hand if she needs to. She's not losing her independence now. She asked around in the hospital and there's a steering wheel gadget she can get installed that'll let her turn the wipers and indicators off. Becky's got it all planned out. She'll be back at LAFS in no time, she tells Sam.

24.3.97

She's glad to be out of hospital finally, but now she's home again she's got the carers to contend with. It's a trial to be surrounded by so much straight-ness, Becky tells Sam. All they talk about is their family, always going on about their husbands or boyfriends, or worse, their kids. She usually tells them she's a lesbian who hates men just to see what they'll say, to shock them a little. Maybe it's mean to say but she wants them to know she's not like them. It's nothing she hasn't dealt with before and she knows she'll break the new ones in, but it does get frustrating. They're quite happy for her to be disabled and talk about that, but the second she mentions an ex-girlfriend or one of her groups she can see their jaws clench up. Or their arses. Sam says that sometimes you can't change the situation you're in, but you can change how you deal with it. Becky's heard it before and it's sounds close to hippy bullshit, but she's promises Sam she'll try, I'm not so angry, though, at least? Becky laughs, she does feel calmer after talking to the women on the line. She rings off as she's waiting for a friend to call.

That's the last call from Becky that I know of.

In a 1994 copy of *Bad Attitude* magazine, a left-leaning feminist and lesbian-inclusive magazine that ran throughout the '90s, I find an article from a disabled lesbian credited only as Aspen. Written around the summer before Becky's first recorded call in the logbook, the article is titled 'Don't expect me to put up with your shit'. I can't help but feel Becky would approve. It opens with a list of the ways that lesbians make spaces and events inaccessible to disabled lesbians: the lack of building access, workshops without sign language interpretation, events held in the evenings or venues changed at the last moment where accessibility requirements are unknown.

Access and sharing of access information was one of the key aims for the group GEMMA, which is mentioned several times in the logbook, both in the logs about Becky and about Carol, the blind lesbian whom Becky helps out and who is another regular caller to the Lesbian Line. Founded in 1976 and still running today, GEMMA aims to provide a space for lesbians with and without disabilities to meet and befriend one another. They wanted to create a network for disabled lesbians through facilitating penfriends as well as in-person groups and meet-ups like the ones Becky went to.[4] It also produced the *Disabled Gays Guide* in 1985 which was instrumental in informing disabled lesbians about available accessibility provisions, as well as encouraging organisations and events to add access information to event listings and flyers.[5]

Disability activism wasn't just about access rights, however, as Aspen goes on to explain. It's also about the way that other lesbians speak to her and the questions which patronise or offer unhelpful and unsolicited advice. I think of the phone workers who take Becky's phone calls and want to believe for themselves that Becky is getting better when Aspen writes, 'One lesbian asked how I was and accused me of having a negative attitude when I told her.'[6] She writes of lesbians who wish to 'catch us out' and see their disability as something they are 'putting on' when, for instance, they are able to do a physical activity that they might not always be able to do, or are having a 'good day' mentally. It's a double-edged sword; if a disabled person appears too well or can mask their current state of being they are seen as fraudulent, but if they are truthful about their state of mind or condition they are accused of being too 'negative'. Aspen writes, 'They [able-bodied lesbians] have no way of knowing what preparation or after payment is exacted for attending a lesbian event.'[7] This sentiment, that disabled lesbians pay the price for an evening of fun, or must mentally and physically prepare themselves before participation in an activity that non-disabled lesbians wouldn't think twice about, is one which I have heard before. I have heard it, almost verbatim, from my disabled lesbian friends. Aspen writes of the pressure by non-disabled people to make herself appear well for their benefit, to be a productive member of the lesbian community. She writes tellingly that such behaviour is 'not living, it's barely existing'.

Aspen, like Becky, is not looking for pity or advice on how to live her life, she is looking for real tangible help on her own terms, not what people assume she needs. She wants lesbians to stop patronising her partner and thinking she is perfect for 'putting up with her'. She writes of her close lesbian friends who understand what she needs, who have been there for her to take her to hospital, to help out with her garden, to host a party in the daytime so that she can attend. The most lesbian detail of these adjustments they make (that I can't help smiling at) is when Aspen writes of the lesbians who 'have stopped burning incense' around her on account of her asthma. As Aspen convincingly shows, access to her community is both a social and political right and she wants non-disabled lesbians to be just as dedicated to fighting for inclusive spaces as disabled lesbians. Reading through the article, the only ground made in the years since it was written is that smoking is now banned indoors, but everything else: the lack of access, sign language interpretation, the stigma towards invisible disabilities, inappropriate and unhelpful questions are all common today both in the lesbian community and wider society. Aspen ends the piece calling for further 'change and more thought', pointing out that for non-disabled lesbians there may well come a time when they too will need a world that is safer and more accessible for them. It's shameful that Aspen has to appeal to able-bodied people's selfishness when it comes to improving life for others, and that disabled lesbians are forced into this role of activist whether they like it or not simply because otherwise much of their queer community is rendered inaccessible.

When I came out it was at a similar time to another friend who had recently left a twelve-year relationship having realised she was queer. We began going on dates at the same time but our experiences were extremely different. My friend is chronically ill and disabled and while we both had to put up with a string of terrible dates (including at one point accidentally the *same* terrible date), her encounters often came with an extra slice of ableism. One date expressed surprise that she brought her walking stick to her date; several people asked inappropriate and invasive questions as their openers over OkCupid. One even having the gall to ask her, 'how disabled are you?'[8] like there was a limit to how much 'disability' she was willing to put up with. My friend felt let down by her queer community, and rightly so. There was a failure to see her as a complex person with intersecting identities and needs, she was both patronised, desexualised and over-sexualised by non-disabled queer people. As the journalist Hannah Shewan Stevens writes:

> To better represent and include disabled queer people, our community needs people to fight for our inclusion. We need allies to listen to us and ensure that our lives are spotlighted too, and not just at Pride events. Disabled LGBTQ+ lives should be celebrated every day of the week, so please don't forget about us. We're here and we're queer too.[9]

Becky's calls in the logbook speak to this sense of exclusion. She is always having to stake her place in the lesbian community and ensure that she is not pigeonholed into subsections of her identity. Becky's last call in the logbook ends with her final complaint about her relentlessly heterosexual carers. She seems to take on the chin their refusal to see her as a lesbian and always having to contend with their 'straightness', but I get a sense from the log that it also wears her down.

There's isn't another entry about her before the logbook ends in July 1998. I have no way of knowing what happened next. It's possible she never rang the line again, but somehow I doubt that. All I know is that on the last call in the logbook she is described as calm and chatty. What happens after is a mystery. Did she go back to Pride? Did she find some new friends, a girlfriend? Did she continue to call the Lesbian Line? The three or so years of Becky's life I can half see and speculate about in the logbook are, despite her circumstances, ordinary ones, lived through circumstances that work to make her life extraordinary and at times difficult. Her life could be, like all of ours, frustrating, harder than it needed to be and lonely, but it also contained friendship, love, humour and a good heap of books. She was clearly someone who enjoyed joining in and helping others, a sociable sort despite the list of grievances she had for friends and neighbours. She found friendship in the phone workers too and they filled a gap that the government allowed to widen with its abrupt withdrawal of support and endless delays. The Lesbian Line provided another way for Becky to access her community and the resources that she needed. Here was a group of lesbians that, when the lines were open, were (for the most part) happy to chat to her for an hour or so. It was an outlet for her complaints and a space to bring her back to herself. It gave her the means to speak to people who, unlike her carers, saw her for who she was and offered a strut of support. I can only hope that she had many others; it would seem that she did. Perhaps there are other logbooks filled with entries about Becky or perhaps that really was the last time she called. All I know is the rest of the logs don't feel the same without her.

You Can't Choose Your Family (Except You Can)

In those early days when I was out to only a few people my queer friends became invaluable. In this space I had temporarily created between myself and my family, I built around me a small circle of queer women: some newly out like me, all of us around the same age. They gave me that sense of community at a time when I needed it most. This is what some people call a 'chosen family' – a group of friends that LGBTQ+ people often build around themselves when their own family has rejected them or forced them to hide their true selves. While I was still close to my family I couldn't deny that I was hiding a part of myself from them until I was ready.

But being around my queer friends allowed me to relax into myself. We went to club nights in South-East London pubs that for one night were transformed into tiny queer oases of pop songs, sweaty dance moves and gentle flirtations. I learnt the awkwardness of rejecting a friend's advances and how your first crush can dissipate without you even realising. I learnt how to joke about wearing Birkenstocks, ex-girlfriends dating other ex-girlfriends, and moving in after the first date. Learning this lesbian vernacular, this new lesbian way of being, was a validation of an identity I was still only just beginning to understand.

I found my queer community online too and used it as a space to 'try out' my tentative lesbian self on Twitter and Tumblr. I tweaked my performance of the person I presented online to one that was a littler gayer; never explicit, but coded to those who would know. I chose spaces online away from close friends and family that knew me in 'real' life. It was a process of learning to exist in relation to a parallel set of selves. Looking back on it now, I used those online worlds in the same way that the closeted women who rang the Lesbian Line did: as a way to interact with other lesbians, to feel a connection to this new way of thinking of myself. It was a way to find a community without exposing myself before I was ready. Grown up and away from home with a supportive group of friends, I had the time and space I needed. Not everyone was so fortunate. Fear of family rejection casts a long shadow in the logbook.

11.5.95 – log by Hannah: ***it quite upset me***

She found the number on the back of a magazine shoved in her daughter's bedside drawer, the one where she keeps her diary – which she would never read, but now she wishes she had. It might have saved her all this upset and anger, could have stopped her daughter from running off like she did and leaving her to pick up the pieces like always. The woman who answers the phone is one of them as well, of course, and she really lets her have it. What is it with these women? If they can even call themselves that. She doesn't care what they do behind closed doors but why do they have to shove it in everyone's faces? Disgusting is what it is. Like that ugly thing who took her daughter away from her.

She's never liked short hair on a woman. She looked like a man, acting like it too from the way she stood outside their house beside the car while her daughter grabbed her things. Well, she's glad to see the back of her, glad she told her never to come back to her house, not while she was with that queer.

She doesn't even realise she's shouting down the phone or that the other woman is trying to talk to her – something about understanding – it doesn't matter anyway, she's done listening. It's not just that her daughter let herself be led astray, although she thought she was better than that, it's that she lied to her for so long. Her daughter doesn't understand how hard this has been for her. She thought she'd raised her right even after her husband left them. Maybe that's where she got it from, this running away and ruining things. Well, good riddance. She doesn't want her anywhere near her home. Bad enough that thing showed up outside the house with her ugly car and her ugly haircut for all the neighbours to see. Disgusting, ugly thing.

She puts the phone down still shaking, she doesn't like raising her voice and in the quiet of the house her anger is left ringing in her ears. The knot in her stomach is as tight as ever. She can't believe she told a stranger all that and vows to herself that she won't speak of it again, not to anyone. Better to forget she ever had a daughter.

While not every parent reacted as strongly to their child coming out as this mother did, doing so for many lesbians in the logbook still risked rejection from their family and expulsion from their home. For others they received a shrug and an acknowledgment that they'd always had their suspicions, and this didn't change anything. Even for my generation and those younger than me, acceptance is not a given. This was never more evident than during the Covid-19 pandemic when so many young LGBTQ+ people were suddenly confined to their homes away from their queer families or a support network. One study by UCL and Sussex University found that during the 2020 UK lockdown the greatest impact to queer people's mental health and well-being was felt by those forced to live with homophobic family members or flatmates with little outlets for expressing their gender identity or sexuality.[1] For many queer people home is not a guaranteed place of safety, with nearly 10 per cent of the respondents to the study saying they felt unsafe in their homes.[2]

Some people will never come out to their family – for some this is a necessary choice that means they can maintain connection to family and culture (despite having to hide a part of themselves) and may not be seen as a negative, while for others it's to ensure their own safety. Rates of homelessness are disproportionally higher among LGBTQ+ people and over three-quarters of LGBTQ+ youth cite coming out or being outed, or a hostile living environment (typically their family home), as their reason for being made homeless.[3] For queer people of colour in particular, especially first- and second-generation children of immigrant parents, home can be a complex state where their queerness, culture and religious beliefs can collide or obscure one another. A report by akt (formerly the Albert Kennedy Trust) on youth LGBTQ+ homelessness found that people of colour were more likely than white respondents to fear that expressing their LGBTQ+ identity to their family would lead to their eviction, and felt less supported by siblings and extended family members.[4] Overall, for all LGBTQ+ homeless youth surveyed, the two highest factors that contributed to a lack of support were their family's lack of awareness of issues that affect the LGBTQ+ community, or their family's interpretation of their faith.[5]

It was rare for parents to call the Lesbian Line but on occasion it did happen. Some sought advice for their newly out child, but unfortunately others were looking for somewhere to direct their homophobic anger. Undoubtedly these calls were upsetting for the volunteers to receive. After one such abusive call, one phone worker notes that she 'hopes no one else gets her'. There was no official counselling policy for the volunteers themselves and they mostly relied on support from each other to get though the hard calls. They would often discuss tactics for dealing with such calls at their regular phone worker meetings.

Much more common were calls from lesbians from within the home doing so in secret, either because they were a young person still at home and didn't want their family members to find out, or because they were married or in a relationship with a man. The need for secrecy here was often a necessary one and some callers were at risk of violence if caught using the lines. As the UCL and Sussex study of LGBTQ+ people during the 2020 lockdowns shows, keeping your sexuality secret at home is something that continues to affect young people today. During the lockdown periods Switchboard reported an increase in their messenger and email services as queer people sought out safe ways to communicate with their community and access support without the risk of being overheard.[6]

Even in the early days of mobile phones many of the women are calling from phone boxes in the street or from a landline when their parents or husbands are out. Sometimes they are only downstairs and often such calls end abruptly. The young lesbians and married women in the logbook are often confined to their home to perform their assumed straight familial roles as daughters, mothers and wives – unable to be their full selves. For many women the Lesbian Line was their only contact with another woman like them.

The majority of queer people will likely grow up in a straight household and even if that environment is not openly hostile (and sadly many were and are) they often, explicitly or implicitly, reinforce heterosexually as the only correct way to construct home and family. This binary poses homosexual relationships as ones that are 'non-reproductive' and 'unnatural', against the 'productive' and 'traditional' institutions of family and marriage, reinforced in the West by both secular society and religion. It's easy to think this was always so, yet in *The History of Sexuality* Michel Foucault explains how the creation of the category of 'the homosexual' as a visible, medicalised identity in the nineteenth century led to it being positioned as a threat to the heterosexual family. This figure of 'the homosexual' brought with it fresh anxieties and perceived threats to the 'natural' familiar order and the noble Christian aim of procreation. Now that homosexuality was an individual 'affliction', it was just as likely to occur within a family unit and so opened up homosexuality to be studied as a 'perversion', which through medical and 'therapeutic' intervention could be studied or even 'cured'.[7] While lesbians did not loom as large in the consciousness at this time (their homosexuality more likely to deemed a symptom of hysteria), women continued to be defined by their role as mothers, wives and daughters. The homosexual now by being made visible was required to keep itself hidden or risk expulsion – the unmarried aunt always catches the eye of any lesbian historian.

This anxiety and false division between family and homosexuality continues well into this century. There's been an attempt to distance the family from unbounded sexuality by replacing it with a nostalgia for a morally 'pure' form of sexuality and family that never existed. *Adam and Eve, not Adam and Steve* as the saying goes. I cannot help but think again of the specific wording of Section 28 which made it unlawful to promote 'the acceptability of homosexuality as a *pretended family relationship*' (emphasis my own). To think that once our government thought that a gay person who was in a relationship, who had a partner, or children, might only be pretending, playing at being a family, is deeply hurtful. That the family they were making was not real or meaningful, that they were clutching at a shadow of the 'real' thing. I think of the homophobic mum who rang the Lesbian Line to call her daughter's partner a 'disgusting, ugly thing' – an outright refusal to acknowledge her personhood. It's a hurt we're still undoing in ourselves.

While today in the UK queer people have more options than ever if they want to start their own family, any legal gains with regard to the 'traditional' markers of family are startlingly recent. The right for same-sex couples to adopt was actioned in 2005; civil partnerships were sanctioned a year earlier for same-sex couples and it wasn't until 2014 that legislation was passed to allow same-sex marriage. Until recently many fertility treatments for LGTBQ+ couples were not available through the NHS and required private funding – a huge barrier to many wishing to start a family.[8] While fertility treatment is now available on the NHS, the postcode lottery of services still limits many queer women wishing to start treatment because of their age, BMI or required number of private attempts before they can even be added to the waiting list. Homophobic rhetoric continues to seep into attitudes towards surrogacy and adoption. I remember crying in anger in 2018 when I read a column by Richard Littlejohn in the *Daily Mail*, in which he argued that a child was best raised by a mother and a father. The pull quote ran: 'Please don't pretend two dads is the new normal', after it was reported that Olympic diver Tom Daley was expecting a baby through surrogacy with his husband.[9] These voices are in the minority in the UK but still they persist, still they knock us back.

While in the archive at Islington's Pride I came across news clippings from the 1980s with headlines like 'Gays Can Work

With Kids'[10] as councils slowly shifted, under improving equal opportunity charters, to actively encourage gay men and lesbians to work with services that supported children and young people. While the tone of the article was celebratory, for me it only brought into relief the prevalent homophobia of that time which thought children needed protecting from gay people. There was still a fear that gay and lesbians might 'corrupt' the British youth into a 'gay lifestyle'. It was the reason the Lesbian Avengers defiantly took as their motto 'we recruit', because at the time it was an accusation aimed at many lesbians – that they were trying to 'turn' straight women and children gay. Homophobia was so engrained that some believed any contact with a gay or lesbian person was dangerous, in part fuelled by misunderstanding and stigma around the HIV/AIDS epidemic.

This fear that homosexuality might destabilise the 'real' family or, shock horror, make people queer, is one that still pervades today, especially around gender identity. It is just as misplaced now as it was then. You see it in protests against organisations such as Mermaids and Gendered Intelligence who work with young trans people,[11] or opposition to better representation of trans people on TV for fear of influencing young people to transition.[12] Likewise, recent protests around drag queen story time events have shown these same tired protestations around the safety of children and are more about hatred of trans and queer people than any gesture to protecting children (who are only in danger of hearing someone read them a story).[13]

The impact on queer youth is stark. Research shows that trans and non-binary young people experience much higher rates of depression, suicidal thoughts and attempted suicide compared to other LGBQ youths.[14] In denying young queer people access to better representation, access to healthcare and connection with older queer and trans people, they rob them of both finding their queer family and of envisioning a happy future for themselves.

There are signs this is changing, but not without a fight. In 2019 protests outside Birmingham schools again used the defence of 'family values' to voice opposition to a school's use of children's books to teach diversity and inclusion, including same-sex relationships.[15] The protests actually had the opposite effect, however, and actually pushed schools into more actively addressing LGBTQ+ inclusivity.[16] In 2021 Scotland became the first nation in the world to add LGBTQ+ history to the school curriculum.[17] These are small steps forward but I worry for any queer or trans youth growing up in today's climate who do not have a caring and loving support network – some kind of family (whatever that looks like) around them.

26.6.97 – log by Ellen: ***Now has a shared house with three other women***

Judy's never lived in a house share before so she didn't know what to expect but the other women seem nice. They all get along, she says. Judy's been waiting to update them all at the line as they helped so much to get her a place. It's not too far from her work, either, and the new bus route gives her plenty of time to read. Ellen asks how she's settling in, and Judy says she still feels a little shy, she only really knows Kylie, although the other two are friendly. It'll just take some getting used to. All lesbians too, if it can be believed!

Ellen asks what she told her mum. Judy laughs and says she told her they met at a church group, which seemed to pass muster for now, at least. One of the girls, Sandra, made a rota for the fridge with a list of jobs for the house which keeps things straightforward. So far, at least. Chores split four ways is still better than when she was at home with just her and her mum. Ellen asks if maybe she was missing home a little? Maybe, Judy says, but she's keeping busy. They've made plans to go out next Friday, once they all get their pay cheques and Sandra's dole money goes in. It feels good to be independent.

While some queer people have little interest in reproducing the heteronormativity they see in parenthood and marriage, others throughout history have created their own ways to marry and have children outside of legal recognition. Like the nineteenth-century philandering 'modern lesbian' and landowner Anne Lister, who infamously 'married' her lover Ann Walker in 1834 at a church in York. Or the 'Ladies of Llangollen', Eleanor Butler and Sarah Ponsonby, who by dint of their wealth and class were able to live together and managed mostly to avoid scandal. Likewise, gays and lesbians have found 'work arounds' to starting a family long before surrogacy or artificial insemination were officially available to them. In many ways there were more options available for gay and bisexual women, so long as they could find a friend to 'help' out and pop over with a jam jar or similar.[18] Although doing so left couples with little legal support should the biological father wish to claim parental rights later on. Lesbian and bisexual couples who had children from previous relationships could look to merge their families, although often not without difficulty. Up until the 1980s it was not uncommon for courts to rule in favour of the father for custody if the mother had left the relationship to be with another woman or was a 'suspected lesbian'. There are accounts of lesbian couples in the 1970s having to undergo psychiatric evaluations alongside their children when fighting for custody. In one such interview, Pauline Heap recalls how her husband stood up in court to denounce the 'evil influence' of her partner during their custody hearing, preferring that his children be taken into care rather than be looked after by two mothers.[19] Thankfully the judge on this occasion did not agree.

But many women were not so fortunate. Indeed, the Cambridge Lesbian Line received so many calls from women who were facing difficult legal battles for custody that they kept on file contact details for feminist lawyers.[20] In the London Friend Lesbian Line logbook there is an account of a lesbian couple who enquired about a support group for prospective mothers called NEST, of which sadly the volunteers are unable to provide much information. They express their excitement that they are looking to start of family but aren't able to help much. Another caller later asks about adoption and if their partner could legally be the co-parent. Again, the phone worker leaves a note asking for hints on organisations she could suggest as she doesn't know any herself. This shows not only how little institutional support and guidance there was for lesbians wanting to start a family (whether through adoption or fertility treatment), even as IVF and artificial insemination became more accessible, but also the lack of knowledge within the lesbian community itself.

No wonder many of us choose to make our own familial relationships that subvert and reject the image of the traditional family and embrace our 'unproductiveness'. When I think of mothers and fathers, I think, too, of the lesbians who call themselves 'dads' – mock-serious in their styling of socks and sandals, baseball caps, tool belts and a sense of protectiveness. I think of the queer 'dog mums' and proud gay 'plant dads' I know. Queers that reject the neoliberal, heteronormative definition of the family and humorously reappropriate titles that straight culture once tried to deny them from claiming. Yet it also underscores that while for some, becoming a parent holds little appeal, for others living more precarious lives than ever, starting a family remains financially out of reach. I know I'm not the only lesbian to discuss with my wife whether we save for a house or IVF. 'Should we just get a puppy instead?' I half joke. 'Yes,' she says.

Not that I was thinking much about adoption (children, dogs or otherwise) when I first realised I was a lesbian. I was too busy finding my feet with my new queer friends, both online and offline, who accepted me without question. A few even told me they had assumed I was out long before I'd even thought about it myself. And while frustrating (could they not have said something sooner and saved me all the angst?) it also quietened my fears that I was making this all up. That somehow I had been subconsciously living as a lesbian long before

I even realised it myself. Identity is not just what you feel, it is also confirmed, reflected and shaped by those with whom you surround yourself. At a time when my family couldn't see the person I was trying to become, these queer women allowed me to see myself through their eyes and align who I felt I was with how I wanted others to see me. My friends. My chosen family.

Lesbian Lifelines

6.1.96 – log by Martha: ***When calmer she does talk about other possibilities***

She calls because she can't think of what else to do. She's never called the phone line before and even dialling the number fills her with terror. There's some change in her pocket lined up and she holds onto the door of the phone box for support. As soon as the woman says hello she starts talking.

It's two years since she fell in love, since her crush refused to evaporate, only hardened and resolved into what it is now – pure yearning and desire for her. It might have been all right; she might have got over it if she wasn't always coming round to their house. Her little sister's piano teacher, of all people. The first time she came over she couldn't stop looking at her, she's so beautiful in this inconspicuous way. She's had two years of looking and now she wants more.

It's not like she's a kid any more, she's twenty years old. She sees other girls sometimes late at night tiptoeing back to their houses, or the students in their flat shares. At least she's not like those girls. She is in love. And it's killing her. She calls the Lesbian Line because she thinks at least these women understand, at least they know what it's like to be in love with another woman. She tells the woman on the phone that only being with her will make her happy. If she can't be with her she doesn't know what she'll do.

I wish I was normal, she says, hating how desperate her voice sounds alone in the phone box. It would be so much easier.

The woman on the phone says it's okay and tries to get her to calm down, but it's all coming out of her in a rush. She's telling her things she's never said before. She's so excited to be in love but sometimes it feels like she can't breathe when she thinks about what her family would say if they knew. She can barely get the words out, but she has to. Her parents want her to marry in May. It's the only thing they talk about. She knows they just want her to be taken care of. They love her, they really do, but there's no way she can do it. If she gets married it'll all be over.

The woman on the phone lets her talk. She feeds another 20p into the coin slot and wonders if she's been gone too long, said too much. The woman on the phone wants to know if she can see another way out of her situation. She asks her to slow down and take a couple of breaths. It's okay, the woman on the phone says again. Have you thought about what else you could do?

She's thought plenty of times about leaving or showing up at the woman's door to tell her how she feels. She could try putting off the marriage, delay it a few months at least to give her more time.

The woman on the phone tells her that she can be a lesbian and be happy, she's proof of that. She's got lots of lesbian friends and while it's not always easy, it is possible. She starts to tell her about a group she could go to, if she could get out on a Monday night, it would help her meet other women like her.

Before she has a chance to reply, the line starts to beep and she realises she's run out of change. She leaves the phone box and heads home.

In an interview for *Radical History Review*, Karl Peder Pedersen, the archivist at the Danish Gay and Lesbian Archive, suggests that the queer archive is another kind of chosen family which can supplant the traditional family unit.[1] Artefacts or material which in a 'straight' inheritance pass down to children are instead entrusted to a queer archive which is then passed on to the next generation. Transforming queer archives, even within institutions, into familial and intergenerational spaces. I like this image of an inheritance that is parent and child both.

This is reflected in the physical space of queer archives also which can blur the distinction between home and institution. Like the Lesbian Herstory Archives (LHA) in New York which was first housed in the apartment of two of the co-founders, Joan Nestle and her then partner Deborah Edel.

Eventually their collection of lesbian 'herstory' became so large they had to raise funds to purchase another house to contain the still expanding archive. This building remains a space which straddles home and archive with a photocopier in the kitchen and a bathroom full of archival clutter. As the scholar Jack Jen Gieseking describes it: 'The rooms, bathrooms, and closets burst with topic collections . . . During my time there, piles of unsorted publications formed a two-foot-high mound in a corner of what was once a bedroom.'[2] In this space any lesbian is welcome to join the collective as a voluntary archivist and it remains open to any who wish to visit. Similarly, all lesbians are welcome to donate to the archive (pending a review by the volunteers), allowing it to function as a constantly evolving entity. Nestle writes that establishing the Lesbian Herstory Archives was done in part to push against the homogeny of lesbian identity through intergenerational collection and curation:

> Our archives belongs [sic] to no one group of lesbians and to no one selected image or formula for liberation; it will eventually pass into the hands of a new generation of re-memberers who we hope will keep the door open to the multiplicities of lesbian identity.[3]

Their focus on collecting the ordinary everyday objects that make up a lesbian life and an openness to donations ensures that it stays close to its grass roots while attempting to capture lesbian life as it changes. Its inheritance is found not in the individual but in the collective as it passes on to the next generation. Nestle and the LHA are ensuring their survival by allowing the archive to be a fluid, homely collection, open to all who might need to access it. A mother and child to all lesbians.

In November 2019, when I first heard about the LHA, I went with my wife to Stoke Newington Town Hall to sit in the cold semi-gloom with fifty or so other queer people and film lovers to watch the documentary *The Archivettes*, about the creation of the LHA and how it continues to survive today. It opens with a young woman, Melissa, who lost her partner, Ellie, the year before, as she drives over to the LHA to donate her belongings. On arrival she hands over boxes and suitcases of Ellie's T-shirts, paintings and photographs. She says, 'It's going to be okay, her stuff is going to be okay . . . I know her spirit is very much alive, but for this now to extend to people who never even met her, y'know, that is so beautiful and such a gift.'[4] Later, two 'archivettes' sort through Ellie's belongings to begin cataloguing. They linger and smile over the pictures of Melissa and Ellie together, the magazines she appeared in, and they read out her memorial card. It's a tender moment in the documentary which often showcases the care the archivettes take over even the smallest objects of a lesbian's life. You watch in real time as lesbian history and community is formed, a bond forged between lesbians who never knew each other, between the inheritance and the inheritor and the hard work that goes into preserving individual stories.

After the screening, Polly, one of the archivettes from the film, told an old lesbian-dad joke:

How many lesbians does it take to screw in a light bulb?

Three: one to screw in the light bulb and two to make an empowering documentary about it.

As dad jokes goes it's not bad, but it does acknowledge that if us lesbians don't record our history, no one else will.

Like many I had no lesbian parent, no queer ancestors in my family to guide me growing up. When the history we learn in schools, museums and from our own family obscures – or straight up ignores – LGBTQ+ history, our queer chosen families become that site of education and shared learning. When I came out, I had only scraps of gay and lesbian history. Everything I knew had been dragged together piecemeal, second- or third-hand. Lesbian knowledge production feels dangerously precarious, and so much of it I had stumbled over by chance. An offhand reference in a book, a stray Tumblr post, a TV show or documentary that unexpectedly featured a lesbian couple, that led to another and another. I searched for my lesbian inheritance in books, TV, films and video games. When that wasn't enough I looked to fan fiction: where straight characters are often rewritten as gay, or lesbian sidekicks unfairly killed off are brought back to life and made centre stage. I consumed as many queer and lesbian stories as I could. I reread Sarah Waters, I read *Carol* for the first time and closely tracked Therese's burgeoning love for a woman. I bought *The Well of Loneliness* and didn't read it to the end (too sad) but having it on my shelf felt affirming. Often, I was looking for lesbian representation in the wrong places. I watched *Imagine Me & You*, *Kissing Jessica Stein*, and *Chasing Amy* – classics in the terrible lesbian-film rom-com canon as written by a man – and cringed. I rewatched teen movies searching for a lesbian subtext, which wasn't too hard to find. *A League of Their Own*, *Bring It On* and *Bend It Like*

Beckham, perhaps starring the most obvious couple Jess and Jules – they are even mistaken as one, prompting the immortal line: 'Lesbian? Her birthday's in March, I thought she was a Pisces.' And that's just the sports-adjacent films.

In 2004 *Mean Girls* took on a different meaning; now I could see Janis Ian for what she was: the coded-emo lesbian that is bullied for it and incongruously paired up with a boy by the end of the film. Twenty years later in the musical remake, Janis is notably an out and proud lesbian, her sexuality no longer vague and played for laughs. I was looking for myself and some kind of lesbian lineage in all that historical fiction and teen rom-coms. A strange combination which left me scrabbling to follow a lesbian web of citations across theory, media and history I'd made for myself. It was, at best, a haphazard mission of self-directed lesbian study.

It reminds me of the experience Paul Polydoris, the literal gender-bending protagonist of Andrea Lawlor's vibrant novel *Paul Takes the Form of a Mortal Girl*, who describes his inventory of the poetry section at the gay and lesbian bookshop where he works. He sorts through the chapbooks and volumes of verse, skimming from poet to poet, following

> a dense web of blurbs, dedications, and acknowledgments. From Delany's memoir, he recognised Marilyn Hacker, then Auden (Auden was gay! He knew it!), who led to Frank O'Hara, who led to James Schuyler, who led to Eileen Myles, a celestial firmament hovering above the pages.[5]

Such discoveries contain great joys. Here is queer

inheritance as a kind of heavenly sky spread out above us if only we know to look up and reach out to it. I had many such moments myself: Susan Sontag was bisexual – of course! (the result of a Twitter Sontag diary bot and one quick google). And Stella Duffy! (Never read her until my wife told me to file her books in the queer section of our home shelves.) And Dusty Springfield! Ali Smith taught me that Tove Jansson snuck her female lovers into the Moomins and wrote a whole book, *Fair Play,* about her long-term relationship with a woman. And Tracy Chapman too! So many years after I sang along with my dad to 'Fast Car' and 'For My Lover' – how had I not seen her queerness in her emotive lyrics, lamenting, 'deep in this love / no man can shake'.[6] So obvious now that it borders on embarrassment.

Every discovery like this is tinged too with sadness: that I didn't see them earlier, that they were so hidden to me I didn't even know to look for them. Coming out to myself was really a process of learning to see that self anew. Accident or fate? Accident that the three closest friends I made at university were all queer? Two out at the time and then me and our other friend coming out only later. They were the ones who sat me down and made me watch *But I'm a Cheerleader, Ginger Snaps* and *Bound.* Handing me pieces of my lesbian inheritance before I even knew I needed it. Sisters showing their ignorant sibling the way. Later I would discover the early 2000s lesbian classics, watching them over and over again in secret: *Saving Face, If These Walls Could Talk 2* (which has a far better cast than it deserves: Chloë Sevigny playing a '70s butch is not to be missed), and of course *The L Word.* You may note these are all American. There were UK equivalents, most notably *Nina's Heavenly Delights* (2006), *Lip Service* (2010–12) and *Stud Life* (2012), but for whatever reason it was the US films and TV shows that I stumbled across first and could access more easily.

'Is she a sister?' another lesbian couple I know years later will ask while we sit watching Eurovision together. All three of us pondering the singer's wide stance at the mike stand and her stylish men's suit. And then later still: *Is she one of ours?* my wife will question me silently in the squeeze of her hand in mine as we catch the eye of a couple walking towards us. Recognition in the closeness of their walk, the way they hold their shoulders, the subtleties of fashion that echo our own. A shared glance, the ghost of a nod as we pass. Whole essays of identity told in a single lesbian look.

We find lesbian life everywhere.

23.4.98 – log by Polly: *I stupidly didn't ask her name!*

This call is easier than the first. They both involve tears but this time it's happy ones. When she rang, a woman called Sam answered and so it was to Sam that she first said it. She'd never said the word out loud before but now she can't stop saying it. Not just to herself whispered late at night in her head, but she's said it out loud to her best mate (who said it didn't matter much either way to her), then to the woman at London Friend who runs Changes and who Sam said would be expecting her. Then again, moments later introducing herself as one of them in front of the other women that were there. And then again the following day at the bar she'd snuck into – on a date of sorts with the cute brunette two years older than her and out six month before her.

It was like discovering a whole other world existed. A world of women that was hidden this whole time until she said the magic words herself. She feels like she is floating on air. She can't wait 'til she turns eighteen and gets a decent job so she can leave home and move in with some mates and all of London will be hers. She hasn't told her mum yet. Maybe she never will, she loves her mum but she doesn't think she'd understand. They're in different worlds now. She'd heard from some of the girls at Changes about how some of their parents chucked them out when they told them.

But she doesn't want to think about that now. She only wants to think about happy things today. That's why she called the phone line in the first place – to share happy news. The woman who picked up the phone today isn't Sam, it's a different woman, she sounds posh, but nice. She's disappointed at first. She'd called back purposely at the same time on the same day in the hope she'd be on shift again. In the end, though, she doesn't mind too much, perhaps it's better this way. She quite likes the idea of staying anonymous, of being one of the many people who've called the Lesbian Line. It got her where she needed to go. It's got her to this. A new future. She doesn't have the words, not yet, she's still a kid, after all. It'll be years until she has the words to know what that call did for her. Knocked the course of her life on a different path, not a happier or a better one, it's hard to know that, but one which is at least closer to the kind of life she's only just begun to dream about. And so for now the only message she has for Sam is ask the woman on the phone to send her a big thank you. That will do for now.

I remember after my first research trip to the Islington's Pride archive I came away with a great sense of longing for community. Two years after coming out I still knew no lesbians from the generation before me. That first trip into the archive I looked through a stack of leaflets from Central Station, a gay and lesbian pub that operated like a community centre, and couldn't help feeling like I'd missed out. The kind of nostalgia for a time and group of people that you never knew had existed until that moment. In my notebook I listed just a few of the LGBT groups that were running in the '80s and '90s, in awe of their variety:

- North London Bridge Club
- The London Blues (all uniforms welcome except Nazis)
- Gay Board Games Club
- New Beginners (group for young queer people)
- Lesbian and Gay Christian Movement
- Roman Catholics
- Stepping Out (coming-out support group)
- Monday Group (a lobby group who then have a quiz after)

- Gay Skinheads
- S&M Bisexuals
- Stonewall FC
- Rainbow Support (group supporting men whose partners have passed away)
- Transgender London
- Star Trek

Reading through the logbook produced many more now familiar to me: Changes and LAFS (Lesbians at Friend on Sundays, a social club for run by London Friend), GEMMA (a social group for disabled and non-disabled lesbians) and NEST (for lesbians looking to start a family). There were groups for lesbians who were grieving and lesbian-specific counsellors, as well as the London Lesbian Centre. The women in these pages worked hard to maintain their community and their contact with one another, ringing round centres and pubs to update details and meeting times. Most phone lines like this had a folder of useful information readily to hand in case of queries.

Finding the logbook was like finding the diary of a long-lost family, this rag-tag, imperfect group made up of phone workers and callers, even the difficult ones. Maybe especially the difficult ones. Venturing into the logbook I could imagine myself as a kind of distant cousin. There was a sense of trespass but also ownership. They're writing about people like *me*. A me that might have been, had I been born earlier, come out sooner. I could have been a caller. I imagine most of these women are still alive but it's their past selves I want to claim as my family. After all I only have what they've left behind.

Part of this project, my need to write about the logbook and myself in one breath is because I so desperately want to find a way to link myself to this lesbian history. To write a community into existence between them and me. To create my own lesbian inheritance.

Lesbians do have a track record in this regard. Audre Lorde's groundbreaking 1982 'biomythography', *Zami: A New Spelling of My Name,* weaves together her own real life history with self-mythology, poetry and politics. And ahead of more contemporary projects like Jenn Shapland's very personal *My Autobiography of Carson McCullers,* Cheryl Dunye, in the mid '90s, made the semi-autobiographical film, *The Watermelon Woman,* which creates a Black lesbian history in the space of absence.[7] I only found out about *The Watermelon Woman* through the mystery of the YouTube algorithm, but it's very much part of the lesbian canon. The main character, played by Dunye and also called Cheryl, is a struggling filmmaker trying to make a movie about Black women because 'our stories have never been told'. She discovers a Black actress from the 1930s who is credited only as 'The Watermelon Woman', if she is credited at all. The film follows Cheryl as she tries to uncover more details about the 'real' Watermelon Woman – Fae Richards – tracing her history back through various archives and people who knew her. Because of her detective work Cheryl learns that the actress herself was also a lesbian and had an affair with a white director and later a long-term partner. Throughout the film the screen is heavy with a sense of archival materiality, often showing close-ups of old black and white film footage or photographs, sometimes held up by Cheryl herself or even lip-synced along to.

The screen constantly reminds the viewer of Cheryl's personal investment in her research and the tangible traces of lesbian history she strives to share. Richards's story appears completely authentic down to the clips of film and archival ephemera shown. Cheryl even visits a parody of the LHA archive, the 'Centre for Lesbian Information and Technology' (lesbians love an acronym) to rifle through a box of donations, illegally filming what she finds before she is thrown out.

Throughout the film the language of family reappears. Richards is a 'sapphic sister', and when Cheryl finds Richards's partner of over forty years, she asks her to confirm she's 'a sister' before they agree to meet. At the end of the film, Cheryl presents the documentary she has made about Richards, retelling her life and showing the archival material she has found. In voice-over Cheryl says, '[Richards] paved the way for people like you . . . If you are really in the family you know we always have to look after each other.' There is a sense of deep archival and familial care in the way Cheryl talks about Richards; it so desperately means something to Cheryl to have found the story of the Watermelon Woman and that she is the one to tell this Black lesbian experience. In her final speech, addressed directly to the camera, Cheryl says that Richards 'meant the world to me . . . it means hope, it means inspiration, it means possibility, it means history'. In finding her foremother in the past she has found a way forward and a source of creativity to finish her film. Cheryl is able to finally, confidently, declare that she is a Black lesbian filmmaker, echoing Audre Lorde's many introductions of herself as a 'Black lesbian, mother, warrior, poet' – because, as Lorde said at a conference address in 1982, 'If I didn't define myself for myself I would be crunched into other people's fantasies for me.'[8] Cheryl too, in making a biographical film of Fae Richards, redefines 'The Watermelon Woman' by returning her name to her and reclaiming her history from a racist stereotype that ensured Richards was never properly credited in her time.

The biographical meta-film that plays at the end of *The Watermelon Woman* is intercut with the end credits, ensuring that the audience knows the names and roles of the people who made this film also. Astute viewers will note that Zoe Leonard is credited with producing the archive of 'The Watermelon Woman'. It foreshadowers the final, devasting text card which reads: 'Sometimes you have to create your own history. The Watermelon Woman is fiction, Cheryl Dunye, 1996.' The first time I read that endnote it hit me like a blow to the stomach. Richards wasn't real.

On the research she had done for the film, Dunye said later that 'what I found was nothing. So, I had to tell that truth. I think that's where the film gets its real depth.'[9] The revelation that Fae Richards never existed is so poignant precisely because of the fiction the viewer has been led to believe and hope in. Here, the layering of a fictional presence over a factual absence reasserts an emotional and historical truth. For Cheryl in *The Watermelon Woman* to find a historical Black lesbian Hollywood actress to create art about, Dunye had to invent her. The real Dunye had no such guide. She exposes the reality that in order to make art about figures from the past who have been repressed and obscured through homophobic and racist structures, fiction is required to bridge the gap in mainstream historical records. The truth that Dunye reveals is not that Richards was fictional – she no doubt existed in some incarnation – but the reason why it was Dunye could not find a record of her story.

I still have doubts that writing about the logbook is the 'right' thing to do. Is this how I should treat family? Would they want me to write about them in this way? Some days I think that writing about the logbook is only a self-serving act, a way to talk about myself. A year before I found the logbook I read an essay by Kevin Brazil called 'The Uses of Queer Art', and a line from it has haunted me ever since I began this project: 'if the past is only being used to tell others who you are, it's unclear whether it is really being remembered at all'.[10] In writing about the logbook, what if all I am remembering is myself? But then I'm not sure how else I can approach this particular history. Not when it's as personal as the logbook has become to me.

As Joan Nestle again writes of the LHA: 'Our will to remember is our will to change the world, to continually reconstruct the words 'woman', 'lesbian', and 'gender' so they reflect the complex creations which we call our lives.'[11] It is lesbians who create the lesbian archive, just as the lesbian archive creates lesbians. Just as I reproduce the logbook here in my own way and it, in turn, reproduces me. Nestle sees a way through the past to the present, a handing over to the next generation. Our lesbian inheritance is not only to ensure we will be remembered but to make ourselves anew, not from nothing, but from what we meant before.

Brazil writes that '[q]ueers need to do without history in order to be queer'[12] – suggesting that 'queer' invites a freedom from definition and the history of sexuality by virtue of being a socially, culturally and historically invented identity. But I would ask, whose identity isn't in part created by the people and environment we surround ourselves with? I would argue that identity is both singular and relational. Besides, it's not a queer history I'm looking for, it's a lesbian one which has already lost so much. Perhaps I am not radical enough to do without history just yet. Perhaps a lesbian inheritance could be something different. One which might both preserve the past while looking to the future.

In the 1980s Adrienne Rich described lesbian existence as one which is lived 'without access to any knowledge of a tradition, a continuity, a social underpinning'[13] – historically erased by the dual forces of compulsory heterosexuality and the conflation of male homosexual experience with lesbian and female existence. Although I would add that much was gained by standing in solidarity with gay men who faced their own specific oppressions. If the 1990s resulted in a paradigm shift for lesbian representation in media and growing visibility,[14] then perhaps it is only now that lesbians can live with access to that history. Something close to the definition of lesbian existence that Rich sought when she described it as 'both the fact of the historical presence of lesbians and our continuing creation of the meaning of that existence'.[15] The logbook is my way of accessing that lesbian existence – a way to create new lesbian inheritances. To turn our absences into a presence as Dunye did through fiction. I think of Michelle Tea, who looks to the future when she writes: '[T]he purpose and point of our political writings, our personal struggles [is] not to change the world that can't or won't be changed. It's to leave traces of ourselves for others to hold on to, a lifeline of solidarity that spans times, that passes on strength like a baton from person to person, generation to generation.'[16]

I think that's what I'm really looking for.

A *lifeline of solidarity*, a lifeline, a phone line, a line, a lineage, a lesbian line.

No More Lesbian Sheroes

3.8.97 – log by Sarah: ***Congratulations to whoever tidied up the ♀ ♀'s line noticeboard – it looks fab!*** London Friend in general is never particular tidy – it's used too much, by too many different people, for that – the small office that is home to the phone line hardly fares any better. If anything, it's often worse off and any mess is magnified in such a confined space. For Sarah that's not usually a problem actually. She's one of those people who can work around mess. Not like Cora, who finds a way to make a comment every time they are on shift together about whoever was on before and how they've left the index cards out of the Rolodex or managed to skip pages in the logbook so now do they go back and have entries out of order or strike through the blank pages? Which to Cora seems like such a waste.

So, when Sarah arrives at London Friend and makes her way over to the kitchen to make a coffee before her shift starts (she knows she shouldn't drink coffee so late but how else is she supposed to stay awake?) and sees that the lesbian noticeboard has been perfectly organised, she has to say something in the logbook. Someone has taken down all the old flyers and out-of-date notices and stuck up the most relevant ones neatly with two push pins either side to stop them hanging down. In contrast to the men's one opposite, still piled high with newsletters and flyers going every which way, it looks far better. For a second she wonders if it's not very feminist to have such a tidy noticeboard. Women's work and all that, but if it means lesbians can better find the information they need then surely the two things cancel each other out. It's not like the men expect them to tidy up their board – now that would not be right on. Perhaps Sarah does like things to look neat after all. But then after what turns out to be a long tricky shift, which she has to deal with alone because Monica had to cancel, when it comes time to put away the pens and the index cards she finds herself sweeping them into a drawer to be put away properly later and just has to hope that Cora isn't on the shift after her.

Not every entry in the logbook concerns the callers; in between the records of the calls are little notes and comments left by the phone workers to each other. Many of the notes concern the trivial day to day workings on the phone line: the answering machine not being plugged in, who's next due on shift, or pleas to keep the office space tidy. These mundane little details always make me smile when I see them.

Because whenever I read an entry in the logbook I am acutely aware that it is not a call I am reading about but the phone worker's experience of that call. Every call I read is filtered through the perspective of that volunteer. And so naturally, my mind often wanders to the phone workers themselves. I have read and reread the logbook so many times now that I recognise phone worker's logs by their handwriting alone. Some of them have an almost print-like neatness to their letters while others scrawl out their words and take time to decipher fully. In their notes to each other especially there is the strongest spectre of the real person who put pen to paper.

Dani is one such instantly appealing logbook keeper. She writes in huge letters which span at least three lines so that her logs easily take up half an A4 page for a short note, or are multiple pages long for something more complex. She makes free and frequent use of exclamation marks and always draws full circles over her 'i's and in exclamation points. She is the kind of person I can imagine you can't help but be drawn to. Dani feels like a whirlwind in the logbook: her notes always give the impression of being hastily written, usually to apologise for missing a shift, messing up the answering machine or to inform others of when she is next in:

5.4.95 *hello again – couldn't reset answer machine – I'm such a dizz with technical stuff! I'll speak 2 someone! or maybe it's the machine? if Rochelle rings for me – I'll be in on Sunday 9th April*

Dani

This is important because there is one caller in particular who only wishes to speak to Dani. The caller is a survivor of sexual assault with a complex history that she has only fully disclosed to Dani. I can't help but admire that chaotic and larger-than-life Dani, who is obviously also such a deeply caring person, has forged such a strong connection with this repeat caller who seems so vulnerable and unsure of herself.

Here are some more typical notes from Dani:

> **13.11.95** *eeeeek! Switched the answer-machine off in a panic not sure its working properly – would someone check? SORRY!!*

> **24.5.95** *If Rochelle phones me – i'll [sic] be on 4th June + 18th June,*
>
> *Dani*
> *Cheers*

> **[date unknown]** *HOPE YOU ALL HAVE A LOVELY CHRISTMAS TIME – MAYBE SEE YOU AT THE PARTY?!!*

Dani's notes end around 1995–6 and I'm sorry to see them go. I miss her big statements and messages that take up three pages. You can't miss Dani and that's something to be proud of. Never mind that she can't work the answering machine or that she often misses her shifts. You get the sense that when she is there she is really *there* and puts her whole heart into being on the phones. In one memorable log she writes about a repeat caller who is waiting on an appointment with a counsellor: 'it's another 3 months before I can get an appointment slot with a female counsellor (aargh)', and then goes on to add that her 'medication [circle over 'i's in medication] is [circle over 'i'] late (???) got to wait another week to get it sorted – (aargh again)'. I find the 'aarghs' so endearing. While other volunteers sometimes express frustration at repeat callers, Dani, for all her seeming haste and hurry, does not. She is instead always on the caller's side, frustrated on their behalf and empathetic to their seemingly never-ending waiting.

I think 'aargh' does express it best. Aargh at the system that makes this caller's life more difficult and aargh that's there's little Dani can do to help, except listen – which she does – noting that 'the caller was down initially but a bit more up towards the end'. Sometimes a collective aargh is what we need to hear, an acknowledgement that it's not just us. The situation really is shitty even if there's little we can do to control it and Dani gets that.

Sam is another frequent note-maker in the logbook at least from 1993–94, during her reign as the person in charge of rotas. She is another favourite of mine (I know it's weird to have favourites). Many of Sam's notes concern either her own shifts or those of others. She is organised but not overbearing. Not to be a total lesbian, but I wonder if, like me, she is a Virgo: we're supposed to be practical Earth signs that love a schedule. Not that I really care about star signs but it's impossible to be a lesbian and *not* care about star signs to some extent. Sam has self-assured Virgo energy. If you need any more evidence, look no further than her perhaps too-gleeful correction of another phone worker on the status of the newsletter *Lesbian London*:

> **19.8.93** *Lesbian London has now closed down – sorry Sam! Lucy*
>
> **26.8.[93]** *No it hasn't yet! Sam*

Another of her notes has a lightly threatening joking-not-joking tone that I recognise from my own experiences trying to organise volunteers:

> *Dear women,*
>
> *Be warned! I'm rota person for February. (Can you hear my whip cracking yet?) Please sign up early 'coz things are looking really empty.*
>
> *Also anyone with ideas about publicity to make Sun/Mon/Tues schedule known should let me know. The publicity group is meeting tomorrow Tues 4th to get things going, but ideas are always welcome.*
>
> *Thanks*
>
> *Sam*

There's not really a hierarchy as far as I can tell from the logbook, but as with any groups there are those who end up taking charge more than others, either by default of having been there the longest, or because no one else is willing.

Anyone who has ever done any kind of volunteer or committee work knows that one of the hardest parts of the job is chivvying people along and having a large enough pool of volunteers rather than the same few dedicated people doing everything. Perhaps unsurprisingly, then, the majority of the notes throughout the logbook to other phone workers are about updating each other on who can cover what shift, or if someone is unavailable.

It's clear that staffing was an issue, as it seems to have been for most gay and lesbian phone lines throughout the years. One regular caller later laments that she keeps getting 'all these new girls' every time she phones up. It's evident in the logbook itself that staff turnover was high, there's a constant stream of new names and logs by someone you only see once or twice. Helen Bishop and Pam Isherwood during their tenure at London Lesbian Line confirm that volunteer turnover was high there also. The average was around two to three years, although some stayed as little as three to six months. They cite the difficult nature of the work as one reason, but also the huge amount of administration support that was needed to facilitate the actual calls, which left some feeling frustrated:

> It takes a whole team of people to support two people on the phones, setting up a rota, filling the rota. We had teams: admin, publicity, training, worker support (when we had funding). It was all shared out so you didn't just come in and just do the phones. But sometimes the women just wanted to do the phones and they wouldn't come to the collective meetings.[1]

And of course, by going solo as women-only lines they were competing with each other over a smaller pool of volunteers. The London Lesbian Line would often set up a table at a lesbian pub or night hoping to recruit more volunteers. Lesbians willing and able to work the phone lines were an important and precious commodity and this often meant demand outweighed supply. With the phones only open two nights a week at London Friend Lesbian Line many women ended up calling the mixed line. There are occasionally notes attesting to this:

> **9.6.[96]** *Had 2 long, heavy calls from women who really needed to talk to a lesbian. I did my best and suggested they rang back tomorrow, Monday 10th. Peter*

At times it can feel like the logbook is unorganised and the shifts rather erratic, but knowing that likely in the '90s they were facing budget cuts and a lack of new volunteers coming through this perhaps explains some of the difficulties they had in having consistent phone workers and schedules. I get the sense they are trying as best they can and volunteers were often juggling work, childcare (one note describes their toddler crawling around on the floor) and family commitments – unpaid labour that historically women have taken more than their fair share of. Not to mention other activism or groups that phone workers were involved in, and the mental toll that the phone lines had on the volunteers. There's at least one note from a phone worker to say she is thinking about leaving the service because of a particularly difficult caller who rings repeatedly.

Speaking to ex-volunteers at London Lesbian Line, several of them commented that in the '70s volunteers were much easier to find because living costs were relatively low: people could afford to live on the dole or find places to squat and had more free time. Thatcher's Britain changed much of this after the '80s and into the '90s when the rush towards neo-liberalism, consumerism and the rising cost of living meant many lesbians who might once have had some free time during the day or evening to volunteer were no longer able. Likely there were other factors that led to a dropping off of volunteers (such as a sense that gay liberation had been 'achieved', and the rise of the internet) but I'm sure lack of time, financial pressure and mental burnout played its part.

In the face of all this a sense of resilience was key. For some, humour was how they coped with the more difficult calls. The phone workers will often make a joke either for themselves or for the other volunteers to find. Like Pauline opening her log one evening with 'I had a call tonight (funny that!)'. After a log from a particularly heavy call from a woman who is very aggressive, Clare writes a P.S. asking the other volunteers if they think velour as a fabric will make it into the next century. She adds: 'Or am I just trying to lighten our collective minds with abstract humour?' Ellen, another phone worker, has written in answer: 'I doubt it but Velcro definitely has a future!' Can't say she was wrong.

It's easy to want to cling onto these little moments of humour and quirks that punctuate the gravity of some of the logs. I know I extrapolate a great deal from not much information, and I'm aware that out there somewhere are the real people, going on and living their lives. Most likely nothing at all like how I imagine them to be. I would hope most of them are still around – I don't know where they are or if they would even want to talk to me if I could contact them. Perhaps they would rather I hadn't written about them at all.

It's why I haven't used their real names and have changed any details which might identify who they are. I have tried to hold the real person and the people in the logbook as two separate things. There is the real person whose life has gone on, and there is the person they left on the page here in the archive, perhaps unknown to them, for others to read. It's a feeling not dissimilar to rereading my old diary – the one I kept when I was questioning everything. Reading it back I don't fully recognise that person any more, who I was then is so distant as to be part of my imagination.

It's a feeling I'm sure many of us have experienced whatever our previous history. There are points in your life where your whole being can change in a moment, and other times when it happens so slowly you don't even notice until you look back. For me coming out is both a definite line and a blurred one. There is my before life, my 'straight' life, but who was that girl? Was she the same person as me now? There's a continuum sure, but connecting the dots is murky territory. I wonder if the phone workers in the logbook would recognise themselves now? The writer in me can't help inventing new futures for them, to speculate on what they are up to. Are they still volunteering? Are they happy? What do they think of their past selves?

29.12.93 – log by Sally: *apologies for not starting on Tues. Somewhere over Christmas among the turkey and festive cheer (?), I lost a day*

Sally address her note to Sam because even though Sam is not in charge, she kinda is in charge and if Sally doesn't say anything Sam will be annoyed if she later finds out Sally missed her shift . . . Again. It slipped her mind somewhere between all the turkey and the chaos of the back and forth between her parents' house and her now empty student flat. Those days after Christmas always feel like nothing days and the slow sad creep of being back at her parents (and therefore back to being straight) meant that it was the 28th before she knew it and she'd already missed her shift. She'd rather not tell Sam in person herself and so the note feels like the best option. She attempts a cheerful tone in her opening, she's sure the women don't really mind – everyone misses a shift once in a while, but she's still fairly new and wants them to see her as an adult. Not as someone who's only just moved out and is still trying to figure out all this university stuff. Everyone else seems so smart and sure of themselves on the phone line. Speaking of which, Sally has a bunch of university deadlines looming over her in January which she spent Christmas ignoring and now regrets. Everyone says the first year doesn't really count but it doesn't feel that way. And because she hasn't even started on her essays it's looking more and more likely that she

> isn't going to make the phone worker meeting on the 12th. Another thing she needs to let Sam know. She hopes they won't kick her off the rota, but she has to put her uni stuff first. Maybe she's not cut out for the Lesbian Line after all? She wouldn't be surprised if soon they ask her to leave before she's even got started.

The experience of reading the logbook, of navigating all the phone workers' logs and notes to one another is, to put it plainly, a messy one. The women in the logbook resist orderliness through their haphazard approach to record keeping and hurried notes to one another. To read it is to plunge into a jumble of handwritten notes, scribblings out and doodles (mostly thanks to Zeenat) which refer to unknown past events, organisations and people. Later on, the logs get further apart in time and there are instructions to look for and record logs elsewhere. I have nowhere else to go, however, this is the only logbook I have. And so it is a mess that I perhaps foolishly have attempted to unpick. Reading the logbook is to reckon with a Gordian knot of unravelling threads that lead to other stories which always remain out of reach because, by their very nature, they are half-heard conversations with unknown conclusions.

It's impossible to approach the logbook straight-wise. I dive into the logs expecting to research a topic, a particular caller or volunteer, but something else will catch my eye: a one-off call whose story intrigues, a little note from a phone worker, and so I spiral off in another direction. Likewise my notes spill over three notebooks and a growing folder of Word documents as I try and impose order. It's a different kind of failure, a very 'unqueer' one, to try to arrange the logbook into a neat narrative. It doesn't stop me writing each topic and log entry onto pieces of paper and sticking them on a board which I rearrange like a jigsaw with no fixed picture. But that's not how real life and real people work.

Queer archives too seek to work with mess – an ongoing attempt to create order out of chaos. Many are constituted out of ephemera – the fancy name academics give to the bits of paper that you find pushed to the back of the drawer, or stuck onto noticeboards, handed out at events and sometimes crushed underfoot. And while ephemera is not unique to queer archives (just ask my dad about his junk drawer), they take on a central, almost holy relic-like role there because of how easily, and often, they are lost.

'Ephemera', Martin F. Manalansan IV writes, 'embodies fleeting nomadic, messy and elusive experiences and processes of self-making.'[2] Ephemera as a history-holding object, is the opposite of the official mainstream archive which seeks to impose order though governmental records and careful categorisations. Ephemera is what the queer scholar José Esteban Muñoz describes as 'traces, glimmers, residues, and specks of things'.[3] I like the idea of glimmering ephemera – a discarded object that could easily be overlooked but which can catch the eye. Something which is more than it appears. They are leftovers of lives that are uniquely queer because they have survived despite existing on the margins. They are the proof that it is possible to exist in a world which seeks to disregard them. A random poster for a lesbian night thirty years ago that was designed to be thrown away feels so momentary, and so it is all the more precious to find it carefully preserved within an archive. I experienced this myself when delving into Islington's Pride archive for the first time and holding in my hands flyers for future events long since past. They are special things.[4]

While Islington's Pride aims towards order in its brown boxes, not all archives are the same. And being queer means that one does not have to shy away from this mess and fragmentation of the self which the queer archive reproduces. If you look at a picture of the infamous Lesbian Herstory Archives you will see rooms overflowing with material for the volunteer archivists to recategorize as they will. There feels something uniquely lesbian and feminist in its non-hierarchical approach to archival work. Archivist and scholar Jack Jen Gieseking defines this as a 'useful in/stability' – a radical positioning to hold together both that which resists change and that which is always in flux to create an 'inclusive and useful space of growth and difference'.[5] Mess in a queer archive is productive and expansive. In writing this, I too am surrounded by my own useful in/stability: a messy archive of stray papers, books and notes that clutter my desk as I type and out of which some sort of order is pulled. This book too exists in fractured digital documents spread out across a computer on the brink of breakdown[6] and in the clouds of the internet. Stable for now but always moving.

Mess and queerness are deeply intertwined – part of being queer *is* to be messy, to go against the norms of orderliness and authority. Accepting this mess allows us to resist the push towards assimilation into heterosexual society through increased acceptance and greater visibility which only places pressure on the individual queer to perform 'goodness'. A 'goodness' which is defined by the standards of straight society to reproduce the social mores and economic status recognised as success by neoliberal society. As Carmen Maria Machado notes, to look at queerness free from moral imperatives or a need for 'good' queer representation is ultimately liberating: 'it sounds terrible but it is, in fact, freeing: the idea that *queer* does not equal good or pure or right. It is simply a state of being'.[7] Such respectability politics manifests both to police queer messiness that might fall outside of the bounds of perceived heterosexual acceptability (SM, kink and polyamory, for instance) but also as an ideology that refuses to acknowledge real harm and biases when it appears in our communities for fear of making queer people 'look bad'.

We don't like to think about the 'bad gays', as Huw Lemmey and Ben Miller describe them on their podcast and book of the same name. They profile people like the first 'out' politician and Nazi leader Ernst Röhm, or 1930s fraudster Marthe Hanau. Through the playful binaries of 'good' and 'bad' their work reminds us that queer people are just as susceptible to corruptions of power and capable of contributing to, or creating, systems of abuse, discrimination and harm. That white queers hold up systems of white supremacy and that upper-class queers exploit the working classes. They reveal the limits of representational politics of 'queer heroes' by demonstrating that queerness cannot be used as a barometer for morality. It's still 'good to be gay', but being gay doesn't automatically make you 'good'.

Instead, such acknowledgement reclaims the narrative of the 'bad' or deviant queer from homophobic rhetoric to show a broader spectrum of behaviours, how such 'bad gays' came to be and how their own desire or sexual preference does not let them off the hook for their harmful actions. Until we reckon with such a history there can be no true queer liberation, only a sheen of queer acceptance which puts all queers under pressure to perform 'goodness'. As we'll see, the phone workers in the logbook were no exception, capable of performing harm or being complicit in upholding racist and transphobic views. How do we reconcile this, then, with the good work they did do?

Perhaps to be queer is to embrace mess. For Manalansan, mess in the archive is a way to reclaim the ordinary, complicated *realness* of queer people from historical attempts to portray a few noted individuals' achievements as unusual, heroic acts. 'I intend,' Manalansan writes, 'to locate discomfort, dissonance and disorder as necessity and grounded experiences in the queer everyday.'[8] This aligns with what Sara Ahmed, writing on lesbian feminism in *Living a Feminist Life,* describes as the 'battle for ordinary. When you have to battle for an ordinary, when battling becomes ordinary, the ordinary can be what you lose.'[9] She argues that reclaiming the ordinary in the face of a society that would work to make our lives extraordinary is political feminist work. This ordinariness can be its own kind of rebellion. Seeing the women in the logbook as ordinary people allows us to find their realness: of how people go about their everyday lives. Trying to make others better, often failing, sometimes succeeding, often not knowing what they are doing or what consequences their actions will have. Radical, yes, because how could they not be? But also imperfect (I doubt any of them would claim to be perfect anyway).

It's tempting to write about the logbook as part of a heroic lesbian history, a story purely about women supporting each other within their community. And there is no doubt that they truly did that, but the reality of the logbook is also a messy picture of this community. The women at the Lesbian Line are not lesbian 'sheros', but ordinary people – and they often mess up. The phone worker's 'messiness' manifests itself in all kinds of ways: forgetting to plug in an answering machine, complaints about callers, or not turning up for a shift, to more serious instances regarding a lack of understanding and care for racialised callers or trans lesbians.

Acknowledging this mess allows us to resist simplistic understandings of objects and people and to hold two contradictory states at once. The useful in/stability of the archive collapses the binary between perceptions of 'good' and 'bad', between order and mess. It allows us to see that there are bad gays and terrible lesbians. That ordinary people are capable of harm to one person and kindness to another. That not every phone call can be an answer to a problem. Mess is real, mess challenges us to unpick the sanctioned, sanitised narrative and root about in the fragments for the difficult and uncomfortable truths that help us understand our past.

White Fragility and the Failure to Listen

7.12.95 – log by anon: *Seems sweet, wants to talk but difficult for me to understand*

As soon as the voice at the other end of the phone says hello she knows it is not the woman she usually talks to. She asks for her but is told, sorry she isn't here right now, but I can help?

She will try her at least; she knows it's rude to hang up straight away without the hellos and how are yous and the chat about the weather, and so she gives the woman on the phone the short version. She thought perhaps when she moved here her feelings for women would go away, but they haven't. She's never told anyone in her real life about any of this. She calls it her real life, but sometimes it feels far from what she imagined as a child growing up in India. It would be too much, she thinks, even to tell her cousin whom she lives with and who is very understanding but prefers things to stay a certain way. She does not think her cousin could keep it to herself and it would bring so much trouble into the family. She loves them very much and doesn't want to make things more difficult for them. They worked hard to get her here and give her a place to stay. She doesn't want to do anything that would upset them. And so she is trapped between her real life and this other life she can only access part of the time.

She's happiest when she comes to Shakti. When she's there she feels more relaxed and like she is where she is meant to be. But as soon as she goes back home she doesn't know if this is right and soon slips back into her other life, her real life. At the group she feels most herself, but then the person she is at home is also her real self and so it's like she is always being pulled one way or another. Even at Shakti she sometimes feels like the odd one out, even among the other Pakistani women because they were all born here.

The woman on the phone is listening very intently but doesn't say much.

She speaks English perfectly well, just like most people her age back home – it's one of their 'official' languages, after all. She has made it a habit to tell British people this when they ask about her accent. Her raised eyebrows and sarcasm are sadly lost on them, you think they would know their own history better ... Still people here struggle to understand her. It would be so much easier to speak to the woman she did before, there is less she would need to explain and she wouldn't worry about what the

> person on the other end of the call thinks of her or her family. She knows what this woman is thinking: what a traditional family she must come from, that she's come from some tiny village. All wrong, of course. She doesn't say any of this, though she could. It won't help her problem, the one that is splitting her in two. She thanks the woman for listening and says she will try again another time.

There are times in the logbook when it feels like the phone workers have failed to respond to their callers in a way that best meets their needs or situation. This is the case at times when they take calls from Black and South Asian lesbians and other lesbians of colour. And while it's true not every call will be a positive one, if my aim is to show what the everyday lives of lesbians was like, I think it's important to acknowledge where the phone workers failed their callers. To not discuss racism as it manifests in the lesbian lines would be to falsely erase it from its story and the experience of the lesbians of colour who called during this time. My aim is not to vilify individuals but to look at how their responses might point to the kinds of structural racism that lesbians throughout the '90s encountered, both in the wider lesbian community and those they spoke to when seeking help.

In considering the ethnicity and racial background of the callers during the '90s we need to be mindful that the language used by, and to describe, racialised people was different from today. And like today, language was not universal or fixed across individuals or organisations, nor was it free from their own biases and contentions. As discussed earlier, well into the '90s 'Black' was used by some people and organisations as a political term to include not just people of African or Caribbean descent, but people from Asia, the Pacific nations, Latin America and the first peoples of Australasia, North America and the islands of the Atlantic and Indian Ocean. However, some lesbians, particularly those not of African or Caribbean descent, felt that as an overarching term 'Black' was not inclusive of their own heritage and culture. 'Lesbian of colour' was used instead by some lesbians at the time to express solidarity, and could include or exclude Black lesbians depending on the context – for others its association to racist language in the UK meant it was to be avoided and was too non-specific. Likewise, in common usage in the logbook, 'Asian' in its British context was typically used to refer to people of South Asian heritage, and less likely to refer to people from East Asia. As a descriptor it risks misrepresenting a diverse group of South Asian countries and cultures, but many British Asian people continue to use it to this day. When writing about the '90s I've tried to be as accurate as possible when using language within specific contexts and with the knowledge I have available to me.

When thinking about attitudes to race within the logbook it's useful to consider Reni Eddo-Lodge's evaluation of how racism operates within the UK as an overarching cultural force when she writes:

> We tell ourselves that racism is about moral values, when instead it is about the survival strategy of systemic power . . . this isn't about good and bad people . . . Structural racism is dozens, or hundreds, or thousands of

> people with the same biases joining together to make up one organisation, and acting accordingly. Structural racism is an impenetrably white workplace culture set by those people, where anyone who falls outside of the culture must conform or face failure. *Structural* is often the only way to capture what goes unnoticed – the silently raised eyebrows, the implicit biases, snap judgements made on perceptions of competency . . . This is what structural racism looks like. It is not just about personal prejudice, but the collective effects of bias.[1]

Looking at London Friend and the Lesbian Line as an organisation with a majority white staff and volunteers, even as members of another marginalised group, reveals the ways in which, as a collective, they failed to account or cater to the specific needs of Black lesbians and lesbians of colour. The consequence was such that often racialised callers did not receive the same specific care and inclusion that was implicit in calls from white lesbians. The organisers of the Lesbian Line's tenure, and London Friend as a whole, were not unaware of its majority white volunteer base and did take steps to make positive changes to enable a more equative and inclusive environment.

I referenced Rani Kawale's work previously, but it's worth touching again on her study on the emotional work by lesbians and bisexual women in London from 2004. Although this is later than the time period of the logbook, many of the conversations and responses are relevant to the experiences of lesbians on the scene in the '80s and '90s (and indeed today). They illustrate how little was gained in the intervening periods:

> On the scene, a group or bar does not need to specify that white people are welcome, this is already assumed because, for example, the term 'lesbian' is racialised and usually refers to 'white' lesbians. Such places may be publicised as being for 'lesbian' and 'bisexual' women but they rarely have room for 'black' women to be 'black' in them. The whiteness of the scene in London was identified to me only by the South Asian interviewees which suggests that the white women did not necessarily see it as racialised.[2]

Whiteness in UK gay and lesbian scenes goes unchallenged because whiteness is seen as inherent. In this assumed whiteness the structural bias of racism that Eddo-Lodge speaks of is revealed – if we cannot see, or refuse to acknowledge, this we cannot address our own privileged position within the lesbian community and complicity in keeping ourselves here. Yet for those placed outside of this whiteness it is all too obvious that such 'silently' white spaces, whether intentionally or not, exclude others unless actively countered. It's certainly true that Black lesbians and lesbians of colour experienced racism in trying to enter these coded-white spaces, or were forced to assimilate or downplay their ethnic background to 'fit in'. During an interview with Femi Otitoju by Fopé Ajanaku for the podcast *Black and Gay, Back in the Day,* Femi recalls a story of being in the nightclub Heaven when she was younger and receiving looks from white queer people at the club who assumed she was straight and in their space. The host, Fopé, then replies with her own similar story from the present of being turned away from a gay club because it wasn't a 'soul night'.[3] Their stories are decades apart but the racism from the queer community is the same: they were seen as Black first, lesbians second and made unwelcome.

To be able to ignore racism within the lesbian community is part of the power white lesbians hold and use to maintain and control the status quo over majority white lesbian venues and gatherings in both public and private. I spoke to the anonymous founder of the Instagram British Asian Lesbians @bal.br, a community project that aims to unite British Asians both online and in person, on how she creates spaces for British Asian lesbians to connect with one another. She set up the project in response to attending a club night and seeing no one who looked like her and realised that this wouldn't change without such spaces working to make themselves more inclusive. Across Instagram and in private group chats the group discuss navigating their British Asian lesbian identities, family, religion, and not knowing how to speak to white people about the issues that affect them. She explained, 'I felt whitewashed in my society and life', and that growing up in Britain with immigrant parents meant that often white lesbians misunderstood many aspects of her relationship to her culture, especially her relationship to her family who do not know she is gay. She described having 'multiple identities that can't mix', with one way of being in London, and another when she is staying with her Muslim parents. The reality of this is more complex than white lesbians often tend to assume. 'It's not wrong, it's just different,' she reiterated when describing the relationship she has with her mother in particular. Coming to understand and embrace both her sexuality and her Asian identity has allowed her to forge connections with her mother through important traditional rituals, her mother oiling her hair or dressing her in a sari for Eid. These moments, as she described them to me, were ones she used to hide away from but were important to connect to her mother and her culture. They are also tinged with a sense of loss – that she cannot fulfil the role her mother wishes for her. This nuance of how British Asian identity and sexuality interact is often misrepresented in the assumptions white lesbians project onto British Asian women – often painting them as passive – and overshadows their own lived experiences. When so many British Asian women are not out to their family, their necessary anonymity, for reasons of safety, also risks these voices remaining unheard as they are not archived and preserved. As a project, British Asian Lesbians aims to clearly state that British Asian lesbians have always been here, and to capture their experiences and voices.

I also spoke to Shirine, a bisexual trans Muslim filmmaker and writer currently practicing in London. While Shirine no longer describes themselves as a lesbian, they still have a deep connection to the word. Both as one which once held a lot of importance for them and as a word still used by many of their friends. It indicates a space of safety and familiarity for them. As they told me, 'the identity of lesbianism and the word itself is quite sacred to me, and I love hearing other people from all life journeys and experiences use it to describe themselves'. For them, language is incredibly important to how they define themselves, even as they question the limits of English to fully describe their identity and spirituality:

> I tend to find the language that I use to describe myself, and the fluidity of that, comes most naturally around my queer

> Muslim community. There's an intuitive understanding of the kind of inherent contradiction and slippages [of gender and sexuality]. I think that this speaks to my identity as a queer bisexual person, and also as a Muslim person and how important that is to my identity and sense of self.

For them, being surrounded by queer Muslim community (including lesbians) allows for the freest expression of themselves, which doesn't require qualification or explanation: 'If I'm in a space where there are people who are queer in different ways, trans in different ways, bisexual in different ways, but there's this common kind of thread of Islam running amongst us, there's this more comfortableness of simply being.'

As Kawale says: 'It appeared that white women could ignore the privileges of whiteness, and experienced the scene differently to how South Asian women experienced it, and while the scene supported sexual diversity, stereotypical notions about "race" and ethnicity remained deep-rooted within it.'[4] Kawale identifies this as a kind of emotion labour on lesbians of colour to perform their lesbian identities in white spaces in a way that is acceptable or 'readable' to white lesbians, often at the cost of their ethnic identities. Essentially forcing them unfairly to choose between their race and their sexuality.

The need for British Asian Lesbians' Instagram shows that this is still a long-term systemic issue. That London Friend was a predominately white gay and lesbian space was something many of its volunteers or users may not even have considered. Nor how unwelcoming or uninformed such a space might appear. They were not alone in being unable to answer the needs of its Black callers, as one lesbian, Dolores, notes in the 'Special Lesbian Issue' of the GLC Women's Committee magazine: 'Meeting other black lesbians was difficult, initially. I didn't know where to find them, and neither did the white people on Gay Switchboard or [London] Lesbian Line.'[5] This, then, was a wider issue across many of the phone lines that they needed to address.

It's clear from London Friend's annual reports, monthly newsletters and flyers that many of its committee were actively trying to diversify their group attendees who mostly skewed towards white gay men. To counter this they sought to encourage more lesbians, Black people and people of colour to volunteer. Flyers from the late '80s, '90s and into the early 2000s include call outs declaring: 'We are specifically looking for lesbians and black and minority ethnic lesbians and gay men.'

Tracking how effective this was is tricky. There is some basic accountably on data collection from the later '80s regarding the ethnic backgrounds of London Friend's service users. In 1988 during their census week they recorded over forty people out of 194 service users that were from an 'ethnic minority',[6] which was a huge uplift from eight the previous year. But given the diversity of London, only 20 per cent seems low. Sadly, I don't have data on whether this trend continued or if these drives for diversity were effective or long lasting. That they continued to make specific call outs into the 2000s would suggest it was ongoing work, but also that they were aware that without explicit moves towards inclusivity for their hosted groups, leaders and volunteers, they wouldn't see positive change.

One way London Friend sought to bring more people of colour and other ethnic groups to their services was through the groups they ran or accommodated. These included Fusion, for multiracial gay men; the South Asian Lesbian and Gay Network (Shakti); Orientations (Chinese and SE Asian gay and lesbian group); Cypriot Lesbian and Gay Group and the Jewish Lesbian & Gay helpline, who all used London Friend as a meeting place at different times. However, there weren't separate groups specifically for Black lesbians and lesbians of colour at London Friend until 1989–90. These consisted of ONYX for Black lesbians and Shakti Women's Group, who met on the first Sunday of every month.

ONYX was formed by a group of Black lesbians who worked at Changes and LAFS who wanted to organise a separate social and discussion group for Black lesbians and lesbians of colour. They met on 10 September and by the following October, ONYX was made official. It aimed to 'provide a warm welcome, in the London Friend style, to all Black lesbians and lesbians of colour. It's for people in all situations and any age'.[7] It took as its logo a globe drawn into the circle of the women's symbol which also formed part of its name. Its time at London Friend proved to be short-lived, however, and in 1991 ONYX moved their meetings to the Camden Lesbian Centre & Black Lesbian Group (CLC&BLG) on Phoenix Road, not far from Euston station. According to Lucy Brownson, an archivist and researcher at the Glasgow Women's Library, the reason for this move may have been because London Friend could only provide a white male facilitator for their meetings. At CLC&BLG, Brownson notes that they:

> hosted monthly discussions and activities centred on a different theme or issue each month, ranging from mental health, to activism on lesbians and HIV/AIDS, through to creative sessions and poetry readings [and] ran workshops on aspects of lesbian life that might otherwise be awkward or difficult to broach – for instance, one of their first workshops at 54–56 Phoenix Road was on lesbian and gay sex for beginners.[8]

ONYX's formation and subsequent move from London Friend is just one example of the kind of structural barriers that groups of Black lesbians and lesbians of colour were forced to navigate in majority white-led queer spaces. By failing to have other Black lesbians on its staff London Friend lost out on hosting the group and contradicted its aim towards creating a more inclusive environment.

The mid '80s and early '90s saw several such groups organise together as well as the creation of the aforementioned CLC&BLG, originally two separate organisations (the Camden Lesbian Centre and the Black Lesbian Group) which merged in 1985 through the establishment of an equally balanced committee of white and Black lesbians. The CLC&BLG gave lesbians of colour a vital permanent physical meeting space. The ongoing creation of such Black lesbian groups was in part a response to a lack of acceptance both in white lesbian groups and from within Black feminist groups. It left Black lesbians doubly excluded and marginalised, despite often being at the centre of such activism. As Lola Olufemi notes in *Feminism, Interrupted*, grass-roots organisations formed in the late '70s and early '80s such as

OWAAD, while united on their stance for racial, class, gender and labour equality, were worried about campaigning for gay rights. They were concerned they might alienate other radical male political groups they wanted to work with or tarnish their reputation as a feminist group. As such the demands of Black queer women in these spaces often went ignored or unaddressed:

> The issues of queer women although urgent and politically relevant, were sidelined because activists lacked the language and conviction to understand queerness' relation to feminist work and questions of state violence . . . As a women's group, they [OWAAD] were required to prove their political relevancy to men who accused them of division; this resulted in a deep anxiety about the presentation of their work and practices, leading to a culture of silence around questions of sexuality, mandating a negation of queer life.[9]

As Valerie Mason-John and Ann Khambatta note in their indispensable anthology of essays and interviews with Black lesbians in Britain, *Lesbians Talk: Making Black Waves,* during the women's liberation movement and in militant Black groups, Black lesbians experienced homophobia in Black spaces and racism in lesbian ones. They remained 'silent and isolated. We were required to break our identities into acceptable fragments: we were Black in Black groups, women in the women's movement and lesbians on the lesbian scene. There was no space to be whole, to be Black lesbians.'[10]

The founding of centres in the 1980s such as the Black

Lesbian and Gay Centre, which opened in 1985 in Haringey, and groups such as Peckham Black Women's Group (1981); Black Lesbian Group (1982); Chinese Lesbian Group (1983); Black Lesbian Support Network (1983); Asian Women Writers' Collective (1984) and Camden Lesbian Group (mid 1980s), as well as many other conferences, newsletters and magazines throughout the 1980s were important and radical spaces for Black lesbians and gay men to meet, organise and express themselves fully. October 1985 saw the Zami I conference held in London, attended by over two hundred women of African or Asian descent. It was followed by Zami II in 1989, this time in Birmingham and again over two days welcomed over two hundred women. The need for such spaces was self-evident.

As well as social and community spaces, discos and club nights were instrumental in bringing Black lesbians together and be themselves. As part of Haringey Vanguard, a Black LGBTQ+ community heritage project, DJ Yvonne Taylor recalled the lack of pubs and clubs that appealed to her during her visits to London in '70s and '80s.[11] She later told *gal-dem* magazine:

> I met this collective called Sistermatic. We ran a monthly club at South London's Women's Centre on Acre Lane, in Brixton. We had no idea what we were setting in motion ... the night gave Black lesbians a riotous space to explore their sexuality as well as their style. We invited all types of women. Whether you were a style queen or if you wanted to wear miniskirts or whatever. We had a representation of all types of lesbians. There were Asian

> women there, punks there, feminists there . . . I think the party changed a lot of people's concepts of sexuality, a lot of Black lesbians back then were living double lives and we wanted to make it okay to just be whoever you wanted to be.[12]

As writer Jason Okundaye notes, it was 'more than just a club . . . it was a community'.[13] The message from Black lesbians and lesbians of colour was clear: if they weren't welcome on the white lesbian scene they would make their own spaces to meet, talk, flirt, debate, dance, protest and simply be their full selves. White lesbians didn't always respond positively to this, seeing such actions as a betrayal of 'sisterly solidarity' and choosing race over sexuality. As if it was a choice they hadn't been forced to make. As if seeing it as a choice in the first place wasn't a specifically white way of looking at things.

Just one example of this from the early '90s is journalist Megan Radcliffe's review of the *Lesbians Talk: Making Black Waves* anthology. The introduction to *Making Black Waves* notes that it's the first book to record the history of Black lesbians in Britain and discuss the issues that have directly affected them. Radcliffe, a white lesbian reviewer, panned the book in *Time Out* magazine, blaming Black lesbians for not engaging in the lesbian scene and preferring the solidarity of Black men. She refuses to engage in a meaningful conversation about race in the review while declaring that none of this is her fault and Black lesbians only speak to make her feel guilty. At all points white lesbians and their feelings are centered. It's not a review to linger over,[14] but I think it's a useful insight into the attitudes from some white lesbians around race during the time of the logbook. We might recognise this today as 'white fragility', a term coined by Robin DiAngelo to describe the defensiveness white people display when confronted with their own complicity in upholding racist structures and ways of thinking.[15] Regrettably, I don't think any of the prejudices expressed in the review are surprising to contemporary ears. It's just one example of racism from white lesbians in the mainstream media, although they did not go unchallenged.

There were more complex conversations happening in radical feminist and political magazines such as *Bad Attitude* and *Spare Rib*, which wanted to make their spaces more inclusive. In the June 1990 issue of *Spare Rib* there was a feature on lesbian representation in the Channel 4 series *Out on Tuesday*. This interview features a nuanced conversation with one of the white editors, Mandy Merck, about the lack of Black representation in the television series. Merck points out that their all-white executive team meant that they struggled to reach Black communities or to gain their trust due to the mishandling of Black representation already on television. She blames being unable to find Black directors and researchers as one reason for the lack of input, but also said they worked to ensure that Black lesbians and gay men were represented on the show outside of issues surrounding race.[16] The interviewer pushes back on this, pointing out that even as one of the more racially diverse programmes on Channel 4 at the time, it still struggled to accurately portray the various attitudes in the Black lesbian and gay community, and without Black members on the production team it will never be truly inclusive of Black lesbian and gay experiences.[17] Again we see how structures of whiteness fail to even see who it is that they are excluding by not having Black gay and lesbian people involved behind the camera as well as in front of it.

Building on the work of the Black feminist movement and anti-racist groups, Black lesbians and their allies had the language and support to challenge these displays of racism to some degree. Radcliffe's review prompted a protest by the London Lesbian Avengers (which Radcliffe herself was a part of) and led to a 'zap' (a public demonstration or intervention) outside the *Time Out* office. Mrittika Datta in *Bad Attitude* magazine responded to the review with a powerful statement of intent and refusal to give up her right to speak into white lesbian spaces and call out the racism she saw there. She wrote:

> I thought about the ways in which the talking space is often assumed to be continuous, whole, so that a provisional safe space is seen as oppressive to that whole. But the 'whole' itself is constructed, exclusive – that black people are overwhelmingly denied a voice there.[18]

Once again we see the language of wholeness invoked, but here Datta inverts this idea to show the ways in which white lesbian spaces that proport to be 'whole' are in fact exclusionary and easily threatened just by the need for separate Black lesbian spaces. She challenges those white lesbians who (ironically) see such separatism as divisive and instead asks them to question how they have made others feel unwelcome. Datta notes that speaking up against these stereotypes is not without cost for Black lesbians and lesbians of colour: 'All these actions bring us slap-bang up against racism ... We grasp or present our Black identities often with a pride that cuts itself off from the mainstream.'[19] For Datta and her fellow Black lesbians to express themselves fully, with all of their happiness, grievances and different selves, they have to create a space away from the racism inherent in structures centred around whiteness.

In the present, events like UK Black Pride and South Asian Pride demonstrate the continued need for these spaces where Black lesbians, South Asian lesbians and lesbians of colour can be their whole selves – doubly so because of the resistance from white queer community events such as that first encountered by UK Black Pride, accused still by other organisations of being separatist. But as Lady Phyll explains, she would not settle for joining the regular Pride. 'I am faced with the lens of whiteness all the time. And when our narrative has been shaped for us, we have to do something, to shape it for ourselves. Hence why UK Black Pride exists ... we have to tell our stories. We really do.'[20] She echoes Datta's final words from almost thirty years ago:

> Often we're tired of the black/white duality created and defined from a white perspective ... We create ourselves in images, familiar, perhaps shocking, that are interruptions into racism and beyond the parameters of its imagination ... The question is, how can we find more and more ways to share all this work, discuss it, see it, flaunt it, enjoy it?[21]

There's a brilliant sense of the richness of Black experience and creativity in this final statement that encourages Black lesbians to take up space and create ways of thinking and being, outside of the racist assumptions others would make of them. To create new ontologies and new worlds for themselves. It also shows how much more work white lesbians need to do to unpick the racism within our community that seeks to limit the bounds of what a Black lesbian can be. Datta's words feel as applicable now as they did then. She refuses to reduce herself to one thing under a white gaze, instead choosing a Black self that is expansive, creative, politically engaged and joyful. She invites others to join her there.

23.2.95 – log by Zeenat: ***She asked me my name and I told her – she said 'that's very unusual'***

She might be the only Asian woman answering the phones but there's certainly more ringing them. She's even had a couple of calls from older women who remind her a bit of her Aunties (not that she would ever tell them that). When she first started volunteering one caller soon set her straight when she said she thought being gay was mostly a white thing since she hardly knew any other Asian lesbians. The caller asked her where she got that idea from and she admitted it was something her mother would say to them growing up, whenever there were gay men on the news, dying in their hundreds.

People think that being Asian and being a lesbian don't go together, the caller had told her, yet here we are. Zeenat had no reply to that, but she's learnt plenty since then, knows now there are lesbians to be found in medieval Islamic poetry and of course there's the groups that run at London Friend. She's not so lonely as she was.

The younger girls who call up remind her of her little sister and her friends, so self-assured. Zeenat feels caught in the middle even though she grew up here. Things are definitely getting better and it's nice to talk to more people on the phones, at least, who understand where she's coming from. But sometimes it feels like things are really slow to change.

Having more Asian women on the phones would help, for one thing. She's tried recruiting a few of her friends but they don't seem interested. She can't blame them, really, they tease her enough about her white girlfriend and being a do-gooder. But at least then the other volunteers wouldn't look to her as the fount of all knowledge for anything to do with race. She mentioned to Clare she'd needed to move a shift around as it coincided with Iftar and she looked so confused. Most of the time it's just friendly curiosity and she honestly doesn't mind but it's always on her to explain. They all live in London, she can't be the only Asian woman they know. But Zeenat likes the work, she enjoys being on the phone, even the hard calls. She likes being able to sit and listen and feel like she's helping. She likes making her little doodles that scrawl up the

> page – it helps her think. There are nights when she wants to quit like anyone, but she really believes what they do here matters. She wants to try.

So what of the Black lesbians and lesbians of colour who called the Lesbian Line looking for advice or a chat? What did they find waiting for them at the other end of the line? There were overwhelming odds that the person picking up the phone would be white. As far as phone workers go, from the few years covered in the logbook, there was only one phone worker who identified herself as Asian. I doubt she was the only non-white phone worker but she is the only person who explicitly talks about her race. I'm certain there were others and while I'm reluctant to assume the rest were white, it's not too much of a stretch to conclude that white volunteers were in the majority from the AGM reports and requests for volunteers of colour. Looking through the pictures I've found of the Lesbian Line (both London Friend's and the London Lesbian Line) in newspapers as well as the small handful of photographs from the London Friend archive at Islington's Pride there are no pictures of Black lesbians or lesbians of colour. I know there must have been others like Zeenat who volunteered, but the record of them has vanished into the white pages of the logbook.

Likewise, I don't know how many Black lesbians and lesbians of colour rang the line as no records on race or ethnicity were recorded and many callers may not have wished to disclose this information had they been asked, nor might it have been relevant to what their call was about. Instead, I'm left to infer from the records and conversations callers had with the line – an imperfect method to say the least that risks tokenising Black lesbians and lesbians of colour as calling only to discuss race. After all, these calls were made over the phone and assumptions and inferences as to a person's ethnicity would have been frequently made. A couple of times a caller is identified as Black, usually as a way to distinguish them from another caller of the same name. Never is a caller identified as white; if they had a regional or European accent this might be noted but it tells me little about the racial or ethnic identity of the callers. There are a few callers identified as 'Asian', and one regular caller who is identified as Black and disabled, who lives at home with her mother who doesn't accept her sexuality.

There is one call in particular which a phone worker identifies as potentially from an Asian woman, but the person making the log is unsure. It seems like an assumption based on the caller's described home life and current situation. The log is from a twenty-year-old caller who is upset and confused and in love with a woman, while her family is pressuring her to marry a man. I have no way to know her ethnicity for certain, nor whether the phone worker's guess is a correct one or based on assumed stereotypes about South Asian families and traditions. Either way it's not much to go on.

There is only one repeat caller identified as Asian, referred colloquially by the moniker 'Angry Asian Woman', which already gives some indication of the nature of her calls and how she was perceived by some of the phone workers. The first recorded call in the logbook is in late December 1995, but this isn't her first call since the volunteer describes her as 'still very angry'. The calls consist of a conversation about what the caller describes as the scapegoating and lack of community in the lesbian scene. She goes on to talk about the ways that she feels she has been alienated from the lesbian community because she's Asian. During her call she rails against what she sees as the elite 'conservative' runners/rulers of the scene. The call ends abruptly. Clare, who wrote the log, is non-committal and the record is more focused on the caller's anger than the subject matter of her call.

Below this entry Cora has added a note with a tone of confusion stating that the caller told her 'she wasn't black when I spoke to her – she'd asked me, so I asked her'. It's unclear if Cora was using 'Black' here in its broader political sense (possibly outdated for the time) and the caller therefore took offence as an Asian woman. This comment does reveal a lack of awareness from the volunteer and how easily misassumptions can be made, especially over the phone.

The next time she calls it's Zeenat who answers the phone and their conversation appears to be much more in-depth; there's a different dynamic between them as Asian lesbians speaking to one another and in many ways the call is more confrontational. The caller uses a racist slur aimed at Zeenat herself for choosing to work on the Lesbian Line, using it to demonstrate how the caller thinks the others will talk about Zeenat behind her back. It could be seen as an attempt to shock Zeenat into understanding what the caller is trying to articulate about the way white women treat her as an Asian woman on the lesbian scene. The caller sees Zeenat as being guilty of assimilating into the white lesbian organisation and abandoning her own cultural heritage.

While the caller here is making some broad assumptions about Zeenat, this pressure to assimilate or tone down their relationship to their Black or Asian heritage is something that other Black lesbians and lesbians of colour regularly experienced. As other writers at the time have already noted, there was no way for Black lesbians and lesbians of colour to 'win' here, since joining the wider (implicitly white) lesbian community meant fragmenting their selves into what was deemed acceptable by white standards and their assumptions about their own culture. Refusing to do so would have them deemed as uncooperative or not wanting to engage. Zeenat doesn't have a chance to discuss her own feelings about this and so they are absent from the log. It's likely that she wouldn't anyway since she admirably tries to keep the conversation focused on the caller rather than respond to the accusations aimed at her. Zeenat notes that any attempts to enter into a dialogue with her are shut down and 'she just kept talking at me'.

Zeenat ends her log with a sense of defeat and disappointment, either at herself for not handling it better, or at being unable to calm down the caller. It is of course upsetting to be on receiving end of such anger and to absorb so much pain and hurt from someone else, all the while knowing the person does not know you or your situation. Zeenat writes: 'I must admit that this call made me feel very uncomfortable – I really felt on the defensive.' This call is a reminder that no community is a monolith and that this question of assimilation around cultural and sexual identities was an active one during this time, as it is today.

Not all the volunteers find the calls difficult. Clare, in the end, seems to rather enjoy the conversations they have, or at least says she finds them interesting. However, the caller hangs up on her because Clare refuses to agree that the gay and lesbian community is 'divisive, political & incestuous', as the caller describes it. While Clare doesn't have to agree with her here, there is a failure to listen to what the caller was trying to say. The question should not be about whether the caller is right or wrong about the inclusively of the lesbian community, but how can the Lesbian Line best support her needs. From her records, it seems Clare often let herself be drawn into numerous debates with callers; perhaps she saw her role as a challenging voice rather than a listening ear, but it has varying results. In this instance it closed down the conversation rather than expand any mutual understanding.

The caller says she is 'glad to be out of it' (the gay and lesbian community) yet she is still calling a lesbian line, she is the one making contact. Even if it's to lash out at them, it's clear she needs someone to talk to and must feel lonely and abandoned. To then have the person who answers the phone deny these feelings or to say the community is not divisive must be doubly frustrating. Clare ends the log by asking others how they are getting on with this caller, indicating that while Clare finds these calls instructive (perhaps) she is still ill equipped to respond appropriately. Clare is looking for a solution to these calls to change her mind rather than support the caller and understand her emotional state. There is a great deal of trust lost here, something I don't think some of the phone workers even realised they needed to establish. All of them respond defensively; admittedly, these calls sounds very difficult to be on the receiving end of, but there is no self-reflection in the logs about making their own lesbian spaces more inclusive. The wider accounts of London Friend show this wasn't the case everywhere, but for this period – as far as I can see in the logbook at least – there's a startling lack of self-awareness.

It's Zeenat again who takes her call next, a month or so later. Tonight, Zeenat notes she is different, whereas before she has been 'aggressive and rude', today she is calmer but the subject is the same. She wishes to talk about the lesbian scene in general, in particular all the cliques and insider groups that make it up. This conversation, though, sounds more positive, at least from the phone worker's point of view. And I do mean conversation – I do not know exactly what was said, of course, only that they 'chatted for a while and then she said she had to go'. As usual Zeenat has doodled around her call log in blue biro, perhaps while they talked. There's a cube, a cylinder, a little hat shape and something like a dagger, as well as other abstract shapes dotted around the page.

There's no doubt that the caller has been marginalised and abused by the white lesbian community, that the racism she has experienced has ostracised her and left her hurt and angry. This pain is the harm that racism – the women, clubs, bars and services that have made her feel like an outsider – has inflicted on her. The women who answer her calls are facing the fallout from this experience as she seeks to defend herself from further harm. Zeenat in particular is seen by the caller as doubly complicit by 'siding' with those who keep her on the outside and so is the object of her anger, while simultaneously being the one person on the line who might most understand her situation. But the Lesbian Line more widely represented the community that had rejected her and was a tangible target at which she could direct her anger. These calls are complex in nature; multiple logs describe her as angry, abusive or aggressive, and many of the volunteers describe being made to feel uncomfortable or attacked and struggle to converse with the caller because of the force of her pain and anger. Some of the discomfort is from the white volunteers having to re-examine their own attitudes towards race and racism within lesbian spaces, something they might not have had to consider previously. This discomfort leads to the defensiveness we see in logs like Clare's.

Without hearing the calls it's impossible to know how much of this anger recorded in the logs was present and how much was interpreted as anger by the person on the end of the phone. How much her identity as an Asian woman might have played into the white phone worker's responses when listening to someone describe problems and divisions within the community. As we've seen, white lesbians wanted to believe the community was cohesive and supportive – and often to them it did appear that way. The majority of the logs describe the caller as 'Angry Asian Woman' – it's not until a few calls later than someone notes in parenthesis, 'We must get her name!' It wasn't unusual to give the callers nicknames like this, but with regular callers the logs often referred to them by their actual name. That no one thinks to ask for her name is perhaps a small example of the way she was seen for her emotional and ethnic identity first rather than as an individual in need of support. Zeenat never calls her this nickname, only once referring to her as 'Asian woman who sounded very angry'. Elsewhere, another self-identified Asian caller's name is misspelled by the person making the log and with a question mark after it. Simple things such as not knowing how to pronounce or record a person's name means that not only did the caller potentially feel uncomfortable and misunderstood during the call, but also that records were not properly kept or as easily traced. As we have also seen, the volunteers themselves were not immune to incidents of racism and racist remarks from the callers. Zeenat notes one instance of a caller remarking on her 'unusual' name, and no doubt there were other instances of such microaggressions.

I want to be clear I think abuse of any kind should not be tolerated but, in the case of someone calling for help and care, as I think this caller is, I can perhaps understand it while at the same time not condone it. Again, this is not a question of moral judgements over who is in the right or wrong, or who has suffered most harm, but how the politics of care work intersect with racial trauma, bias, white fragility and a lack of understanding and empathy. The needs of this caller were not met over and over, both by the lesbian community and the phone workers who often did not know how to respond; it was their job to listen, but the caller felt unheard and, sadly, too often she was met with defensiveness and disbelief.

*

Like all the calls there are layers of distance between myself and the caller, but here there is an extra distance in my position as a white reader, seeing this small insight into the life of another lesbian speaking about exclusion from a community I myself have been unquestionably welcomed into. I am reminded of Danielle Brathwaite-Shirley's work and the need to be aware of one's own position in relation to history and access to knowledge. There are layers of bias inherent in my reading of these notations and it's one I have attempted to resist and question.

The history of Black lesbians and lesbians of colour is far more wide-ranging and complex than I could ever fully capture here – and I don't wish to relegate their lives to one small chapter in a book. There are others telling this Black queer history more fully and I would encourage you to seek out their stories and archives, such as the work of Paula Akpan, Bernice Mulenga, Veronica Mckenzie, Shivani Dave, Sue Lemos, Sabah Choudrey, British Asian Lesbians, the Haringey Vanguard archive and the rukus! Black, Lesbian, Gay, Bisexual and Trans (BLGBT) cultural archive, as well as the academics and writers I have referenced in this chapter. As Paula Akpan writes: 'So much of what forms the slim official record of Black lesbian history in Britain emphasises political organising, rather than how the community lived, loved and whiled away their free time.'[22] There are so many more stories to be told and our history is incomplete without them.

What Happens When a Lesbian Makes a Move

14.12.95 – log by April: ***I said 'don't worry nothing will ever come of it, & there's probably a lot of feelings around at the moment'***
She's just such a good listener, this woman at the Lesbian Line. I feel like I could tell her anything, everything. Sometimes you just get that instant connection with a person. Like a spark. Isn't that what they say? It's exciting of course to feel like you can say all the things you've never been able to before. Or had been too afraid to say out loud. I could tell she was hanging onto every word I had to say. Like it was only the two of us in the whole world. I hadn't told anyone else before, I suppose it was a coming-out call of sorts. I told her about the affair at work – the whole thing from start to finish. Over really before I could blink but I don't regret it.

I never thought I'd be the one with another woman either, but you know how these things happen. Another spark she was I suppose. We shagged in the office. Is that the right word for it?

It sounds bad saying it out loud. Well, one thing led to another, we were both a bit drunk and next thing you know we were pushing ourselves into the stationery cupboard. I guess you could say she shagged me, or I shagged her? These things are all new to me. We kinda took turns. So what does that mean? I ask the woman on the phone. If her hand was . . . ?

The woman at the line interrupts me before I can finish my train of thought. She says, You don't have to go into details actually, that's quite enough. Suddenly sounding so prim! Honestly though I can't help it, my mind is all over the place. I feel like I'm still spinning. Maybe she doesn't want to hear about another woman if she thinks we have something of our own going on.

I tell her not to worry about her – that's long since over now. I know what it's like to listen to some bloke drone on and on so I ask her questions about herself. How long has she been on the phone lines for? Does she know any good places to go out? Y'know, gay-friendly places? She reels off a few but I've never heard of any of them so it doesn't mean much to me.

Well, where do you like to go on the weekends? I say. What do you do for fun? Her answers are getting shorter and shorter, she sounds a little suspicious. It's not like I'm looking for anything long term – I just want to get a sense of her. Feel her out, y'know, see if there's a decent club night that

> maybe one time we could accidentally-on-purpose bump into each other at. I hope she feels the same spark I do. I've almost convinced myself I'm half in love with this woman already and I've not even seen her! She must know what it's like, must remember when she first came out, it must have felt the same. Like a whole new world opening up.
>
> There's all this lesbian stuff to get to grips with, I say, not to mention all these women to get a grip on! Haha. No, don't worry, I tell her, just my idea of a joke. The woman on the phone gives me the brush off then and tells me she doesn't think anything is going to come of this. Which, hey, is fair enough. Plenty more fish in the sea as they say.

For lesbians the line between friendship and relationship can be a blurry one. Friends become lovers, lovers become friends. I know more than one long-term couple who didn't realise they were dating well into what the other considered the start of their relationship, thinking they were just 'really good friends'. I've had more than one intense friendship with another queer woman where we've flirted with the idea of it being something more, before mutually deciding we're much better off as friends. Female friendship has long been a helpful cover for women wishing to conceal the true nature of their relationship to the outside world. Nowadays, 'just good friends' or 'gal pals' has become something of a cliché, used to expose the ways in which lesbian and gay relationships have been erased historically. Another pejorative we'd turned into an in-joke. Seen from the inside this blurry line between friendship and something more is, I think, one of the great joys of being queer. Far from the stereotype of the predatory lesbian, creeping on her friends, it is more about the unique way that lesbians have learnt to build community. Out of the wreckage of a failed relationship a friendship can emerge. Not always, of course, but sometimes.

That friendship is as important as a sexual relationships is also borne out in many of the small ads you find in the women-seeking-women section in old magazines. In the back of '90s issues of *Spare Rib* you are as likely to find a request for friendship as you are a relationship. Sometimes it was both, the writer wanting to hedge their bets. When you know your kin are few and far between you learn to take what you can get, I suppose, and who knows where it might lead? The small ads under 'Relationships' might list things like:

> Lesbian, 42, professional, sincere, non-smoker, animal lover, varied interests, seeks friendship/ relationship.

> LONDON. Gay professional, 40s, sensitive, caring, seeks counterpart.

> Non-scene lesbian, young 37, professional. Love countryside, music. Sincere, genuine seeks same for friendship/relationships. Photo appreciated.

> Essex lesbian, young 36, quiet sense of
> humour, non-scene, professional, seeks
> friendship with similar, pref non-smoker.

There's usually a lot of descriptions of lesbians as being 'non-scene' in these ads, e.g. not part of the lesbian scene – usually to mean going out to clubs and pubs. Which would make sense; the lesbians that weren't into going out would need other avenues to find friendship or relationships and depending on where you lived there might not be social groups or easy places to meet other lesbians. Often the small-ad writers were from outside of London or other big cities. Long before dating apps became the norm, posting a small ad in a feminist or lesbian magazine was an effective way to find a friend (or maybe more).

For London Friend, however, the line between friendship and relationship was by necessity an incredibly strict one. As the name suggests, London Friend, which ran not only the Lesbian Line but also a Mixed Line, plus various in-person services and groups, was (and is) at its core a befriending service. Their existence highlights the vital role friendship plays in the health and well-being of LGBTQ+ people. Its service creates space for its surrounding queer community to meet each other and facilitate friendships. What it is not is a dating service, and relationships between the volunteers and users of the service are strictly *verboten*.

London Friend had official policies in place to prevent callers or volunteer phone workers from overstepping their personal boundaries. In the same archival box that holds the logbook there is a 'Befriending Statement and Guidelines' from December 1992, right around the time of the logbook. In it the rules are direct: phone workers should not interact with callers outside of the phone lines unless absolutely necessary. 'The aim is to help the caller to make their own friends', the guidelines emphasise. As a last resort volunteers may provide in-person support to a caller; for instance, if they felt they wouldn't be able to go to a group by themselves, though ideally they would be referred directly to a counsellor or in-person service. Any meet-ups have to be recorded and other volunteers informed of the arrangement. The guidelines clearly state that it's considered a form of abuse to have a sexual relationship with the person you are befriending and any violations will result in the volunteer being asked to leave. They stress the need for 'clear and firm boundaries between you and the caller', and as far as I can see from the logbook the phone workers took this very seriously.

But while at London Friend relationships with callers were a serious no-go, their social groups like Changes and LAFS encouraged lesbians using their services to make friends, and of course some did end up romantically involved. As Annette told me during her time volunteering at Changes she saw several successful relationships form between service users, both romantic and platonic, and they would actively encourage the women to go out together as a group. 'People developed really good friendships and supported one another when they were going to bars, nudged each other on to get people up to dance. You'd hear about it the following week . . . that was always lovely.' She says, most importantly, 'they had each other's backs'. Annette herself started volunteering after a ten-year relationship she was in ended, for her it was an important way to reconnect with the lesbian community and help others. Sometimes on nights out she would spot women she recognised from Changes but she always kept her distance. Even now there's a sense of pride and wonder at seeing women she had supported out on a night out: 'They'd be changed women . . . they'd get their confidence. Whether they were twenty, thirty or forty, they'd start to come out as *them*.' It didn't always go so smoothly, however. Indeed, one caller rings the Lesbian Line depressed because the woman she met at Changes has stopped being interested in her and she needs some advice. Managing the group's dynamics required a steady hand from the volunteers.

Other lesbian lines didn't have such a strict policy of interaction between volunteers and callers. Some operated as an incidental dating service and events like the London Lesbian Line discos or the Cambridge Lesbian Line's informal parties helped callers (some of whom lived in rural spots) to meet up with other lesbians. What they got up to from there was their own business. As we saw in Cheryl Slack's account of interacting with the London Lesbian Line, the phone worker there had no qualms about taking her to the West London Women's Centre and they even ended up dating for a few weeks. There aren't many calls in the logbook from women explicitly asking about dating services, but there are plenty asking for the details of lesbian groups they could join and pubs and bars to go to that were lesbian friendly or likely to have a high female contingent.

There's one curious call from 1995 that hints at just how small the lesbian dating pool was in London at the time. The call is from someone who, ironically, is complaining about the lesbian scene being too insular and cliquish. The call goes on for a while until the caller asks for the name of the person they are speaking to and once they have it, very quickly rings off. The volunteer simply notes: 'Bizarre!!!' It seems likely that the caller perhaps knew the volunteer, or at least knew *of* her (an ex of a friend perhaps?) enough to panic and hang up as soon as she found out her name.

Similarly, there's one instance in the logbook of a new phone worker writing to let the others know she has had a sexual relationship with one of their regular callers and they remain friends. She requests that no information about her is discussed with the caller, including when she is next volunteering, but that the caller does know she is working on the line. She stresses she will 'keep my friendship with J– outside of L.F. separate from any contact I have with her on L.F.'s phone lines'. For this volunteer, at least, she certainly took the separation between the helpline and their personal lives very seriously and wished to maintain a professional relationship while at work, without having to break off their friendship.

It's maybe a stereotype that all lesbians stay friends after break-ups but there is plenty of anecdotal evidence to indicate it's fairly common. On a practical level a local lesbian community can be small and so distance between you and your ex might not be possible or desirable if it means finding a whole new group of friends. No doubt this was amplified before social media and digital communication, when the majority of social interactions were in person. Lesbian events for gay women would likely attract the same people – especially where they crossed over with other subcultures that form around music, sports, kink or activism,[1] as well as intersections across lines of race, class and disability.

There's a reason Alice's infamous chart from *The L Word*, which tracks the interlocking dating histories of the queer women of West Hollywood, is an enduring lesbian cliché. There's a more up-to-date equivalent to be found in Maddy Court's excellent zine *The Ex-Girlfriend of My Ex-Girlfriend Is My Girlfriend*, which dispenses dating advice to queer women on topics such as long-distance relationships, broken hearts and how to tell your girlfriend you're faking your orgasms. It's a kind of mini Lesbian Line in book form and its title sums up plenty of queer women's dating history. Even as a baby gay, newly out onto whatever remains of the London dating 'scene', I quickly discovered this fact for myself, discovering hours before a date that my friend had been on a disastrous night out with the very same person the week before. Often there is little more than one degree of separation between you, your date and another queer you both know.

For me, entering the world of lesbian dating was a raft of new experiences and anxieties around my status as someone so newly out. Big-time imposter syndrome. When it comes to relationships, flirting or making any sort of move I'm more likely to be the person calling the helpline than the one handing over sage advice. Before I realised I was a lesbian I had never really dated. Not like *dating* dating, like actually trying to go and get a date. I'd had a boyfriend in my teens and while I suppose you could say we went on dates to the bowling alley and the park (where else can teens under eighteen go?), we mostly hung out at each other's houses. Fumbling at each other in our bedrooms, talking about deeply intense teenage things or, in an extremely cool twist, writing a fantasy novel together on the computer in his family spare room. Eventually, as horrible as it sounds, I just didn't want to be around him any more. I was bored, I think, and realised that I'd rather be doing anything else than hanging out with him. I broke up with him in my local park. He cried, I didn't. I'm not even sure I felt that bad about it. I thought he would be the first of many boyfriends. Most of my friends were onto their second or third by this point and I felt like I had some catching up to do. In the end I never dated a man properly again – not for want of trying on my part, although even at the time I think they sensed my enthusiasm was rather lacklustre.

I thought I had crushes on plenty of guys when I met them: a housemate at uni, a guy from the Christian Union committee, a co-worker, a friend of a friend at a party. My attempts at flirting were unsuccessful. This could be because my definition of flirting was to try to make them laugh at my jokes and talk about video games. Or as I prefer to think, because somehow, unknown to myself, I gave off such dykish vibes that the men knew to steer clear. It's nice to suppose that my subconscious was protecting myself even then. But who can say. Of course, at the time I assumed that there was something wrong with me because that's what I understood it meant if no one (no man) wanted me. I had plenty of friends so I knew I wasn't unlikable, but I was perhaps un*lovable*.

After a while I simply stopped trying to find someone, happy to be single. I told myself not to worry, the right man would come along at the right time. There were stabs of incredible loneliness at times, but when you've been single for long enough that even the old ladies at church stop asking you when you're going to find a fella it becomes an easy, entirely normal thing. I had a loving family and good friends around me, my life in London kept me busy. To me, being single was my default and I was fine with that.

It's strange thinking about my former self, someone I hardly recognise now. How embarrassing that I thought I was *straight*. Sad too that I wasted so much time, that I thought there was something wrong with me. It's odd to think the majority of my life I didn't know about this whole other part of myself, or that when I failed spectacularly with dating men, I never considered the alternative. Instead, I assumed I simply had to keep at it or accept it just wasn't for me. I never even considered I might be a lesbian for so long because everything I knew had taught me that I must be in want of a husband. I just hadn't met the right 'one' yet. And so, the steps involved between dating my first boyfriend to going on my first date with a girl were agonisingly slow and fraught with confusion, self-doubt and shame.

In the end it was a friend who inadvertently got me on Tinder. It was April 2017, not too long after I'd tentatively come out to a few of my close queer friends but before I'd told my family or even kissed a girl. We'd been out-out and that particular night ended with a chilly confession outside and an awkward misalignment of flirting. A friend told me they had a crush on me which unfortunately I did not reciprocate and so fumbled my way through a reply to let them down as gently as I could. They then told me that they thought my friend's friend was flirting with me the whole night, which I knew for a fact was not true because my friend, whom I actually did have a crush on, fancied *her* friend and they ended the night together. This was perhaps the closest I have been to the plot of *The L Word*. I'll draw you a diagram:

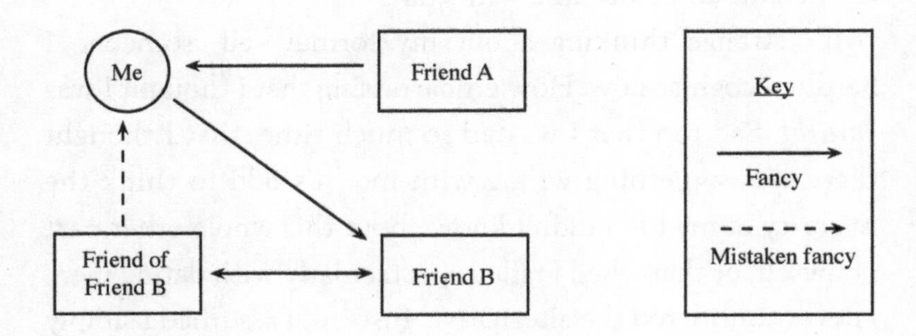

I made a hasty retreat and left them to it, yelling goodbye as I ran for the bus and spent the journey texting my best friend from home the cliché of the lesbian evening I'd just had. I felt happy, giddy with an adrenaline rush of emotions, a little guilty, embarrassed (as always) but alive with the knowledge that my lesbian identity had been affirmed in some strange way. Someone fancied me, which honestly felt like a revelation despite it being unreciprocated (I'm entirely grateful to them for being so gracious and kind about it), and they had even thought someone else had been flirting with me. If one person fancied me, the odds were someone else would, right?

12.3.98 – log by Linda: *lasted for 2 mins on info*

Hiiiiiiiiiii, is this the Lesbian Line? Is anybody there?

Hahaha, no not you, Stella, shhhhhh, no no, shut up I'm on the phone.

Hello, hi, hi are you still there? Yeah yeah, I'm all

right, I'm in Brighton on ummmmm thingy street, you know the one round the back streets? Near the vegan café? I dunno the name sorry, there was a payphone and I just need . . . no shush, Stella, get offffffffff. Yeah sorry, I just need the name of a lesbian pub cos it's early but we went a bit too hard maybe before we went out and I dunno know where we are now or where to go. You got any ideas? Hellooooo?

A good queer night, one where you feel welcomed and accepted and the music hits just right, is a very special thing. It's one thing to go to any old pub with your gay friends, but it's another to be screaming the lyrics to Britney's 'Toxic' at 2 a.m., sweaty and happy, shoulder to shoulder with a bunch of people who just *get it*. A good dance night should be hot in every sense of the word. Ideally there should be ample opportunity to find someone to fuck or fall in love with if that's what you're after, or just as equally the option to ignore everyone else except your best mate and dance until your chest hurts and your feet are sore. A good night out should feel like possibility. It should feel like escape. It should feel like freedom.

It should be all of that, but of course LGBTQ+ clubs and bars are not perfect; like any queer space that aims for inclusivity they can also feel exclusive. Often, they are 'cliquey', and who is counted as being on the 'out' can range from being the (perceived) wrong class or race, or how you dressed. The emergence of lesbian and gay nights run by and for Black people or actively trans-inclusive nights speaks to the need to ensure there were spaces everyone could go out to and find their community in. It's why, when you find the right queer night that feels tailor-made for you and your pals, you hold on to it tight, well aware that it could be taken from you at any moment.

The history of lesbians bars offer a snapshot of how lesbian life and dating has changed over the years. One of the most well-known lesbian clubs in England was of course the Gateways on King's Road in Chelsea. It opened in 1930, and then became a members' club in 1963, but didn't restrict itself to women only until 1967. It was infamous for being full of butch/femme couples, split by strict dress codes: suits and short hair for the butches, skirts and lipstick for the femmes. Annette O'Connor recalls being introduced to Gateways on only her second time going out as a lesbian. She told me, 'I lived there. I'd literally go down four or five times a week, Sunday lunch, Monday, Wednesday, Friday, Saturday night. You just lived there, basically, because it was such a good vibe most of the time. Not all of the time, but most of the time.' For many 'the Gates', as it was known, was their first foray into lesbian culture.

Other places took a more haphazard or relaxed approach. Many of the early gay and lesbians bars were just that: for both gays and lesbians and their histories are intertwined, overlapping with drag and trans histories. Gay clubs were more than just places to dance and drink; for many LGBTQ+ people they were safe havens where for an evening they could dress how they liked, flirt with whomever took their fancy and even organise politically. As Clare Summerskill notes in *Gateway to Heaven*, a collection of oral histories from gay men and lesbians, 'the discovery of those bars and clubs was often nothing less than a life-saving event . . . By even setting foot in a gay bar or club we were doing something extremely important, we were seeking out other people like us . . . One of the main reasons for seeking out such a place was that we wanted to know we were not alone.'[2] In her interviews with lesbians she records not only memories of 'the Gates' but other clubs active around the 1960s such as the Fiesta in Notting Hill Gate, and gay pubs such as the Boltons and the Coleherne.

Like today, many of these pubs or clubs were open to all queer people or had specific lesbian nights. In the 1970s more clubs started to appear as gay liberation gained traction and public acceptance. Soho, of course, remained a hub for queer nightlife. One lesbian recalls 'Louisa's supper club', a mixed club run by a French drag queen which brought in a female European crowd. More followed: the White Raven in Bayswater, the Mother Redcap in Herne Hill, the Black Cap in Camden.[3]

The 1980s saw the closure of the iconic Gateways in a shift away from members-only spaces, which were deemed too old-fashioned and stuffy, to discos and clubs with a more public persona. When I spoke to Lisa Power, Diana James and Annette, they all reeled off the clubs and bars they used to frequent: Lemons in Acton, June's on Oxford Street, the Fallen Angel and Rackets on Islington High Street, Minories pub in Tower Hill and of course the Ace of Clubs in Piccadilly. A quick scan of *London Lesbian* magazine from 1988 lists plenty more: the Drill Hall, Venus Rising, the Duke of Wellington pub on Balls Pond Road and Gingers at

Spats (also on Oxford Street). Joelle Taylor captures the joy and recognition of dyke bars during this time in her poem 'A Lesbian Walks into a Bar', writing, 'we share a root language a lesbian / walks into a bar or / a bar walks into a / lesbian how it is to / arrive what it is to / become o holy'.[4] In the preface she explains how the poem is an amalgamation of her experiences when she was younger: 'I wanted to recreate that sense of belonging, especially in terms of an indistinct outer threat. The bar is safe ground and a space for those within to examine their lives.'[5] Going out wasn't just about having a good time and a good flirt (although it was also that), it was where community and selfhood was forged.

As well as pubs and bars there were home-grown nights like Sistermatic, which made space for Black lesbians to meet and dance; Club Kali, founded by DJ Ritu and Rita, which shone a light on South Asian music and culture; or SM dyke nights like Chain Reaction at the Market Tavern. Not to mention the one-off nights and discos organised by places like Black Lesbian & Gay Centre or the Camden Lesbian Centre, and the various lesbian lines, of course. Many of the lesbian nights worked hard to be accessible and inclusive; Eddie Lockhart of Sistermatic, for instance, recalls creating spaces so women could bring their children, and of keeping admission prices affordable for all with a sliding scale of entry costs.[6]

In the '90s the opening of Candy Bar and G-A-Y (formally BANG), both in Soho, indicated something of a revival of the gay club that always seems to be on the brink of dying out. As the '90s identity politics of gay and queer moved more mainstream, lesbian bars had to compete not just with gay bars but straight bars also. Likewise, gay bars began to target a more lucrative straight clientele now they were more public. Jeremy Atherton Lin in *Gay Bar: Why We Went Out* describes this as a 'post-gay' mindset, as '90s postmodernism moved its way from academia to identity, the idea of separate gay and straight clubs lost some of its appeal. He writes: 'One potential reading of this new gay liberation: to be liberated from gay.'[7] While Lin is writing mostly about male gay bars the sentiment extends to lesbians also: maybe we didn't need gay clubs now that gay people could go anywhere. Maybe we didn't want to hide ourselves away in rainbow-flagged pubs. Maybe they were a bit cringe? As the lesbians migrated to their local microbreweries and mixed gay bars, what little lesbian spaces there were began to decline.

However, we should not underestimate the impact of rising rent costs, taxes and overheads that made many lesbian-only venues difficult to maintain. Candy Bar closed in 2013 partly due to a huge increase in its rent. Because I came out too late I never actually went to Candy Bar and so I have to ask my wife what it was like. She thinks for a moment and tells me a story about going upstairs with a girl and getting fingered on the sofa they had up there, before a disappointing snog and goodbye into the night. She shrugs. Everyone who went to Candy Bar has a story like that, she says.

Talking to older lesbians, and even those my age who were out much younger than me, made me realise just how much I had missed. Too trapped in the straight world to be much aware of many of the gay bars during their early 2000s peak. And then by the time I did come out in the late 2010s most of the lesbian bars had vanished anyway. By now even the early

2000s sound like the glory days. But perhaps every generation of lesbians is doomed to think this. Even in my short lesbian existence I'm already nostalgic for clubs that have long since ended. Where could I go to meet lesbians?

For me it was Passionate Necking (RIP), hosted on the last Friday of every month at the Montague Arms (RIP) in Peckham (still going). The door was staffed by friendly looking dykes, it cost £2 to get in and the dance floor was overlooked by taxidermied animals (RIP) and surrounded by a bunch of other random pub junk. The music was wall-to-wall pop hits, queer anthems and dance and R&B music to move your body to. It was a good time. By the standards of the 2010s it ran for a respectable three years from 2015–18, but like many independent queer nights it burned fast and bright and was stopped too soon by the machinations of capitalism. It described itself as 'Peckham's favourite LGBTQ+ friendly pop/R&B/alt/everything dance party'. It was *the* place my small group of queer pals and I would go to dance and flirt. I mostly stuck to dancing, despite desperately wanting to do more of the flirting.

To get there from where I was living at the time in South-West London I had to take a bus, a train and then another bus and then a short walk. It was over an hour in total to get there, but so few were the queer- and lesbian-friendly club nights that I happily made the journey. I had to time my departure for the last train home, jumping sweatily onto the night bus and jamming my headphones into my ears to blast whatever pop song had been playing as I left. From the outside it looked like any other semi-run-down London pub on the corner of the busy Queen's Road in Peckham, its name picked out in gold text along the square Georgian top.

Like many other female and non-binary-focused queer nights and inclusive spaces at that time, Passionate Necking didn't have a permanent home, popping up once a month before disappearing into the internet until it was ready to re-emerge. Not much has changed, to be honest. There's still only one dedicated lesbian bar in Central London, She, which to my mind at least most closely resembles an Anderson shelter and is a mixture of old dykes, baby gays and hun-bun sports lesbians on the prowl (at least it was last time I went). The pandemic saw these nights move online (which for many meant they were accessible for the first time); however, this proved to be temporary and most, if not all, are back in person.

I think we're seeing a reaction to the postmodern shift Atherton Lin describes and a move back towards hyper-localised nights tailored to specific identities and experiences. Certainly, when I was newly out (and single) with a queer female friendship group mostly formed around going out, lesbian and dyke nights were where we wanted to be. At the time of writing this, Aphrodyki, Lick Events, Butch Please, Butch Revival and Pop-Up DykeBar are still going strong. Bethnal Green Working Men's Club continues to host a variety of queer nights as does the Royal Vauxhall Tavern. This is just a small snapshot of the ones I know about. I'm sure there are much cooler nights happening unbeknownst to me and new ones being planned as I type. In January 2024 a new lesbian bar, La Camionera, caused a viral sensation when over five hundred queer women showed up at its launch in Broadway Market.[8] It now has a permanent home in East London, alongside 'big FLINTA*-gay living room' Goldie

Saloon. It's prompted a wave of reporting that there's a 'lesbian renaissance' of club nights and pop-ups for lesbians and dykes[9] alongside a slew of lesbian and queer pop stars: girl in red, Kehlani, MUNA, boygenius, Reneé Rapp, SZA, Peach PRC and Chappell Roan, to name but a few.

I'm cautious of such claims – reminded of how we were a 'trend' in the '90s. The death and reanimation of lesbian clubs and dyke nights is an endlessly told story that's never quite true – they will never fully disappear nor reach a sustainable peak because they continue to hold a precarious position. Often they are pop-ups and as such have to move from venue to venue at the whim of the club owners or promoters. In-person club nights and bricks-and-mortar spaces with a specifically female focus have long risen and declined. Perhaps it's their nature that these nights can only last so long and then slip away for someone else to fill the gap. There are various theories as to why this is the case.

The most likely point to the inequalities of women's wages to fund such events or even attend them, and likewise the rising costs of rent, astronomical in London but rapidly increasing elsewhere, mean permanent homes are difficult to maintain. Within a capitalist framework lesbian-only spaces are seen as risky investments: a limited clientele who are more likely to be both time-poor and economically less well off when compared to their male or straight counterparts. As such, clubs are reluctant to host lesbian-only nights because they are seen to offer a lower economical return.[10] As Beverley Skeggs describes it, 'Gay men have a greater volume of and access to different forms of legitimate capital which can be spatialised, unlike most lesbians and straight women.'[11] She notes that historically, exclusion from public spaces runs along lines of sex, race and class and is dependent on who feels safe being visible in such public spaces, let alone if they want to be visible in the first place. For smaller, moveable nights, even promoting them can prove difficult when words like 'lesbian', 'dyke' and 'lez' are blacklisted[12] on social media and female nudity (unless it is considered art) is usually removed.

It's also been argued that lesbians tend to settle into relationships quicker and so stop going to club nights, preferring to stay home. It's a broad stereotype that I'm not sure really holds water, but it is certainly true that women are more likely to have care-giving responsibilities that might make going out inaccessible even if they wanted to. Whatever the reason for the continuous ebb and flow of club nights there are always young lesbians waiting in the wings for their turn to go out and meet each other. That much hasn't changed over the years.

While I was never much of a 'scene' lesbian, when I was at my peak of going out, the owners of the pub where Passionate Necking was hosted decided to sell. The rumour was that it was destined to become a gastropub like every other gastropub in London and be stripped of all its most interesting features (e.g. no more taxidermy animals and scooters overlooking the dance floor). In the end the feared gastro gentrification never came to be; it briefly opened as a kind of cocktail bar but closed again in 2019. I never went again. All that remains of Passionate Necking is its now defunct Facebook page, an abandoned Spotify playlist and many memories in the minds of happy queers.

Perhaps I'm part of the problem. These days I'm much

more likely to be in a mixed group of queer and straight friends, not to mention I'm an old married lady[13] and my going out-out days are pretty much over. Now, whether or not the venue is tailored towards queer women is less important to me than the quality of chips they serve and how many buses I have to take to get there. But it's a welcome bonus. If we're in a new place or different country we might seek out a gay bar for our own sense of safety, but otherwise any pub with a decent-looking IPA will do.

I still highly value the role they play in lesbian life and recognise the importance of even the most forgotten and decrepit rainbow flag lurking in the corner in making you feel welcome. Stepping back into an exclusively inclusive queer space, whether that's a bar, a theatre show, a festival or a talk, is like drinking fresh cold water when you didn't even know you were thirsty. It still holds a special feeling: there is a sense of your body relaxing. As an ex-bartender of Candy Bar noted of its closure, 'You can't necessarily go into any straight pub and kiss your girlfriend, because you know you're going to get stares. Women can come here and be who they want to be.'[14] To not have to be on your guard is a precious thing. It's a relief to shrug off the sometimes unacknowledged, sometimes overwhelmingly heavy pressure of the heterosexual world. The popularity of such newer bars and club nights is indicative that such in-person spaces are still vitally needed, especially as newer lesbians come out and seek ways to meet together. Jeremy Atherton Lin sums up succinctly the draw of the gay bar when he says, 'We go out to be gay. We crave this when once again growing bored with the straight world.'[15]

*

Now that I finally felt ready to attempt my first gay lady date and having failed to find anyone to flirt with in the real world, I turned, like most millennials, and like many of those newly out and lost queers calling the Lesbian Line, to my phone. In my case an iPhone rather than a landline, but a phone nonetheless. In 2017 finding a date through an app was so normalised, at least in my age group, that it was *almost* unheard of to get picked up at a bar. At least if you were looking for something more long term. Out of my friends that were in a relationship half had met through apps and the other half had been together since uni.

I'd tried going out and that hadn't got me anywhere. I think I needed the certainty of a dating app where everyone (at least in theory) was, if not looking for love exactly, looking to make some kind of connection. One night, after much agonising, I downloaded Tinder. Among my straight friends Tinder had a reputation as an app for casual hook-ups and skeevy men, but there was still at this point hope in the 'women looking for women' category.

I approached setting up my Tinder profile like a true Virgo and studied for it as if taking an exam. I researched several Tinder bios before refining my own into something which I hoped was informative but not overly keen: namely a list of emojis of things I liked and my job (to make me sound cultured). I wanted to curate the impression of a woman who knew what she was doing – not a baby gay who was terrified of being found out. I scrabbled together enough pictures of myself to meet the requirements and limited myself to just one featuring a Snapchat filter, and set my preferences to women only.

This, however, proved not enough to remove men from my feed. As any queer woman who has used a dating app in the last ten years can tell you, these apps are overrun with couples looking for a threesome (me and my boyfriend are just *so open-minded!*) and the straight men who have adjusted their settings so they pop up in the feed of lesbians and bisexual women (*ladies, I can change your mind!*). Like the prank calls to the Lesbian Line, you see that men continue to find their way into queer spaces not for them. They did not get a swipe right.

Other profiles I did swipe right on and I surprised even myself when I made several matches. It was then that I discovered another common hazard of lesbian dating: who was going to make the first move. Usually neither person. That was what most of my matches in the first few days of using the app were like. A lot of silence or conversations which quickly petered out. In the end I decided to go all in and use only my best lines. 'Hi,' I would message, 'how's your day going?' And if that didn't work I don't know *what* would.

In fact it did work, and I did begin to talk to women, and because it was online and in a format that was familiar to me it didn't feel scary. It held the sheen of unreality that all interactions on the internet do. I spoke to strangers online all the time on Twitter. I spoke to women all the time in real life. And here I didn't have the added worry that these women might think I was trying to flirt with them, or that I might (shock) mistakenly think they were trying to flirt with me. An advantage of dating over an app is that you know roughly why the person is there – it might fall along a spectrum of long-term girlfriend to one-night stand, or even just looking for a friend – but to a degree the parameters were set. And because of how Tinder worked – requiring both people to swipe right to get a match and start talking – the ones who weren't interested, well, I didn't even know they existed.

Over time I learnt the best way to use Tinder or OkCupid, or any dating app, really, was: a) to lower my expectations, and b) if they were not a walking red flag move as quickly as possible to 'do you fancy getting a drink?' to reduce everyone's time faffing about asking 'what are you up to?' and learning each other's emoji etiquette. Still, I much prefer text messaging than the thought of calling someone up over the phone. With a text the stakes are lower, you have more time to compose your answers and while you can find out certain clues about a person (do they write in full sentences, can they spell, do they use that creepy dead-eye smile emoji?) it's still no substitute for speaking face to face.

Anyone who has even flirted with online dating knows that you can't judge a person by their messaging style. Someone who texts you back immediately may be an awkward conversationalist in real life. Likewise, that person who sends you six seemingly random unrelated emojis after ever message can be dour and serious IRL. Not to mention the danger of forming an idea of what the person looks and sounds like from a handful of pictures taken at the best angle, which if you really like the person you have studied far too often late into the night. It can take a moment when confronted with the actual person to mentally readjust your view of them. Better, I think, to meet them face to face while your idea of them in your mind is not fully formed.

And so I began to go on actual real life dates.

On my first ever date with a woman, the woman does not show up and so I don't even know if it counts as a first date. We had agreed to meet after work at the V&A by the tunnel entrance and so I sat for half an hour or so, nervously glancing between the bright white of the sculptures for signs of my date. Occasionally unlocking and locking my phone after checking my WhatsApp messages. The two grey ticks showing my message had been sent but not read. I had told no one I was going on this date for precisely this reason. The only one, therefore, who was embarrassed and disappointed was myself. It wasn't like I thought she was the one, but she was the first one to want to go on a date with me. Or so I thought. Later she texts to apologise and say she lost her phone and her number changed and could I give her a second chance? I sent back *no, sorry, let's just leave it* and deleted her number off my phone.

The next woman I meet is tall and beautiful, Black with short Afro hair and plays football at a pitch near me. I make her laugh over a couple of pints. We tentatively hug goodbye and when I text her two days later to arrange another date she says that it's unexpected but an ex just got back in touch to say that she wants to try again. She's apologetic and kind which makes the disappointment sting a little less. I try to tell myself that it's a milestone of sorts, which I know from friend's dating stories, losing out to an ex. Or perhaps it was the kindest way she knew to let me know she wasn't actually interested.

The third woman is northern, white with large blonde curls around her face, both cuter and smaller in real life than in her photos. She is also miserable with a job in music which I pretend to know more about that I do. Our first date is in a pub up from King's Cross Station. I'm early and nervous and so I nip inside to use the loo before bolting back out to the entrance where we agreed to meet, just in case she spots me and thinks I'm leaving. The only thing we have in common is that we are both wearing denim jackets. We hunt around for shared interests but come up short. Despite this I agree to go on a second date with her because she has free tickets to a Josie Long gig, in stark contrast to her apparent lack of humour. The next day she asks if I want to meet again. She is the first (and only) girl I ever ghosted, and when I tell my friends about this on another ill-fated trip to the bar She they yell at me over the bad music about how terrible I am, until I text her there and then to say I'm sorry but I don't think it's going to work out.

The fourth woman is the person one of my friends went on a date with a few weeks before and the date got so trashed she could barely speak. This skews the whole evening and all I can think of is the money I'm wasting at the National Theatre bar on a woman I know I'll never see again, but I am too polite to leave after the first drink. I think she senses this and when she asks if I want to get a third I tell her it's getting late, even though it's 10.30 p.m. On the way home I text my friend to compare notes on our dates and ask her if this finally makes me a 'real' lesbian.

The fifth date is on a rooftop bar at Waterloo one week after my twenty-ninth birthday. Her long hair is bottle blonde but in her profile picture it was bright pink. She wears wire-framed glasses and the tail of a bird tattoo pokes out from under her shirt. It rains and we crowd under her umbrella with our 2-4-1 garish pink vodka cocktails which have so much fruit juice in it I can't taste the vodka I don't even like. A double rainbow appears. We joke about signs from the gay gods and stop to take pictures until the sun comes back out. She suggests another pub down the road and buys me a rum and coke and I feel happily, floatily drunk when she puts her hand on my knee under the table. After we say our goodbyes, at one minute to eleven she texts *definitely wanted to kiss you*. Our second date a week later ends up in an agonisingly long taxi ride home from a Kate Bush night in Benthal Green to her tiny flat in Croydon. I don't know it yet but nearly seven years later I will be writing this on a Sunday morning while she sits next door, knitting while watching YouTube videos, our dog asleep in her lap. We have been married for just over a year.

The sixth woman I go on a date with is sweet and shy, the kind of slim white bisexual who supports PETA and goes rock climbing. We wander around the Photographers' Gallery and discuss art and the kitten she is looking after for a friend. I text her afterwards to say we should stay friends but after a few shared cat pictures the communication stops and we never speak again.

> **17.10.96 – log by Ellen: *N.B. She became really angry when I refused her!***
> She thought these lesbians would at least be a bit more open-minded than all that. Of course she's not a lesbian (heaven forbid), she's been happily married to Nigel for twenty years next year. Happily, that is, except for one thing which

she thought these women of all people might be able to help her with. Why should they care that she's isn't one of them? Truth be told she did think about it once in her youth, sex with a woman and all that. But the thought of sleeping with someone who had the same bits as her just made her feel terribly self-conscious. The whole lifestyle of it isn't for her. And then along came Nigel and it became only ever a passing thought. Until now that is, when it finally occurred to her that lesbians might be the best people to ask on this particular subject. Surely, they're the experts, so to speak. She just wants a few pointers – a bit of guidance in the downstairs area. To put it plainly, she's never had an orgasm and she would quite like to try it at least once before she shuffles off this mortal plane of existence into the great beyond. *La petite mort* she read the French call it. Well of course they would, they have to be so dramatic about everything, don't they? The thing is, although Nigel is attentive and caring in most respects, when it comes to the bedroom department he hasn't got a bloody clue.

Anyway, the lesbians certainly weren't what she expected. It's supposed to be a helpline but she'd barely got halfway into her questions about who does what where and how much and how often, and suddenly the woman at the other end of the phone is spouting off about how this is a gay help-line and no one here is prepared to 'talk dirty' to her! Really quite rude. How stuck-up! She thought

> lesbians might be a bit more open-minded about these things. And anyway what happened to women sticking together? She thought they were all feminists. She only asked a few innocent questions and it set the woman on the line spluttering and slamming the phone down on her. Perhaps she's never figured out the knack of it either. Oh well, she'll have to wait a while longer . . . she's put up with Nigel for nineteen years, what's a few more?

When it comes sex and lesbians there is a both an overabundance and a void of information depending on whom you talk to. Likewise, stereotypes around lesbian sex fall into two extremes: we are either serial womanisers and sexual experts, or once we are in a long-term relationship we are sexless beings, suffering from so-called 'lesbian bed death'.[16] People love to quote facts such as how lesbians have the most orgasms compared to heterosexual or bisexual women.[17] And to be fair, lesbians often boast about this because, well, why wouldn't we? There's an inherent assumption that lesbians know how to treat a woman in the bedroom: that they make better and more attentive lovers, rid of the male ego and a singular idea about what sex should be like.

As lesbians we've long been told what our sex lives should look like; it's both fetishized by men and a source of judgement from other lesbians. Should it involve sex toys or dominant positions and penetration? Is sadomasochism okay without a man involved and should lesbian sex last for hours? Are you a pillow princess (someone who only likes to receive) or are you a stone (someone who only gives and may not liked to be touched at all)? Do you switch? Do you even have sex at all?

These questions are typical of the kind of debates that were happening in the late 1980s but which continued to influence conversation into the '90s. Dubbed the 'lesbian sex wars', there were broadly two camps which could be over-simplistically labelled 'pro-sex' and 'anti-sex'. Those 'anti-sex' might view lesbian sex that included any type of penetration as reproducing the same power imbalances that they saw in heteropatriarchal sex. In the documentary *Rebel Dykes*, which explores some of the history of these debates, especially around the SM and punk scene, poet Roz Kaveney jokes that for some radical anti-sex feminists 'the authentic version of lesbian sex was holding hands in twenty passionate positions'.[18]

For similar reasons some lesbians argued that sado-masochism and butch/femme dynamics were inherently 'unfeminist'. In the US, the movement was notably led at its peak by Andrea Dworkin and Catherine A. MacKinnon, who opposed all forms of pornography and erotica. 'Pro-sex' lesbians were opposed to the policing of how lesbians chose to have sex and censorship of SM and butch/femme identities from lesbian and feminist spaces. Lisa Power told me how she had to smuggle in sex toys for her mail order business (Thrilling Bits), and erotic lesbian magazines like *On Our Backs* (with photography from Jill Posener), but once in the UK they could be sold openly. Feminist and lesbian shops, even Silver Moon Bookshop – the feminist bookshop that was *the* place to go for lesbian literature – refused to stock them. However, Power points out that this was a sensible decision since they were much more likely to be raided and prosecuted. As the author bell hooks noted, such attitudes from conservative feminists were born out of an underlying prejudice: 'Whenever any woman acts as though lesbians must always follow rigid moral standards to be deemed acceptable or to make straight people feel comfortable, they are perpetuating homophobia.'[19] This moralising extended to the enjoyment of pornography, erotica and kink even when created and practiced by lesbians themselves.

In *Lesbian Sex Wars* Emma Healey notes that by making the personal political, the second-wave feminist movement set the stage for defining lesbians solely by their sexual acts.[20] Thus, those lesbians who wanted to explore the boundaries of sex between women, or indeed any bisexual women, were seen as politically incompatible. Such arguments quickly became deeply personal. Healey sees the 1990s as a period in reaction to the lesbian sex wars which had sought to depoliticise and reprivatise sex, writing in 1996 that 'if in the 1980s the typical dyke about town owned a cat and a bicycle, her 1990s sister seems much more likely to possess a dog and a dildo'.[21] She characterises the '90s as a period of greater lesbian visibility and acceptance but one which had been heavily commercialised for the straight gaze, pushing the image of a sexier, more confident queer woman:

> [T]he lesbian is no longer bad and sad or drearily political, she is a sassy 1990s fashionable gal . . . Lesbian chic is dependent on one image of the lesbian, the one heterosexual society feels it can control: the feminine.[22]

Lesbians were not immune to the appeal that this stereotype might promote, or from replicating misogynistic ways of viewing other women in this way. When I was newly out and in my early days of dating I was at a party of some mutual friends and somehow got cornered into a conversation with the most intimidating lesbian I'd met so far. She was tall and confident, clearly keen to show off her experience and flirting aggressively with every woman within the radius of her eye line (which was all of them because she was so tall). I don't know how it came up but she began to boast about how she could 'turn' any straight woman. It was an uncomfortable conversation – I was with a friend and both of us remained quiet throughout the recital of her conquests. Perhaps she wanted to impress us, sensing we were new at this, or simply wanted to show off or elicit reassurance from us that her behaviour was to be applauded.

When she didn't get the reaction she wanted she began to quiz me and my friend on whether we were 'gold star' lesbians. A ridiculous term for women who have never slept with men, as if there is a hierarchy about who gets to claim the title of the best lesbian. I recall our answers were vague and she thankfully soon gave up, stalking off to find someone more amenable to her charms. It's a conversation that has always stuck with me – meeting this stranger who had seemingly reduced her whole being to who she had fucked and would fuck in the future. Which I don't have an issue with per se, you could argue she was flipping the patriarchal narrative, or conversely that she was making herself complicit in a society which views women solely as sexual objects. Either way, it didn't make her a very stimulating conversationalist.

*

Lesbian sex, in the mainstream at least, is often shown, written about and discussed by everyone *but* lesbians. In the media explicit lesbian sex scenes are often presented to appeal as much to straight men as they are actual lesbians. In *Lesbians Talk: (Safer) Sex,* writing in the '90s, Sue O'Sullivan and Pratibha Parmar describe how the presentation of lesbians as objects of male arousal has led to a lack of shared language around lesbian sex:

> We have tended to have few public places in which to develop distinctly lesbian subcultures and have too often been invisible to each other. Recognising the titillation value of lesbianism in the straight world has made us fearful of developing an explicit and popular lesbian language of lust and sex.[23]

And without that language to talk about sex, lesbian desire is erased and misrepresented by everyone, even by lesbians themselves. In the mainstream, lesbian sex remains the domain of male fantasy even today. Take for instance the controversy around the filming of 2013's *Blue Is the Warmest Colour* with its uncomfortably long sex scenes, featuring what was supposed to be a young teen. The lead actors would later describe the experience working with the male director as 'horrible' and disrespectful.[24] The source material, Julie Maroh's graphic novel of the same name, doesn't shy away from depicting lesbian sex, however the emphasis in her panels is often on the characters' emotions, pleasure and relationship to one another. The graphic novel is far sexier, funnier and closer to real life.

Likewise, the 2016 adaptation *The Handmaiden*, based on lesbian writer Sarah Water's Victorian novel *Fingersmith*, provides another example of lesbian desire made for a straight audience. While in many ways a faithful and thoughtful adaptation, the final scene recreates one of the sexual acts depicted in the pornographic books of the villainous father figure. Some argue this is a reclamation of their sexual independence since the scene is only for the two of them, but as Verity Ritchie points out in her video essay 'The Lesbian Gaze', the women are arranged in an unnatural position so that we, the viewer, can observe them better, questioning the complicity of the viewer and the (male) director in presenting this scene.[25] Lesbians in mainstream media are still regarded as a vehicle for offering an assumed male viewer a slice of titillation. Compare this to how lesbian and queer sex is portrayed in films directed by queer women such as *Portrait of a Lady on Fire* by Céline Sciamma, *Stud Life* by Campbell X, *Appropriate Behaviour* by Desiree Akhavan or *Saving Face* by Alice Wu. In all these films you will find nuanced complex characters having sex in ways which are tender, sexy, funny and honest.

It's almost too obvious to state, but lesbians consistently feature highly as the most watched porn genre (from both men and women – but with men overwhelmingly making up the majority of the views). In 2022 Pornhub reported that 'Lesbian' was its most popular category globally, beating 'Ebony', 'Japanese' and 'Threesome' for the top spot.[26] Everyone on the outside seems very interested in what lesbians get up to when we're alone.

If only we knew. There's a sort of wilful and self-mythologizing mystery surrounding what actually happens when two lesbians have sex. Perhaps it's self-protection, perhaps it's because we simply have more options. But for many newly out lesbians this mystery is hardly helpful, and lack of good representations of lesbian sex can create harmful assumptions. This is true today but even more so in the pre-internet era when information was harder to come by. As sociologist Cindy Patton noted in 1990, when it came to talking about it, 'even lesbians didn't know what it was that lesbians did in sex'.[27]

In *Lesbians Talk: (Safer) Sex*, there is a chapter devoted to defining lesbian sex which the authors describe as an non-exhaustive bullet-point list: 'It's a start-out, a warm-up, and definitely to be added to.'[28] The list encompasses everything from looking at another woman, holding hands or talking to finger-fucking, fisting, dildos and orgasms. It runs a wide gamut of experiences and emotions and acknowledges that while lesbians will all give different answers about what sex is (and means to them), we recognise it when we see it. Even if we can't talk about it. They also allude to the hangover of the lesbian sex wars as part of the reason why lesbians were so reluctant to talk about sex. There was a fear of being judged, either for being into SM or butch/femme dynamics, or the opposite – for being too 'vanilla' and traditional in their sexual activities, or lack of. In addition to this, the ongoing HIV/AIDS pandemic and biphobia within lesbian circles made some lesbians and bisexual women reluctant to speak about their experiences of sleeping with men for fear of being stigmatised.[29]

Not talking about lesbian sex means that even into the '90s sex education for women who slept with other women was scarce, and knowledge around sexual health for lesbians circulated primarily through word of mouth or in lesbian and feminist magazines. Many newly out women may not have had access to such information either because they were too young, didn't know where to find it or couldn't afford to buy protection (like dental dams) and even if they could, might be scared of discovery or didn't know where to get them. If under Section 28 even talking about gay relationships was illegal, there was certainly no 'official' education on how to have safe gay sex. Regarding HIV/AIDS and lesbians, there was a lot of misinformation and misunderstanding due to a lack of research into and attention to how transmission occurred. Writing in the '90s, Sue O'Sullivan and Pratibha Parmar laid out the dividing opinions over how to have safe lesbian sex:

> Today, some are saying that safer sex for lesbians is a red herring: it detracts from the real ways lesbians are affected by HIV and obscures the need for safer-sex education and practice in the communities and groups who are really at risk. Others say this position is irresponsible: no one knows for sure if the virus can be transmitted by oral sex, for instance, and it is better to be safe than sorry.[30]

Not to mention the multitude of other sexually transmitted infections and risk of cervical cancer that were under-researched and underdiscussed. With lesbians divided on the use of dental dams and sex toys when it came to safe sex, it's no wonder than many lesbians simply ignored advice or were unable to make informed choices when it came to sex. One caller from the logbook who discloses she is HIV-positive does so only after several repeat calls and describes how other lesbians now view her with suspicion as she was infected after sleeping with a man. This refusal led to many lesbians hiding their HIV status for fear of being ostracised. Similarly, awareness and information for trans lesbians and sex was scarce or rarely discussed, and so sexual health advice for lesbians at any stage of transition was often absent or lacking within lesbian support groups. If it was available, it was more likely to be within transsexual groups or guides rather than LGB ones.

The idea that lesbian sex is central to what it means to be a lesbian is, I think, up for debate. I suspect there are as many answers as there are lesbians. Sex can be an important part of our identity, as Katherine Angel explains in *Tomorrow Sex Will Be Good Again*: 'Sexuality is lived, learnt, developed over time, in a particular context; this is why sex means something to us – it is never pure function, but always rich with, and burned with, significance.'[31] To say it doesn't matter who you have sex with and when and how is perhaps to throw away the significance sex can play in our lives, but we should also acknowledge that it changes over time. It can change moment to moment. It can become insignificant. Who you do sexy stuff with can be a vital part of being a lesbian but it's not for everyone, or at least it's not always the main part. Lesbian sex is far from a rigid standard of gold star lesbians – it's more fun and wide-ranging than that and a lot of the time no one else but you should give a fuck who you (with consent) fuck. I don't think you can define 'lesbian' just by whom you hop into bed with. Not to mention that such a definition erases asexual people or those who choose not to have sex. Sex can be as central to a lesbian identity as you want it to be, we just need to get better at talking about it. It's not like it's a new invention.

I Don't Want to Talk About Wanking in That Way

When it comes to sex as it's talked about in the logbook it's both everywhere and nowhere. However, for the phone workers it could be a challenge to tell the real questions from the ones trying to trick them into some version of dirty talk. Most lesbian lines would happily discuss any issues around sex provided the caller was genuine and didn't ask the phone workers personal questions about their sex life. Those with honest questions or concerns about how to have sex, how to be safe, what it means if they have sex with women, or with women and men, would be answered and listened to. However, those who were trying to get the volunteers to talk about sex to – I'm trying to think of a more delicate way to put it – get themselves off were not tolerated. Distinguishing these type of calls from one another was a skill many phone workers had to learn and quickly.

It was a fine line to tread between accepting every call at face value and risking indulging in someone's sexual fantasy or inappropriate queries. They risked missing a call from someone with genuine questions about lesbian sex or safeguarding concerns. There are seemingly legitimate calls from young lesbians in the logs that recount stories of sexual relationships with teachers or older lesbians which the phone workers take extremely seriously. There are also calls from women of all ages nervous about having lesbian sex for the first time and as we've already seen there were (and are) so many misconceptions about lesbian sex floating around. Such questions around sex were not unusual for the line to receive and I can imagine there was a sense of responsibility to help those genuine calls.

Overwhelmingly, however, when the subject of sex comes up in the logs it's because the call is deemed abusive or inappropriate. The majority of such calls are from men. Even in a logbook for a lesbian line aimed at queer women, it's men who somehow still dominate the conversation around sex. These calls the phone workers cheerily name 'wank calls'. A typical log for one would be something like the below:

> Lots of calls from men tonight inc. 2/3 wank calls. Perhaps the number has been advertised incorrectly.

The wank calls take various forms. Some are men calling to ask explicit questions about lesbian sex; occasionally they will get inventive and say they are trying to keep their wife or girlfriend happy, or their girlfriend is bisexual and looking for advice. In this case the phone workers will ask to speak to said girlfriend who usually fails to materialise. Then there are more elaborate wank calls from men who pretend to be women. One particularly tenacious repeat caller uses a variety of accents but never changes his story about coming out and having sex with lots of women, which he likes to describe in great detail.

One of the most persistent and recurrent wank callers rings the line intermittently from 1994 to 1997 and is given the nickname 'Miss Penetration' – a jokey nod to the lesbian sex wars and the caller's penchant for questions about whether it was 'normal' for lesbians to enjoy penetrative sex. The impression I get from the logs is that they think the question rather behind the times. Always denoted with the pronoun 'she' in quotes, or 's/he', nearly every volunteer is convinced 'Miss P' is a man posing as a woman to gain access to the line, but this is never confirmed. Miss P's story changes from call to call but generally it begins with her coming out after being married and wanting to know how to have sex with women. This leads to asking 'intimate' questions about lesbian sex and probing into the phone worker's own sexual experiences.

Miss Penetration is looking for specifics. It's Sarah that first names the caller Miss P in the logbook and is the most insistent on using that nickname for them. Because the volunteers were the only listeners to the calls there's no way to be certain that this was the same Miss Penetration that rings up each time. But the similarities of story and accent, which is described variously as 'lightly European' or 'Dutch or German', seems to indicate it is. Sarah treats Miss P like the irritating kid next door who won't leave you alone. They become a fun anecdote to tell your friends about. Sarah writes, 'my fave rave – "Miss Penetration" (or is that "Mr"?) may be back', or she'll note with a sense of glee that she 'got Miss P!!!' In 1997, when Miss P calls again after a long gap,

Sarah excitedly instructs the other volunteers to look back over the earlier entries three years before for the history.

For Sarah, the wank calls are something to lighten the mood between the more serious calls and she appears unbothered by them. She hails Miss P as a kind of minor celebrity, such to the extent that another volunteer, Ellen, jokes that she 'feels like she's missing out on Miss P' since they never call her on shift. Wank calls like these to phone workers created a sense of shared camaraderie – all the women had to put up with such calls, and likely they weren't so different to comments and invasive questions they received in person. At least on the phone lines they were in charge.

Understandably, some phone workers remain unamused by Miss P and those like them – frustrated that the calls take up valuable time on the line and were an invasion of their privacy. These unwanted interruptions trespass on the boundaries and mission the Lesbian Line had set for itself as a space for women to seek information and community away from male-dominated spaces like the mixed phone lines. To the phone workers it was bad enough that gay men called sometimes when the mixed line was busy, but the wank calls were an even greater encroachment into their space. One volunteer writes after a wank call that she is 'very angry and pissed off – a complete abuse of me, my time & everyone else who's trying to get through', and ends the entry by asking how they should deal with such abusive calls. Ultimately, there was little way to stop the men calling. They simply got better at spotting them and ending the call, since as a rule the phone workers themselves tried not to hang up on anybody.

The volunteers had their own techniques for ending calls.

Hannah turns the questions onto the callers themselves and reports that asking them about their own sex life 'seemed to flummox them'. Rachael too is less than impressed with the wank callers, writing that they 'didn't get very far; convinced one was a man and a 'bit dodgy', she hangs up on him as soon as she can. In one long call that a phone worker describes as becoming uncomfortably sexual and personal, another volunteer has written (I think in retrospect, rather unhelpfully), 'I would have hung up earlier'. After a particular strong spate of wank calls, Cora requests that they discuss the 'hoax calls' at the next phone workers meeting, explaining with a bit of experience it's usually easy to spot the genuine caller from the wank call.

Hoax callers and wank calls were a common hazard of working on LGBTQ+ phone lines and I've yet to find a single history of a lesbian line that didn't include such calls or those thinking it was a service that catered to men. Like at the London Friend Lesbian Line, volunteers on other lesbian lines developed their own methods to deal with wank calls. Lorraine, the co-founder of the Bradford Lesbian Line, explains in an interview recorded for the West Yorkshire Queer Stories project that they had a novel way of dealing with this particular problem:

> Men ringing up tossing themselves off, we had a police whistle that we used to – you could just [sighs] you could just tell. I mean [sighs] . . . You know, they'd ring up and they'd say, 'do you do shows?' and you could hear them jerking off and you'd just [sigh] and then [makes a whistle noise] bang the phone down.[1]

It's not hard to imagine those sighs echoed by many a volunteer. Paulina encountered similar issues with her own solution at the Cambridge Lesbian Line she founded:

> We had some funny calls too. Because of how lesbians were seen then, some thought the line was a kind of booking service for brothels. Some man rang up trying to 'book a girl', so we gave him the number for the local police station instead.[2]

When I spoke to Diana James she told me that the volunteers learnt to take wank calls in their stride at Switchboard. She soon became well practised at spotting the men who rang in and would clearly much rather talk about sex with a woman than with a man. At Switchboard they had a policy in place to say that the phone line wasn't for those kinds of calls, but if the caller did have something serious to discuss they were welcome to call back later. Or as Diana put it, 'Phone back when you've finished.' Later she told me that sometimes, having been caught out by a wank call, the volunteers might stick a Post-it note to their head saying 'wank' to let everyone know they'd been 'got'. Clearly a certain amount of humour and resilience was required if you were to work on a gay and lesbian helpline.

While the majority of the wank calls to the London Friend Lesbian Line were from men, there are a handful of logs from women that the phone workers categorise as 'wank calls'. These calls tend to tread a finer line between being fantasies or masturbation aids and genuine enquires about lesbian sex.

Because of their seemingly honest nature, as Diana explained to me during her time at Switchboard, it was much harder to spot a wank call from a woman:

> [S]ometimes you'd get caught and that, you'd be talking, discussing, like, different procedures and stuff, that sort of thing. When it started to get into, well what do *you* do? Do you have a girlfriend, how do you fuck her? Do you use two fingers or three? It was all that kind of thing and then you would hear this sort of [high pitched] ooh [laugh] and you'd go, 'Caught again!'

On the Lesbian Line the wank calls from women were treated very differently than those from men. There's one woman who threatens to take over from Miss P in her regularity of calls and whom Cora notes is her 'first wank call from a ♀'. Initially, the caller wants to talk about her negative body image, but moves on to talking about masturbation. Cora writes that 'I (naturally) didn't discourage', but once the caller goes into details Cora becomes uncomfortable and asks why she felt the need to tell so much. The caller denies that she meant to say it, at which points she hangs up. Cora ends the entry saying that she hopes she calls back as she clearly needs to talk.

When the same caller next rings, Nise answers the phone and tells her she has just been masturbating and felt good about it. Again Nise explains that they are a helpline and politely asks why she is calling. The caller hangs up. Nise writes that it '[f]eels very strange getting a wank call from a woman . . . It doesn't feel as abusive as when a man does it.'

In both Cora's and Nise's logs they express a desire to help the woman, or feel that she does really need to talk, but won't discuss masturbation in detail with her. They wanted to reassure them that such desire did not need to be quashed or hidden again, but there were boundaries to be respected. The volunteers for the most part aim to encourage a sex-positive attitude but were cautious of becoming an outlet for closeted lesbian's sexual fantasies.

It can be incredibly useful to be able to explore desire through fantasies and through unrealistic crushes on unattainable people – provided it does not become obsessive. This was true for me when I was coming out – I developed red-hot crushes on celebrities, musicians and people I passed in the street like I was a teenager ripping through *Smash Hits* magazine. It was a way to compartmentalise my newly discovered capacity for finding women hot as hell without any possibility of having to act upon any of it. The key part for me and my crushes was not only that they were never going to happen but that they remained within my own self, not unfairly imposed on others without consent. And like all good crushes they soon faded to nothing.

Other wank calls from women follow a similar pattern, some calling just after masturbating, or masturbating down the phone, or describing overt sexual acts and asking personal sexual questions of the volunteers. One woman even calls back to apologise afterwards, explaining that she was 'feeling frustrated'. What's most evident is that the phone workers stay on the line much longer with the female wank callers. They are far more willing to give the female wank calls the benefit of the doubt and try to steer the caller towards other issues they feel may be underlying their real reason for calling. One volunteer even suggests they direct the female callers to a sex line: 'some kind of "wank line", whatever is appropriate for her "needs"', Cora writes of the sensitivity required to explain that the line was not to be used in this way but that masturbating in itself wasn't wrong.

However, it cannot be denied that the wank calls from women often had the same abusive consequence as the ones from men. While the phone workers were more willing to help the female wank callers, the impact on a personal level for the volunteers was often the same. There is one telling note from a phone worker after a wank call from a woman who writes the experience was 'frustrating and depressing and just lowers morale'. While the wank calls from women demonstrate the capacity for lesbian sexuality and desire free from the gaze of men, they do so in a way that was coercive and left many phone workers feeling abused or uncomfortable. Leaving little to be celebrated of such expressions of desire. As one volunteer wrote, 'I don't want to talk about wanking in that way!'

Stop Making Us Look Bad: Lesbian Break-Ups and Abuse

Of course with all these lesbian hook-ups, dates and relationships comes the flip side: the break-up. Whatever the time period, the fundamentals of breaking up remain the same: heartbreak, rejection, loneliness, anger, depression, sometimes relief, sometimes freedom and perhaps the will to try again. In the April 1992 issue of *Spare Rib* there is a feature called 'Make or Break: Love in the 90s', with a personal essay from a self-described thirty-two-year-old 'rusty lesbian'. The piece is illustrated with a sketchy cartoon of a giant rotary telephone, a women cowering behind her armchair. The author of the article describes the agony of having to wait for a call from her now ex-lover: 'The telephone has become a monster lurking in the corner, mocking me as I move about the room and eyeing me from every angle.'[1] While the small-ads with their snail-mail correspondence seem to me now to have a certain slow charm about them, it's oddly reassuring to know that lesbians before me have been likewise terrorised by the spectre of the phone. In this case tying you to your home waiting for it to ring with no way to know who was calling. Was it going to be your crush on the other end of the line or an ex-lover demanding her stuff back?

After her first break-up of a long-term relationship the author writes:

> When my first lover left me after seven years I went mad with grief – quite literally. I had what is euphemistically called a 'breakdown'. It wasn't one of those sensitive artist-gone fragile jobbies ... no, it was a ranting, raving, RAGE at the world for abandoning me. I didn't want the loving to end.[2]

She then goes on to blame, in what seems like a very '90s feminist lesbian moment, post-Thatcher era neo-liberalism and rising late stage capitalism for the break-up. And I have to say she makes a compelling case:

> We used to bath [sic] together until she got a shower fitted. Maybe that's when the rot set in. It's modern society that rocks the boat. We've turned into cheap consumers in a fast and furious throwaway world. The pressure to succeed, to make it, to make money, and make more money, has stopped making sense. How can anyone sustain a long-lasting, loving and fulfilling partnership when we're programmed to consume and dispose? This society does nowt to support the concept of real love and care. I live off you and you live off me, and the whole world lives off of everybody.[3]

'Gotta be exploited by somebody', she concludes. I'm not sure what point I'm illustrating here about what happens in a lesbian break-up aside from: I think it's complicated and that the way women are constructed within society plays as much a part as does the other person being a dickhead. So let's unpick the stereotype that all lesbian break-ups are amicable and friendly. Because as many calls in the logbook demonstrate, plenty end pretty horribly.

There is one caller in particular who is really going through it. She's known only as the 'woman from Todmorden', and over the course of a few months manages to turn even the most patient of the volunteers against her, despite her obvious need for help. She certainly fits the bill when it comes to raging at the world and has a tendency for histrionics – but in her defence, it sounds like it was not without cause.

5.11.95 – log by Cora: *to be honest I find it really boring because she goes on for ages*

Her heart is shattering in two, has been for months and months now but the pain is still fresh and hot in her chest and so she does the only thing she can do, the only thing that has brought her some relief after having her heart stamped all over and smashed to pieces: she rings the Lesbian Line. The woman who takes the call says she remembers her. She's from Todmorden, isn't she? Spoke to Monica a week or so ago? It means she doesn't need to go through the whole thing again, but she does anyway. It's good for her to be able to talk it through with someone. To tell her side of the story cos her ex is certainly running her mouth all over town to anyone who will listen. She starts at the beginning even if Cora has heard this particular side of the story already from Monica, she's doesn't care. It's her turn to be selfish for once.

Cora will just have to deal with it cos when your heart is wrenched in two all because of another woman surely it's not too hard to let a woman talk about how she feels? Her side of things goes like this:

My ex-girlfriend is an utter cunt.

Cora, who has been mostly quiet up to now aside from occasional umms and ahhhs makes an audible inhale.

I'm sorry but it's true. You know I'm a prison officer, right? You should hear the things the men say to one another. I'm only telling you the truth. She is an utter cunt. Everything has gone to crap since she left. I say left, but really she stabbed me in the back and fucked off with some other woman ten years her junior. An artist apparently. 'Left' is too mild a word for what she's done to me. She didn't leave so much as rip up every happy thing in my life and explode a giant hole in my total sense of being.

Cora interrupts with a question.

Yes, I read a lot, she replies. I like poetry actually – why do you ask? That's not important right now, what's important is that you understand how much of a bitch my ex is and her new girlfriend. She's taking her to all the places I took her! All my favourite pubs are now polluted with the two of them, kissing and grabbing at each other in some dingy corner. I'm constantly looking over my shoulder in case I see them. I never want to see her again but that doesn't mean I should stop going to my pubs and my hang-outs. I'm not going to be the one who leaves. The stupid cunt can. And so what if she hates the sight of me as much as I hate seeing her. Let her hate me – I hope she feels uncomfortable and awkward and as unhappy as she has made me.

What? I don't think that's petty at all Cora. I think it's being practical. Aren't lesbians supposed to all be about reciprocal care and understanding? I'm just making sure she understands and reciprocates all of the shittiness she's made me feel. I think that's only fair.

Oh, we only get an hour? I didn't realise you time stamped these things. When did you say Monica was next on? Okay I'll try to call then. All right. Yes well thanks for listening I do feel a little better I think. All right. Bye now.

16.11.95 – log by Clare: *Really quite mixed up, I tried to set some goals with her but she can't see a way out.*

She's a sick fucker who's sick in the head and fucking someone who is fucking young enough to be her child for fuck's sake. Look, I'm really sorry to shout and be so fucking angry but this is how she makes me. My ex is deranged if she thinks that's normal and the rest of our fucking friends just go along with it like it's perfectly fine. I feel like they've totally taken her side when she was the one who left me! Can you imagine?

If she was a man everyone would see how weird it is that she's shacked up with a twenty-year old. I hope the sex is good because when we were together she barely had time for a quick fumble with the lights out before she took her sleeping pills and conked out. But then that's lust for you, isn't it? Makes you feel young.

I can't believe she'd do this to me. We were together nearly fifteen years. We fostered cats together for fuck's sake and now she's acting like I was the one who wanted them in the first place. Can't stand the bitch but you know what? If she came round to my house, OUR house, right this minute on her knees begging me to take her back. You know what I'd say?

There's a pause on the line – it's the first breath she's taken probably since Clare answered the phone. She doesn't want to cry. Not in front of a stranger.

You know what I'd say? I'd take her back. That's the worst thing about it. I hate her so much, she makes me so unbelievably angry still, even after all this time, and yet if she wanted to I'd let her waltz right through the door as though nothing had happened and curl up on the sofa like she used to in the evenings with a cup of tea and one of the cats on her lap. I wouldn't even complain. Isn't that awful. She fucked me over – fucked me right in the heart – and I wouldn't even hesitate. That's proper love right there, isn't it. That's how you know, I think. You don't really know if you love someone until they betray you, stab you in the heart and fuck some younger model – if your love can survive something like that. But I know now, I really do. I love her so much and I can't stand it.

Look, Clare, I like you, I do, but if you try to talk to me about setting some goals one more time I'm really going to blow a nut. This isn't some fucking work appraisal, this is my life. I'm not bloody Pelé, am I – I don't need to set some goals. I just need to get the love of my life back or if I can't do that find a way to stop fucking thinking about her all the time and that cunt of a girlfriend she has now. They're still together you know? I know, I'm surprised as you are. But then she always was a bit of a serial monogamist. Jumped from serious relationship to serious relationship. Not like me, I did my dating and then found the one. Well, I thought I had. Ha fucking ha right. More fool me.

Get this, she called me the other day, the new younger model, asking if we wanted to be friends. I didn't know what to say. I wanted to tell her to fuck off but then I heard myself say "okay". I'm such an idiot. I can't see a way out of it. I've tried ignoring her, I've tried not ignoring her, I've tried hating her – trust me I've got that bit down. I've tried forgiving her for what she did but I can't. I can't do any of it and whatever I do hasn't mended my pathetic broken heart now has it? God she's such a cunt, calling me up like that asking me to be friends. Where does she get off? I doubt it was my ex's idea. I bet it was that ditzy blonde's plan. That's the other thing that drives me mad – she doesn't even look like a lesbian. You could hardly call her femme, she looks like a normie. Like some straight twenty-something boring woman. Who looks like that at her age? When I was her age I had my DMs on and a shaved head. At least that was a look. She's not even a real artist, she just takes pictures now and then.

Honestly, 'let's be friends'. That seems like something a twenty-year-old would say, doesn't it? Let's all be friends ... piss off. I suppose you have to laugh really, don't you? Who would have thought at fifty-six I'd be going through heartbreak all over again?

All right I'll think about it. My goals, if you insist, so long as you promise to stop asking me about it. Maybe my first goal can be to stop feeling so angry all the time. Wouldn't that be nice?

2.2.96 – log by Cora: *I have really not got a lot of sympathy with this caller any more – not moving on etc etc*

You'll never guess what my ex has done now. I'm so angry I can't even begin to tell you ...

9.2.96 – log by anon: ***I've taken calls from her at least twice in the last 4 months***
Hi, Sarah – it's me again. I wanted to talk about my ex, I think maybe I've turned a corner . . .

3.3.96 – log by Monica: ***To be honest, I'm getting fed up with her too! (Doesn't that sound awful!)***
There isn't much that I haven't said already but I need you to know. My ex is a bitch and I hate her. She has made my life miserable.

10.3.96 – log by Monica: ***She seems to be moving backwards instead of forwards!***
Maybe she imagines it but when she says hello she thinks she hears Monica who answers the phone let out a sigh. For a second it pierces through her anger and she wonders how this woman she has never met, has never even seen her, thinks of her. Does she know her favourite poet is Yeats and she only went into the prison service because the pension is so good? That she came out when she was fifteen to her best mate who didn't even blink. Gave her the tightest hug in the world and told her they'd always stick together. That she didn't even so much as kiss anyone until she was twenty-one, newly arrived in Manchester from Chorley, sitting in a lesbian bar on Canal Street and totally taken in by the first beautiful butch who spoke to her. But thinking about her first kiss leads her back to her ex, and her easy white hot anger that has been her

> constant companion all these months surges inside her and so instead of telling Monica that she wasn't always like this she says, my ex is such a cunt and I'll never forgive her for what she's done to me and doesn't stop for another hour after that.

The calls stop there – I'm left to hope she found some professional help or time helped her get over such a huge break-up. From the logs they all seem somewhat overwhelmed by the amount of support she clearly needs. Talking it through on the phone can only get them so far and they are unable to make much progress towards helping her find an equilibrium. She's seems resistant to any suggestions of counselling or techniques for moving on and looking to the future.

The lack of empathy here from the phone workers feels somewhat surprising (their messy selves on display) but then again I wasn't on the end of those calls, which sound extremely difficult. Where is the line between understanding someone's anger as a manifestation of their heartbreak and damage to your own well-being having to absorb so much rage? The anger of the caller leaps off the page and once again I wonder about the care that the phone workers received afterwards – if they had a way to look after each other after what must have been emotionally draining calls. The volunteers seem more frustrated than anything that their calls aren't making much difference. For now, this caller is stuck and nothing the phone workers say can help her move forward. It's a reminder of the limits of what the volunteers can do and also that they themselves were not perfect listening angels. They had bad days too. They struggled. They did not have an infinite amount of patience. And like all the calls they took they can only listen, offer a little advice here and there. The care they can provide ultimately depends upon the caller to initiate it – they are always in the role of responder and sometimes, no matter how much they can listen and advise, it isn't enough. At least not in that moment and I imagine that would also have been difficult to deal with.

As well as break-ups there are also calls from lesbians experiencing, or with experience of, abusive relationships. Some disclose that they are survivors of sexual assault or emotional and physical abuse from both men and women. Some are dealing with violent ex-husbands or parents, or current relationships with coercive or abusive female partners. The phone workers' role in most of these cases is to offer support with a sympathetic listening ear and to encourage callers to attend groups for survivors of sexual violence or intimate-partner violence. One of the greatest barriers for lesbians when speaking up about lesbian-on-lesbian violence is simply that they are often not believed or listened to. As authors Joelle Taylor and Tracey Chandler, themselves both survivors of abuse, note in *Lesbians Talk: Violent Relationships*, the topic of lesbian violence during the '90s was still very taboo:

> Surviving the survival process can be as painful and demoralising as undergoing the abuse itself . . . The silence stifling discussion of violent lesbian relationships has been ubiquitous. Silence not only signifies the absence of debate, but also active disbelief – from close friends as well as professionals.[4]

There still remains a great reluctance to talk about abuse perpetuated by women in both heterosexual and queer relationships. Intimate-partner violence within lesbian relationships carries with it an additional stigma of a fear of tarnishing the reputation of all lesbians. For other lesbians it's easier to pretend that it simply doesn't exist, that it's a male issue, and to maintain lesbian relationships as some utopian ideal. As Carmen Maria Machado succinctly writes in her memoir *In the Dream House,* as a survivor of abuse in a queer relationship: 'if I could say anything to her, I'd say, "For fuck's sake, stop making us look bad"'.[5] This concern over appearances means that often disclosure of abuse is ignored or downplayed. Often the abuser is still welcomed within the lesbian community and as we've seen, the pressure on lesbians to have amicable break-ups or remain within small localised circles could lead to the survivor having to deal with such experiences alone, or to remain in contact with their abuser. Many lesbians didn't want to believe that women could be perpetrators of abuse, both physical and emotional. For Black lesbians and lesbians of colour in relationships with white women, where the white woman was the abuser, they were even less likely to be believed, especially by their white friends.[6] Already a minority group within another minority group, many lesbians of colour feared further isolation if they attempted to out their abusers and the loss of their only support network.

The Lesbian Line, then, held an important function of being an anonymous way that survivors could talk about the violence they had experienced without the risk of being disbelieved or brushed off. They were also able to offer free phone counselling and face-to-face counselling through London Friend, which would allow many working-class, low-income lesbians (including those who did not have control over their own finances) to access services they otherwise couldn't afford. The phone workers took all disclosures of abuse seriously, whether they were one-off calls or a repeat caller. They even changed their policy for one survivor who couldn't afford to call the phone line by allowing her to reverse the charges so she could speak to the one phone worker she trusted when she was on shift.

It wasn't easy for lesbians to access appropriate services that would be able to cater to their specific experiences. While there were women's shelters and Women's Aid, there were no specific refuges for lesbian survivors of abuse from other women, and shelters would vary on their inclusivity and awareness of lesbian abuse issues. Many lesbians wanted to avoid Women's Aid or public service channels as it posed a risk of having to out themselves and face not only disbelief but homophobia, both from staff and other service users.[7] Providing aid to lesbians within women's services was still a contentious issue in the '90s, with some refuge workers fearing that more actively promoting their services to lesbians could spread their resources too thinly or might risk their funding. Taylor and Chandler note the need for better training and awareness across both women's groups and gay and lesbian organisations, including Switchboard, which at the time of writing did not provide core training for survivors of women-on-women violence.[8]

The early '90s saw the first established self-help groups for lesbians; however, these were both based in London and so had a limited capacity for whom they could support. At the end of *Lesbians Talk: Violent Relationships,* Taylor and Chandler write of the barriers that need to be overcome to better support lesbian survivors. Funding is key, as well as a national helpline or better provision (and a greater number) of groups across the UK. They note too that breaking the silence around lesbian violence is crucial, but that speaking up is not enough, they also have to be properly heard: 'We need to slice through the silence. It begins with belief.'[9]

There is an assumption, that still persists, I think, that sex and romantic relationships between women are more 'equal' (in the feminist sense) because there aren't any men involved dragging with them a legacy masculine patriarchal power. This was in part a response to some of the conversations around at the time of the 'sex wars'. As Rebecca Jennings notes in *A Lesbian History of Britain,* the perception was that 'relationships between women [are] essentially caring and supportive'.[10] I've had it said to me plenty of times by straight women that I'm lucky to be in a relationships with another woman: 'they must just understand you better', 'I bet you don't argue about who does the housework', 'it must be nice having someone to take care of you when it's that time of the month'. It perpetuates the assumption that even within lesbian or queer relationships, two women will still perform the role society has assigned us within a heterosexual paradigm: that as caregiver and homemaker. It dangerously also paints women as being incapable of harm. And so intimate-partner violence as well as financial and emotional abuse between women largely remain taboo subjects. And for women who do experience it, it's incredibly difficult to even acknowledge that their relationship is abusive, or to disclose to others what is really going on.

The sheen of social media and the pressure on queer people to present a happy and united front means that for those experiencing abuse there is little recourse or language to speak to others about what is happening to them and access help. The sentiment that abuse between women is 'only emotional', or that it can't be that bad because they are physically 'weaker' are dangerous, ingrained biases both within lesbian communities and wider society which must be overcome before abuse can even be recognised or named. Galop, a UK LGBTQ+ anti-abuse charity, noted in their 2022 report on sexual violence that women often reported being unaware that other women could be perpetrators, citing a lack of awareness and discrimination in society and media contributing to an inability to recognise their experiences as abuse.[11] As the few calls recorded in the Lesbian Line demonstrate, just being able to talk about female-perpetrated abuse is a powerful and courageous act. The first step towards a better future.

Trans Lesbians Exist: Get Over It

'I am trans because the world made me so, not because I was born different. I am trans because the systems the world operates through force me to be so, not because of genetics. I am trans because of you, not because of me.'[1] So writes Travis Alabanza in their insightful memoir *None of the Above* on life as a Black, mixed-race, non-binary person. Their perspective helps us reorientate the perception of trans people within a majority gender-conforming society. It is a challenging statement to cis readers. To be trans is to fall outside of the norms of gender created by society, but as Alabanza skilfully and playfully reflects with this statement, that is not due to be person being trans but rather the barriers the world places around them. All of our learned ideas about gender are formed by our upbringing and our culture. In the UK this is a society defined by patriarchal, heterosexual, colonialist and Christian centres of thought that govern our politics, schooling and media. The world around us conceives of gender as binary and unchangeable. For the majority of cis people this feels so obvious as to go unquestioned. Encountering an alternative to this mode of being is what creates the otherness Alabanza speaks about.

An otherness aimed at trans people but not created by them. They are just existing.

For trans lesbians this othering can be twofold: 'I used to reject calling myself a lesbian publicly too because it made me feel like a fraud. Being a trans lesbian made me feel like I was only a lesbian by technicality or a completely different, incompatible species of lesbian.' These are the words of Alessia, a thirty-year-old trans lesbian whom I spoke to online. She lives in a seaside town in the UK, where she likes to cook, play video games and watch films with her best friend. However, these days she says she doesn't think about being trans that much. 'It feels like just another integrated attribute of my whole self. I'm not saying I'm ashamed of it or I try to hide it or anything like that, it just feels less important than it once did, or maybe less all-consuming.' Like many queer people, our sexuality and gender identity can feel at times like the most important thing in the world and sometimes, conversely, quite inconsequential to how we go about our daily lives. It's part of coming to accept ourselves for who we are. It happens when we find our family and where we belong. For Kit, a gender-ambivalent queer person who once identified as a cis lesbian, being trans 'feels like I finally have a home after decades of not feeling myself. I'm no longer playing a part. It's expansive and I love that feeling.' It has allowed them to connect (and disconnect) with womanhood in different ways and how they relate to others; they find joy in 'the curiosity of what womanhood can feel like to partners. There's common themes but nothing is ever the same cookie cutter. With plurality comes more understanding of the niche and specific.' They hint at the ways in which lesbian history and trans history have long overlapped, diverged and developed alongside one another as we have found both common ground and difference.[2]

Just as our conception of our self changes so does the language we used to talk about ourselves. During the '90s 'transsexual' and 'transgender' were both terms which were in common use and overlapped as terminology and personal preference changed over the course of the decade. As noted in *Lesbians Talk: Transgender*, 'transgender' at the time of writing in the mid '90s meant both 'a full time "cross-dresser or non-surgical transsexual" as well as "the group of all people who are inclined to cross the gender line. Sometimes used as a synonym for transsexual."' 'Transsexual', meanwhile, was defined as 'anyone who wants to have, or has had, a sex change operation, including non-surgical transsexuals'.[3]

Today 'transgender' has entered common use as the collective term which includes trans men, trans women and some non-binary people. It should be noted that not all non-binary people would describe themselves as trans. Likewise, some intersex people may identify as trans but the two should not be confused or conflated. In *The Transgender Issue* Shon Faye offers the following contemporary definition of 'trans', noting that terminology changes rapidly and that umbrella terms such as 'trans' are useful for political organising and contain a multiple of different experiences and identities. She writes: '["Trans"] describes people whose gender identity (their personal sense of their own gender) varies from, does not sit comfortably with, or is different from, the biological sex recorded on their birth certificate based on the appearance of their external genitalia.'[4] Kit Heyam expands on this definition to make clear that being trans is not solely about medical transition or moving from one fixed gender to another: 'Talking about being trans as an identity, rather than an action, helps us to understand transness as relating to *who you are*, not *what you do* . . . talking about moving *away from* the gender we were assigned at birth, rather than from male to female or vice versa, helps our definition to be clearly inclusive of non-binary people.'[5]

Both these definitions are useful to consider in their broadest terms when speaking about potential trans callers to the Lesbian Line, not least because without a record of a caller's gender identity I have no way of knowing how many trans lesbians rang the Lesbian Line and how frequent such calls were. There is only one caller in the logbook who identifies herself as a 'transsexual lesbian'. I have no doubt there were other calls from trans women and people of other gender identities outside of cis womanhood, but if so they did not identify themselves as such, either because it had no relevance to their call or because they were not comfortable to do so. Trans identity throughout history is often hidden and only accepted if the person disclosed it during their lifetime or it was discovered after death (and even then it can be contested). As Heyam explains, 'Historical methodology . . . tends to demand a much higher standard of evidence to "prove" that someone in the past can be called trans than it does to "prove" that they can be called cis.'[6] When transness is viewed as a deviation from the norm everyone becomes cis by default unless there is evidence to the contrary. The ironic implication being that misgendering someone as trans could be deemed offensive, but assuming someone is cis is not. As Hayem points out, 'Our sense of what we need to be cautious about has been insidiously shaped by homophobia and transphobia.'[7] I am reminded of a badge made by the Gay Liberation Front in the 1970s that reads 'How dare you presume I'm heterosexual', which articulates a similar sentiment.

The phone workers in the logs often did make presumptions about a caller, including assuming they were speaking to cis callers. Because of the nature of the Lesbian Line as a phone service there was great emphasis placed in the logs on a person's voice. Whether that was the emotion it conveyed or their accent. This also extended to the assumed gender identity of the caller. There are several calls from self-identified lesbians or women that the volunteers note 'sound like men' and which do not neatly fit into the trend of the sexually explicit wank calls where often men would put on a 'feminine' voice to trick the phone worker. It's impossible to know but I can't help but wonder if some of those calls, where the volunteers were unsure whether they were talking to a woman, were from trans lesbians – it's a complex assumption in many ways for me to make, not least because there is no way of 'sounding trans', and likewise perceptions of what a 'woman' sounds like come with various biases and stereotypes around pitch and intonation. Like facial features and the distribution of fat around the body, a voice's pitch is another ingrained marker of gender binaries that we have been trained since birth to identify, and which is reinforced by society and media around us.[8] For trans women in particular their voice can be a source of anxiety when it comes to the concept of 'passing' as a woman. If a trans person does decide to take oestrogen this will have no effect on their vocal chords.[9] For this reason some trans women choose to pitch their voice higher and train it (either self-taught or professionally[10]) to sit within a more stereotypical 'female' register.[11] Likewise, many cis women have voices with a naturally lower pitch which might place them in a perceived 'male' register, especially after the menopause. Conversely, it's possible some of the 'male'-sounding lesbian callers were trans men or transmasculine lesbians, whether or not they were out at the time or on testosterone (which does affect the vocal chords, resulting in a lower-pitched voice).

There is such a wide spectrum for misgendering here because I can base my information only on the assumptions of the phone workers making the log. Without a fuller picture it's perhaps better I don't say anything, but every time I come across a voice that the phone workers are unsure of I can't help but wonder. Take, for instance, one caller who rings the line who's only just come out and is looking for advice. The phone worker thinks the caller might be male and asks if she is a man and then notes that '*he* hung up' (emphasis my own). Perhaps it's a reach to imagine that these calls were more than the pranks some of the phone workers took them to be. Or perhaps a trans woman was calling for help and on being immediately challenged on her gender identity she put down the phone in fear or frustration.

Conversations around gender have changed greatly in the thirty or so years since the logbook was written and while trans and non-binary identities are nothing new, there are more ways than ever to talk about ourselves and our relationship to gender. The one definitive call from a trans lesbian in the logbook highlights how far such conversations have come and how much further we still have to go.

2.2.96 – log by Sam: *I wish the sexual health training day hadn't been cancelled due to lack of interest!*

She calls the Lesbian Line because her doctor was less than useless and besides he always asks all sorts of questions that are hardly relevant. She's not one to mince her words and prefers to get it out the way at the start of a call. She's transsexual. It's more efficient that way and if they can't help her, well, it would hardly be the first time. She explains about how she usually she sleeps with men, well, only since she started to transition. Before she'd always dated women but it seemed natural to switch to men or so she thought. But that's not why she's calling, well not totally, she sort of accidentally got involved with another woman, a good friend of hers, who's been such a great support through all of this. She doesn't know quite how she feels about it yet. They're taking it slow. They've known each other for so long and she doesn't want to risk their friendship. It all feels so new to be talking about it, it's not like she hasn't dated women before but this is different of course. It's why she rang the Lesbian Line in the first place, she wants a lesbian perspective on things. They've only slept together once, she tells the woman on the phone, but they spend most of their time together, she calls her every day and they talk on the phone for hours. No one's said the word 'girlfriend' yet but she's sure she feels the same way about her. It really feels like the start of something and she wants to turn this into a proper relationship.

So that's why she's calling. It's rather a delicate matter and she isn't sure who to ask. Before this relationship becomes something serious she wants to know if there's anything she should be worried about when it comes to having sex? She hates talking about this sort of thing normally. She's pretty mouthy about other stuff and so people think she's open about everything but talking about sex has always made her feel shy. She's always hated the way men talk about sex when they think women aren't around. Most people mistake her for confident because she's proud of who she is, but a lot of it is bravado. She's had to be to get to this point. Had to get good at making new friends and working out quickly which ones she can trust. She likes to keep a certain amount of loudness about her for her own protection but there's plenty she's quiet about too. Isn't every one? When it comes to certain parts of herself that's only for her and someone she cares about to know. In an ideal world she could keep such things private, but that's not always possible now, is it.

In what way, the woman on the phone asks, in what you're doing or . . . ?

How can I keep us both safe? she blurts out.

Oh, yes, I see the woman says, and pauses.

She knows where this question is going and so beats her to it and lets the woman on the phone

> know she's pre-op, on the waiting list for surgery but it's going to take a while.
>
> The woman on the phone doesn't really tell her more than she already knows: it depends on what they do but they should use a barrier if they can, condoms or dental dams. It lowers the risk of transmission. She should check if her friend takes contraception. Fingers can come in handy, she jokes. She talks about cleaning any sex toys they use and regular testing if they can get it. She apologises she can't tell her more, they don't get a lot of calls from transsexuals and so there's not much info to hand. She does recommend a couple of transsexual organisations who might be able to help, but it feels a bit like a fob-off. The woman on the phone encourages her to call again and she says she'll think about it. Maybe she didn't get all the answers she needed, but speaking to another lesbian has helped in its own way.

From the logs this would appear to be both a successful and unsuccessful call. Sam is able to answer some of the caller's concerns about coming out as a lesbian and being in a new relationship for the first time. Topics which as another lesbian and phone worker she is used to discussing. However, when it comes to the questions specific to the caller's transgender identity, in particular sexual health issues and being sexually intimate before medical transition, Sam is lacking information and resources to adequately answer her queries. Her main recourse is to refer the caller to other trans organisations who might know more. I get the sense that Sam is trying her best but is rather out of her depth. In her notes on the call she writes, 'I wish the sexual heath training day hadn't been cancelled!!' Such a comment highlights the gaps in training and knowledge within such volunteer-run helplines. Training which could easily be missed or cancelled due to various circumstances, or might vary in quality depending on whether they were professional-led training sessions or more informal on-the-job training from peers. While Lesbian and Gay Switchboard had a very clear training schedule and rigorous induction process, I know from speaking to ex-volunteers at the London Lesbian Line that they were almost proud of their lack of formal training and saw their peer-supported experienced-based sharing of knowledge an asset. Regardless, there was little such training (formal or informal) which focused on transgender healthcare, sexual heath and well-being.

Diana James was the first intersex trans lesbians to join Switchboard in 1988; as one of the first intersex trans phone workers, when she began she was both coming to understand her own experiences and trying to help others who called. During her interview for Switchboard Diana let them know she was trans as well as a lesbian, a word that at the time she felt best fitted her experience, since being intersex was little understood or written about then unless in a harmful way. Before she was invited to join the helpline she had one final chat with a current lesbian volunteer: Lisa Power. Diana recalls that Lisa told her, 'You're exactly the sort of woman we want at Switchboard, but you do realise you could face some trouble?' When Diana joined as a volunteer, four lesbians left in protest. When they left, the women's group that helped to recruit more volunteers collapsed with them. Diana, once she was fully trained, started it back up again. On the whole Diana remembers her early days of coming out as a lesbian with great fondness. She came out in 1986 and threw herself into the London lesbian scene, often going to her local pub, the Fallen Angel, to catch the eye of one of the butches that frequented the place, or to an all-nighter in Dalston. She told me, 'That was the times, it was a different time, it was new-found freedom for a lot of lesbians then, there were places to go, there so many women to meet, so much to learn. It was just a wonderful time.'[12] In the lesbian community Diana had found solidarity, going on dyke strength marches, hanging out at lesbian bookshops and venues. She stresses the freedom and options they had, relative at the time and especially in London. There might be a different woman every weekend if she so chose (and she often did).

At Switchboard Diana was seen as a lesbian first when on the phones as she had been recruited primarily because Switchboard needed more women – being trans or intersex was still little talked about in cis lesbian and gay spaces. When speaking to callers who thought they might be trans or intersex she often had scant information or knowledge outside of her own experiences. As one of the only trans callers for a long time, Diana often led the training for other volunteers at Switchboard. They were at least trying to change.

In the '90s there were only a few groups that transgender people could be referred to. One, Transgender London, was based not far from London Friend at Central Station in Islington. They aimed to be a new and inclusive space for people who 'challenge traditional assumptions on gender including transexuals, cross-dressers, androgynes, drag kings & queens and friends and allies'.[13] There was also the group Press for Change (formed in 1992) which provided legal advice, training and research for transgender people, their representatives and public and private bodies. The charity Gender Trust (formed around 1988) also produced a newsletter, 'GEMS', that was widely circulated, and from 1992 ran Gendys Conferences every two years that covered a range of topics on transgender issues. Specific support for gay and lesbian trans people, however, was still few and far between.

It's possible this caller turned to the Lesbian Line because the questions she had about lesbian sex she felt were best answered by other lesbians. Likewise, she may have been cautious about outing herself as a lesbian to healthcare professionals for fear of further stigmatisation. As Zachary I. Nataf writes in *Lesbians Talk: Transgender* at this time, 'The gender clinics reinforce[d] conventional, conservative, stereotypical gender behaviour', and to receive treatment many doctors expected a heterosexual binary transition narrative and fixed gender expression, which is so often not the case.[14] During the '90s coming out as gay or lesbian during transition could potentially risk losing access to treatment and healthcare. Both Travis Alabanza and Kit Hayem write about a similar sentiment that pervades today, where access to treatment is easier if a more straightforward narrative of transition can be produced.[15]

All this assumes that a trans person could even access that healthcare in the first place. It was only in 1999 that transgender people won the legal right to NHS treatment and even then, as Christine Burns notes, 'there were problems across the board – not just with obtaining referrals to gender identity clinics but in dealing with the country's hundreds of thousands of general practitioners and hospital doctors. Research by Press for Change showed that at least a fifth of doctors had no idea how to help trans patients even if they were disposed to do so.'[16] Trans healthcare has hardly advanced in the years since.

The early '90s has been described as a key period in the advancement of trans rights in the UK, especially in 1992 when Press for Change was established. As Burns explains, 'There was a sense of possibility in the air. Things were no longer totally, overwhelmingly hopeless. People could see that maybe – not right away, but soon – there might be a way to change the status quo.'[17] Although the Gender Recognition Act (2004) would take over a decade to come into law there were several legal achievements during the '90s which advanced trans people's rights significantly in the UK. This included the creation of a cross-party Parliamentary Forum on Transsexualism (later changed to Gender Identity) in 1994 and the legal protection for trans people against unfair dismissal in the case of *P v. S and Cornwall County Council* in a ruling by the European Court of Justice (1993–1999). The impact of this was a change to the UK Sex Discrimination Act and in 1999, the Sex Discrimination (Gender Reassignment) Regulations were instated, giving protection under the law to people who intended to have, were undergoing, or had undergone gender reassignment treatment.

Such gains were hard won. Writing of her time in parliament during this period while working to set up the Parliamentary Forum, helped by Press for Change, MP Dr

Lynne Jones writes, 'It has to be concluded that unthinking prejudice was rife within government at this time.'[18] However, the involvement of the Parliamentary Forum on Transsexualism and Press for Change, alongside trans people becoming more visible to their representatives in Parliament, had the effect of putting civil servants in direct contact with trans people, often for the first time. Eventually building on this work by trans activists and a dedicated group of pro-trans MPs, the Gender Recognition Act was passed in 2004. While I think no trans person would describe it as perfect, and it has since become the source of contention for so-called gender critical feminists, it was 'the best legislation in the world for its time'.[19]

The '90s also saw an increase of awareness of trans representation in the media and the press, both positive and negative. In *Coronation Street* in 1998, Hayley Patterson became the first trans character in a British soap. Despite being played by a non-trans actress it would prove to be an important piece of television and won over much of its audience, cis and trans alike.[20] It ran in counter to many of the other '90s narratives of trans people in film and television at the time which often portrayed trans people's lives being either a tragedy or the punchline to a joke.[21]

The feminist journalist Jane Fae notes that the '90s was a time of building awareness of trans rights' issues and stories in the national press which were commented on occasionally. While they varied in terms of positive and negative representations, however, '[a] common thread emerged in this period of trans issues as fair game for non-trans commentators to talk and write about. Trans matters were a story – but not one that belonged to trans people.'[22] Not much has changed, as Liam Konemann notes in his excellent essay-book *The Appendix: Transmasculine Joy in a Transphobic Culture*: 'Historically speaking the public attack on transgender people is enacted through false and insulting narratives about trans women. They bear the brunt of the cruelty and take most of the fallout.'[23] In *The Transgender Issue* Faye writes, 'Trans people have been dehumanised, reduced to a talking point or conceptual problem: an "issue" to be discussed and debated endlessly. It turns out that when the media want to talk about trans issues, it means they want to talk about *their* issues with *us*, not the challenges *facing us*.'[24]

That trans people don't get to have a say in the very issues that relate to them is played out in microcosm in the logbook. There is a P.S. to the call that Sam took from the transsexual lesbian that explains she spoke to her because 'she identifies as a woman', but then asks, 'do we need to think about a policy for accepting calls from TSs [transsexuals] on the lesbian line?' Sam and another volunteer, Josie, who later takes a possible second call from her, both seem concerned more that the line is not equipped to answer calls regarding specific transgender queries rather than to question the caller's gender identity. Josie acknowledges the limitations of the question of taking calls from trans lesbians when she writes, 'all these "boxes" are so inadequate to put people into'. It's the first acknowledgement in the logbook that a separate phone line for lesbians perhaps isn't best placed to serve the needs of its community and the limits of a non-intersectional approach to care. I see these responses as positive ones: both phone workers are aware of their inability to fully meet the needs of trans lesbians who may call and want to find a resolution.

Opinion was divided on this, however. Another volunteer has written a reply in favour of making a 'personal choice' so that they don't open what she describes as a 'can of worms', as she's sure there will be a difference of opinion across the volunteers. Writing that she wouldn't support any official policy as it's such an issue that 'a significant number of us might disagree'. Again, I do not think the 'issue' here is regarding the caller's gender (everyone refers to her by she/her pronouns) but rather whether the line should be accepting calls from transgender people in general and that the two were seen by some as very much separate in terms of their needs and what advice could be provided. It's an overspill from some of the separatist thinking that was the foundation for many of the lesbian lines around the country. Some believed that the focus should be on lesbians; implicit in this thinking is that they mean only cis lesbians, and that issues affecting trans lesbians were not within their remit of care. It's disappointing that even by the mid '90s London Friend had no official policy or adequate training for its phone workers on such topics.

At the time of this call, queer theory and 'LGBTQ+' as an umbrella term or way of describing a queer community were not really in the mainstream, and many organisations – while moving towards inclusivity – were still segregated into lesbian, gay, bisexual and trans groups. So where did that leave trans lesbians? Once again, because of an intersection of identities there were few services that could support their full selves. Without trans and intersex lesbians working on the phone lines (as Diana James did at Switchboard), education, training and knowledge was scarce and could be a source of contention. Yet contemporaries of the phone workers on the lesbian lines, such as Lisa Power, vocally supported – and continue to support – trans rights.

It highlights that without trans representation or a cis person actively advocating for trans inclusivity, services could excuse away such conversations, citing a lack of time or funding or the desire to avoid division (arguments that the women's movement once made about why they didn't want to support lesbian issues). It's disappointing to find a lack of solidarity with trans lesbians and the refusal to make a pro-trans policy for fear of creating division within the Lesbian Line. There were individuals who clearly felt differently, but in the logbook the Lesbian Line as an organisation appears unwilling, or too cautious, to make a statement either way. Likely they would have lost some volunteers over this 'issue' – and funding too, I know, was difficult at this time – yet their silence speaks volumes. Perhaps the phone workers felt they weren't equipped to serve the needs of trans lesbians who called the line and felt they would be best referred to transgender services instead. If they didn't get many calls from trans people (which as I've already mentioned is an unknown, but it would appear they weren't frequent judging from the phone worker's reactions) then I can see how this might have felt a waste of resources, although of course such a stance is self-fulfilling. If you fail to make a space proactively inclusive of trans people how do they know they will be welcomed there and know to call? In continuing the silence around trans inclusion on the line they failed their trans lesbian callers and ensured they remained in separate worlds. These conversations within the logbook expose the way in which the separate lesbian lines (away from collective gay, lesbian or trans helplines) could create a helpline that, without saying so, served the needs of only a select group of lesbians whose identity they silently policed. It left a wide margin for error and exclusion.

You may read the above and think I'm being too hard on the phone workers at the Lesbian Line; others may think I seek to absolve them of responsibility. I've spent a long time reading the call logs of these phone workers. I've seen the incredible difference they've made to the lives of many lesbians. But I've seen their failures too, I've seen the times they've lost patience, got fed up, disagreed with callers and missed shifts. And here, whether through ignorance, fear or a lack of understanding or training, I've seen the ways in which they didn't adequately provide empathetic care for at least one trans lesbian who called, and closed down even the suggestion of making more positive provisions for other potential trans callers.

It's a history I have to reckon with myself, and sadly not one that was unexpected given the anti-trans rhetoric that runs through the history of some lesbian communities in the UK. From the rise of TERFs (trans-exclusionary radical feminists) in Britain in the 1980s[25] to 'gender critical' lesbians of today, there is a misconception that lesbians and trans women should be at odds. One reason for this, Faye argues, is that while there has been progress towards a broader understanding of gender difference, it has also led to what she describes as a 'disquiet' in some people through a lack of understanding or fear of a less rigid gender structure or broader spectrum of human sexuality.[26] Faye notes that true trans liberation aligns with similar demands from socialists, feminists, anti-racists and queer people: 'They are *radical* demands, in that they get to the root of what our society is and what it could be. For this reason, the existence of trans people is a source of constant anxiety for many who are either invested in the status quo or fearful about what would replace it.'[27] For some lesbians this fear and perception of themselves as now part of this status quo means that they would rather align themselves with those who once sought to oppress them. When taken in bad faith or without nuance in the media and online, this disquiet is easily exploited to centre cis people's 'concerns' and often ignores the real material conditions that affect the daily lives of trans people. At its most extreme it should come as no surprise that TERFs and gender critical feminists often express views that reinforce a gender binary, are racist, anti-sex work and pro-policing.[28]

The current environment for trans people in the UK is one which leaves much to be desired. Trans people are hounded by the press and on social media; transphobic hate crimes are on the rise, reaching a three-year high in summer 2020 during Covid lockdown restrictions.[29] During a recent visit to the UK in 2023, a UN-appointed human rights expert highlighted the rise in hate speech towards LGBTQ+ people in the UK and pointed to the 'toxic nature of the public debate surrounding sexual orientation and gender identity'.[30] Meanwhile waiting times for gender identity clinics are vastly behind schedule, with many waiting years rather than the legal requirement of eighteen weeks on the NHS.[31] Likewise, there is a lack of access to gender confirmation surgery, partially down to a dearth of surgeons trained to perform these operations.[32] When I spoke to Alessia I asked her what she thought were the main issues most impacting trans lesbians today. She cited the long waiting times and lack of access to care on the NHS, as well as the profiteering by private healthcare that has arisen to fill the gaps in need, which for many is still inaccessible. She also spoke to me of the isolation that can come as a trans lesbian without any peer support. Growing up she knew some lesbians and some trans people but no trans lesbians – going to Pride when she was younger left her in tears because even within a large group of queer people she felt alone in her identity. Nowadays she feels very differently. 'I don't think we're such rare creatures that any cis lesbian isn't going to have a trans person in their network somewhere.' When I spoke to Kit they also mentioned the difficulties in accessing healthcare and the rapid spread of misinformation, noting, 'The freedom to just be everyday and ordinary shouldn't feel so hard fought.'

The mainstream media paints a very different image of trans people. As Lola Olufemi writes:

> Trans Exclusionary Radical Feminists [or Gender Critical] have not only created a false dichotomy between cisgender and transgender women, they have managed to distract our attention away from the structures that determine the conditions of our lives and most importantly, ensure that all women are not free.[33]

Such anti-trans arguments seek also to divide lesbians and trans people and hide the many ways in which the experiences of trans men, non-binary people, lesbians (trans and cis) and trans women overlap, and the long, complex history between such identities.

Lesbians have often been used as a scapegoat in transphobic rhetoric to argue that women are being pressured into having sex with trans women against their will,[34] or that the growing number of trans men are a threat to young girls who might once have identified as lesbians. With one journalist claiming that lesbians are being erased by trans activists, likening them to the Taliban.[35] Meanwhile trans men, if they get a look in in the media, are described as 'fragile or deluded women who have fallen foul of internalised misogyny – often framed as self-hating lesbians pushed into transition by a society intolerant of masculine-presenting women'.[36] It's a sly argument, since while it's true that society punishes masculine women this does not make lesbians become trans men or invalidate cis lesbian identities. The actual threat to butch lesbians, or any woman who 'looks more masculine', is so-called 'gender-critical' women who believe themselves to be the arbiter of gender and womanhood.

For butch, masculine-presenting or gender nonconforming lesbians and queer people, attempts to further ingrain a gender binary only increases the risk of real-world harm for them. For a trans lesbian in particular this can add an additional layer of awareness about how you are perceived by others. As Alessia told me, 'I consciously try to project an image of myself that appeals to other women rather than men. Does it work? It can feel like a bit of a tightrope, projecting a certain level masculinity so people know you're a dyke but not so much that they start looking at you as a man.'

An increased policing over gender as something which can be morally correct will only lead to increased harassment, abuse and a rolling back of rights for all women who are deemed to sit outside of the definition of what a woman is. And as I've already shown, such definitions are not stable or helpful. We have to ask who is doing the defining and why. Lesbian feminists worked hard to disentangle the identity of womanhood and femininity away from the patriarchy, not to erase it but to claim it for themselves if they wanted – it would be a shame to undo all that work.

Likewise, that young lesbians are being pressured to transition is another tactic of anti-trans rhetoric to divide and distract. Being trans makes you trans, nothing else. Here's Liam Konemann again: 'You cannot make a gay kid trans, just like nobody could ever turn me into a lesbian, no matter how many times the world told me that that must have been what I was.'[37] The danger here is not listening to young people when they tell you who they are (even if that changes later), not a moral panic about a small rise in the number of young trans people able to express their gender in a way that makes them happy. Nor does this weak argument address the many barriers young trans people face trying to access gender affirming care. That the number of trans people in the UK is increasing is likely due to a growing awareness and acceptance of trans identities and should be seen as an important step forward.[38] Seeing a broader representation of gender non-conforming and trans people is a positive sign of inclusion, especially in the face of such anti-trans rhetoric in the media.

When cis people discuss trans 'issues' the conversation so often stops at 'should we provide or make space for trans people within our organisation', and not 'what are the needs of trans people and how can we best educate ourselves to support them'. Many trans people were involved in the gay liberation movement and fought for gay and lesbian rights, yet historically this support has not always been returned. Much like the history of lesbians in the women's liberation movement, trans people have been asked to put their demands for liberation on hold. That some lesbians should not recognise what freedoms are to be gained in standing with trans women, non-binary people and lesbians of all genders is to me a great shame and we have greater battles to fight together.

Acclaimed activist and writer Leslie Feinberg knew this in 1992 in hir rousing manifesto *Transgender Liberation*, which argues the need for solidarity across racial and gendered lines: 'Like racism and all forms of prejudice, bigotry toward transgendered people is a deadly carcinogen. We are pitted against each other in order to keep us from seeing each other as allies.'[39] This is as much true now as it was then. As Shon Faye powerfully concludes in *The Transgender Issue*, showing how the liberation of trans people goes hand in hand with improvements to how society approaches work, education, state violence, healthcare and prison abolition. Goals which, historically, the gay and lesbian movement have also supported:

> We are not an 'issue' to be debated and derided. We are symbols of hope for many non-trans people, too, who see in our lives the possibility of living more fully and freely. That is why some people hate us: they are frightened by the gleaming opulence of our freedom. Our existence enriches this world.[40]

If there are any positives to this push by the media and a small vocal minority of an anti-lesbian and anti-trans agenda, it is that cis lesbians are becoming more active than ever in their support of trans rights across all genders and sexualities. In response to the lesbian anti-trans protestors at 2018's London Pride, a group of lesbians and queer people got together to organise #LwiththeT to reclaim their identity from lesbian anti-trans rhetoric. Their group garnered support online with the hashtag trending on Twitter, and *Diva* magazine and publisher Linda Riley offering their full support to the campaign. At Brighton Trans Pride that same year the group was invited to lead the march in a beautiful display of solidarity as Rachelle Foster, co-founder of #LwiththeT, wrote for *Vice*:

> [A]s diverse as the LGBTQIA+ community is, we won't be divided and the majority remain united. Supporting every facet of the community and reminding the world what the Pride flag really stands for – inclusivity – is crucial to improving our fight for equal rights.[41]

The simple fact is most people in the UK, lesbians included, support trans rights.[42]

I owe a great debt to trans writers, thinkers and activists – I think all queer people do. Just as I owe a similar debt to the lesbians who came before me. Everyone benefits from thinking about their gender more deeply even if it is to affirm the gender they were assigned at birth. Here's Alabanza again: 'if transness is working correctly, it is pushing for a world where anyone can express their gender in any way and not be deserving of violence'.[43] It only takes a moment, but for me it's reassuring to know that the lines of gender are not immutable. This too isn't new, but were conversations happening within lesbians communities during the time of the logbook. As Zachary I. Nataf wrote in 1996, regarding the category of lesbian and trans people, 'The issue is no longer simply one of proving that lesbians exist as an identity, as that lesbians have common cause with other category-disrupting subversives.'[44] Some radical stances in the '90s argued that the category of lesbian no longer held any use, or that a breakdown of gender would mean that lesbians would cease to exist, and along with it transgender identities and that 'queer' or no-label labels would take its place. I can see how such statements would be the source of anxiety for some lesbians who had fought tooth and nail to set up such services as the lesbian lines, especially during a time when even the word 'lesbian' was so taboo.

These fears proved to be unfounded. It's been over thirty years since these 'concerns' were first raised and we've yet to see anything close to this manifest. Ironically, to my mind the largest threat to lesbians are transphobes who attempt to create a schism between our communities and push the narrative that lesbians are not trans-inclusive.[45] Yet despite this we continue to proudly call ourselves lesbians and each generation adapts and expands the label to suit their needs. As we'll see in the next chapter, lesbians are stronger than ever, and as a word and identity it shows no signs of falling out of use for cis and trans people alike.

It would have been easy never to mention that short exchange in the logbook. After all, it's a few sentences between two phone workers and the topic is never brought up again. How much easier it would be if I simply ignored the issue like one phone worker wanted to. But I felt that staying silent on the matter would also be to condone it. I set out to find my lesbian inheritance, a lesbian history, and this is part of it too.

There's a direct line between conversations such as these, which were happening in lesbian spaces across the country, and with these same 'debates' raging today. It's not that I think the phone workers hated trans women or didn't acknowledge their gender identity, but that in refusing to even discuss a policy or training for potential trans callers, through their silent prioritisation of (cisgender) 'unity' they effectively cut off the trans lesbian community from their service. While some phone workers were happy to take calls from trans people it would seem others were not, and this lack of solidarity creates a structure that works to keep trans people away from the line. It's transphobia by omission. Today I hope that support for trans people and lesbians of all genders is more vocal, expected and accepted than ever and we must continue to show that support lest the hard gains that trans people and their allies have made over the last forty years be lost. I can admire the vital service the Lesbian Line provided, but acknowledge that for their trans callers they fell dreadfully short.

Gobs of Lesbians Online

26.2.96 – log by April: *She's now wanting to meet* ♀
She calls from a payphone down the street from the hostel she's staying at in Camden. And while she hates having to talk about this stuff outside at least it's a break from the stares and endless questioning of the women she shares a room with. They all say she looks too young and too like a boy to be there. They're right about one thing but she's not a boy, she just cut her blonde hair short and wears a big baggy denim jacket because that way she doesn't get bothered so much at night. When she calls the Lesbian Line she talks in a whisper even inside the phone box, just in case anyone passing by can hear. In the orange glow of the street lamp she can almost kid herself she's someplace else. Not in a strange city with no real friends or family to call. She tells the woman who answers the phone that she left home because her mum found her stash of letters from a girl at school and immediately figured out something was going on between them. She left the next day with as much as she could fit in her duffle

bag and caught the coach to London. Camden was the only place she'd heard of, so here she is.

She's pretty sure she can call herself a lesbian now. Getting thrown out of home must be some sort of rite of passage? She tells the woman on the phone as quickly and as quietly as possible that she'd like to meet other lesbians. Where are they all? She has no idea where to look and is too afraid to say she doesn't even really know what a lesbian is, she knows she should call herself one because she likes women, but she's never met another lesbian. She's never even really seen one. Not that she knows of. Well there was that one on *Brookside* once but her mum turned it off before she could find out what happened. London feels like the place to find them if only she knew where.

The lady on the phone sounds old, older than her mum even, and almost unsure what to tell her. She asks if she has a place to stay for the night. Then gives her information about a group called Changes. They meet weekly in the evenings and it's mostly a place to talk. Usually there's tea or coffee and semi-decent biscuits. She gives the address and explains it's not too far from Camden. She could catch the bus down or walk if she can't afford the fare. They'll be other women there like her and it's a good place to meet people. The lady on the phone tells her to call back again if she needs anything else.

It's a lot to take in and she doesn't know what

> else to say. Just as she's about to speak a group of blokes walk by and, although they don't say anything, the stares they throw at her are enough to make her hastily whisper a goodbye and hang up the phone. She rushes back to the hostel, hopping between the orange glow of the lamp posts, wanting to stay in the light for as long as possible.

The video I'm watching is only a few seconds long. In it a lesbian removes a small set of keys from a tiny black bag over their shoulder and fakes opening a door. They are dressed in a white tee and pink cargo-type trousers, multicoloured hair hair in a partial updo. Their expression is blank. Above them the text reads 'straight gals and their keys'. Jump cut to 'lesbians' in which they (dressed in same outfit minus the bag) lift up their shirt to unhook a ridiculously large collection of keys, lanyards and ID cards attached to their waistband with a carabiner. They sort through the keys for a moment before the video loops and we start over again. Some of the comments below the video read: 'We really out here walking around like janitors', 'I'm straight and I do this . . . wait', 'I'm a lesbian and thats [sic] how i [sic] carry my keys . . . without knowing it was a lesbian thing *laughing face emoji*'.

This video I'm watching is on the social media app TikTok. For those lucky enough to have avoided its clutches thus far, is a social media app made of short videos, usually self-filmed, and featuring overlaid text or lip-syncs to popular sounds and songs. It's infamous for starting viral trends and for being the natural home of Gen Z. This video has over half a million likes and is tagged with hashtags like #lesbians #lesbiantiktok #wlw

#fyp. The last two short for 'women loving women' and 'For You page' respectively. TikTok's For You page is an unsettlingly accurate algorithm which supplies your feed with videos it thinks you'll be interested in based on your profile information and watch times of other videos – creating a kind of feedback loop of content it thinks you'll like. As TikToks go this is a fairly standard entry in the subgenre of 'LesbianTok' as it's known: a loose network of lesbian content creators, writers, 'celebians' (celebrity lesbians) and your average everyday lesbian like me. The videos feature mostly young, Gen Z-looking lesbians mugging to the camera, showing off 'fits' (or 'outfits' – don't worry I hate myself for typing that out as much as you hate me explaining it), dancing to popular songs or recreating the popular meme of the moment. On #LesbianTok you will find everything from tomboy-femme lesbians – athleisurewear, long hair in a bun, a thick gold chain across their neck – to masc lesbians in tweed suits or backward baseball caps, to femme lesbians in pretty dresses sharing make-up tips, to non-binary lesbians with dyed hair and septum piercings. Some videos feature overlaid text poking fun at classic lesbian stereotypes, tropes such as masc and femme dynamics, doing DIY, or being so in love with a woman you're physically incapable of talking to them. We've already seen how these stereotypes and tropes can help to create a sense of shared identity and in-jokes, and TikTok is no different. Trends on TikTok are almost impossible to keep up with and most of the lesbian micro-trends I saw when first on the app (eyebrow slits, the 'buss it' challenge and the 'glamour filter' on masc lesbians) now seem like something from the prehistoric era.

Other videos are more serious in nature or educational.

There to dispels myths about being a lesbian or queer or debate and respond to topical issues. There are TikToks that invite lesbians under twenty-five to ask 'older' lesbians over twenty-five[1] their questions in the comments, and people do. They write things like 'Will I ever find someone who will truly love me for who I am?', 'Does it get easier to find queer places to make friends?' and 'Can my sexuality change over time?' Sounds familiar? There are TikToks about sex and dating, about lust and desire, about getting a girl and what turns a girl on. Some of the other suggested searches after I type in 'lesbian tiktok' are 'need a gf i'm a lesbian', 'uk lesbian studs', 'lesbian thirst femme' and 'lesbian tiktok thirst'. The latter a mix of femme and masc lesbians licking their lips and flexing to the camera (this is research!!) or fancams of current celesbian crushes. There are videos giving out relationship advice or simply showing what being in a loving lesbian relationship is like. As well as actual celebrities on the app there are, of course, influencers (both single and couples) and content creators from other platforms. It's even used by some lesbians as an unofficial dating site.[2]

The hashtag #lesbian on TikTok has over 11.5 million posts. Unlike on Google when I search these terms the top results are much more likely to be content created by lesbians, usually for an intended lesbian audience, rather than pornography for the male gaze. And while many of these content creators use a variety of hashtags such as #lesbian, #bi, #queer, #sapphic, #lgbtqia, #wlw and #gay to describe their content, they often speak about themselves specifically, proudly, as lesbians.

Anyone who has been online for a while will recognise

much of this from other social media platforms and forum sites before that. The memes change but the meaning is often the same. From the early days of Usenet in the 1980s to GeoCities in the '90s, Tumblr in the 2000s and now TikTok, lesbians have been using the internet to express their lesbian identity and find each other ever since it began. And before that, of course, there were the lesbian lines, alongside a whole network of newsletters and in-person groups that served a similar function. So how did we get here? From the Lesbian Line to TikTok lesbians? Did one have to die so that the other might live? Is this really a new type of lesbian or one we've seen many times over just in a new form, with new technology?

To find the answer I need to go the end and the beginning. The twilight of the logbook and the dawning of the internet age.

Unfortunately, few lesbian lines made it into the next millennium. The London Lesbian Line shut its doors in the late 1990s. The Cambridge Lesbian Line hung on a little longer, reportedly closing in 2002, when 'other forms of technology replaced the connections the line had once created'.[3] Many lines suffered a similar fate, as Patrick Halls recalls of the Leeds Gay Switchboard and Leeds Lesbian Line: 'I think probably in the era of the internet and mobile phones, with so much information around, and a much bigger gay scene, so to speak, maybe it was felt that it wasn't needed.'[4] It's impossible to talk about the end of the logbook, and the eventual closure of the lesbian lines all over the UK, without talking about the internet.

The five-year span of the logbook, from 1993 to 1998, saw an explosion in the popularity of the 'net' as it gained ever more content and users. Yet strangely, in the logs it's as if it doesn't exist. I can find no mention of the internet or even computers within the entries. The logbook remains squarely analogue. What technology there is be found is in the references to noticeboards, filing systems and the dreaded answering machine which was more of a hindrance than anything. For them pen, paper, Rolodexes and of course the telephone did the job just fine. A computer and a reliable internet connection wouldn't have been cheap in the late '90s and perhaps they thought it best to wait and see how this whole 'internet' thing panned out.[5] While the Lesbian Line continued to receive calls and create their handwritten entries, the internet only grew in scale and accessibility. The Web came to hold more information than one community-run phone line ever could and promised to connect you with lesbians not just in your city but across the globe. To many new lesbians hearing about the internet for the first time this proved irresistible.

At the opening of the logbook the internet is still in its infancy, and it's just a few years since Tim Berners-Lee launched the World Wide Web and the first website in 1991. In 1993 it now has around 130 websites to its name. By the end of the logbook five years later this will have grown to around 2.4 million. As of February 2024 it's closer to a staggering and unreadable 1.1 billion.[6] In 1993 we are still a long way from the internet as we know it and well before the unstoppable rise of social media. This is Web 1.0, where most pages are static and consist primarily of text, hyperlinks and basic images or a jazzy font if you're lucky. Better perhaps than the black and white bulletin-board style Usenet which preceded it but not by much. We are still in a time where 'surfing the net' is a hip new phrase. This is before GeoCities (1994), Yahoo (1994), Amazon (1995), MSN (1995), Hotmail (1996), Wikipedia (2001), MySpace (2003), Facebook (2004), Reddit (2005), YouTube (2005), Twitter (2006), Tumblr (2007), Instagram (2010), Snapchat (2011) and TikTok (2016). Google's search engine doesn't launch until 1998. Search engines in general being a relatively new concept – just Ask Jeeves (1997). Until then finding information on the internet requires some knowledge of where you're trying to get to and a place from which to start.

Early accounts of lesbians 'dialling in' to the Web are filled with wonder for this new technology. With no other points of reference they often compare it to older forms of communication technology: letters, newspapers and, of course, the telephone. In *Assaults on Convention*, scholar Lisa Haskel begins by introducing the internet. This text was written the same year we got our first computer, 1996, and when understanding of what the 'net' even was could not be assumed. She writes:

> The internet is a global network of computers linked by telephone lines which – with the simplest of equipment – allows the exchange of text either by 'mail' (just like the old-fashioned post, but requiring no paper and with a guarantee of instant delivery to the right address) or in 'real-time' discussion spaces, where a limitless number of users can come together, like a telephone chat-line, but where dialogue is only conveyed through typed text.[7]

Similarly, a few years earlier in 1994, *Diva* featured an interview which, when speaking about the internet, required the following explanation: 'It taps into the phone system via a modem and you type instead of speaking. It's cheaper than using a phone as it's still the cost of a local call to use it internationally. It's immediate and you can leave messages.'[8] In both descriptions the internet is hailed for its ability for instant communication across great distances. Noted too is the cost: it's a (relatively) inexpensive way of meeting people, gathering information and exploring globally, provided you have access to the right equipment in the first place, of course.

Unlike the lesbian lines, distant communication no longer needed to be one-to-one but potentially with an infinite number of people. Indeed, Haskel, while describing how she herself uses the 'net', is not immune to its charm: 'I plug my computer into the phone socket. As I dial, my adrenalin starts pumping at the sound of the data crashing through . . . I'm in. I'm connected.'[9] It feels almost quaint now to hear the internet described in this way. There's a joyful naivety and sense of discovery in this new(ish) technology as it hits the mainstream. The internet, here in the mid '90s, is not yet its own universal, all-encompassing medium, but something which must be framed by the technology that preceded it. It's just like a phone but text-based, it's like the post but instant. It's like the things you know already, but *better.*

Every lesbian-adjacent article I have found from the mid '90s onwards that mentions this new thing called the internet is adamant about one thing: lesbians, bi and queer women should be on it. As one journalist at the time concludes, 'With more than forty million computer users in the world, it's safe to assume there are gobs of lesbians online. So stake your claim in cyberspace as audience or author and add to the constantly expanding, electronically queer world.'[10] Who wouldn't love the idea of 'gobs of lesbians online'? I love the optimism of this statement, the go forth and multiply-ness of it. That the internet really was this new frontier for lesbians to explore and stake a claim over. The article's reasoning for this is twofold and interconnected: by getting online the visibility of lesbians will increase and help others to join them there. And by more lesbians claiming ownership of cyberspace it would also defend against the risk of the internet reproducing the structures and inequalities of 'meatspace'. As Australian new media artist Linda Dement says in *Diva* magazine: 'Dykes should battle for access to new technologies. It's really important for people on the periphery of mainstream culture to use these toys because they are the new site for knowledge.'[11] Lesbians and bi women were well aware by now that if they didn't stand up for themselves and in solidarity with other marginalised identities, they were at risk of being left behind or ignored once again.

Lesbian identity in the '90s was at a divisive time: never had lesbians been more 'mainstream' yet still misunderstood and widely misrepresented. 'Lesbian chic' may have been on trend but the reality for lesbians was an ongoing lack of consideration for their everyday rights and fighting discrimination across multiple fronts: Section 28, safety from sexual violence, access to childcare, homelessness and better representation in the media, to name a few. There were still many battles to be won. Perhaps this is why lesbians were well aware of the potential for cyberinequality right from the off.

It wasn't all wide-eyed excitement at this new technology and many academics and users urged lesbians to fight for a corner of the 'net' or risk missing out. The internet had the potential be a more democratic and equalising space, if only lesbians could get to it in time.

Enter the cyberdykes.

The term 'cyberdyke' shares its origins with the growing interest in 'cyberspace' and 'cyborgs' from the '80s onwards, with concepts like cyberfeminism developing out of seminal texts like Donna J. Haraway's *A Cyborg Manifesto*, which explored the way the women's movement and technology might come to interact in a new kind of human/machine hybrid. The term 'cyberspace' itself as a concept for the Web was inspired by William Gibson's 1982 book *Neuromancer*, which featured a computer network not dissimilar to what the internet would become. 'Cyberdykes' then became a name some lesbians, bisexuals, queers and dykes online used to describe themselves as they explored the internet and 'met' other lesbians. For some it simply described any lesbian online, for others it carried with it a more radical set of views about how lesbians could exist online politically. They adopted a '90s counterculture riot grrl and DIY aesthetic, now with a cool digital twist.

For some '90s cyberdykes the internet was almost a purer form of lesbian identity and communication. As they saw it the internet at this time allowed for a disembodiment of the self as it was communicated across time and space. As one cyberdyke put it, the internet allowed them to, 'think in words, so this is like a direct line to their thoughts. Pure imagination, a pure connection.'[12] Here, written communication allowed for a more intimate form of exchange, unfiltered perhaps in the moment-to-moment anxiety of articulating oneself in person or over the phone and without the delay of a written letter. Here the foregrounding of text as the primary form of communication allowed the body to disappear, something some cyberdykes revelled in: 'My identity floats as words that flow through my fingers onto my liquid-crystal screen and rush through the telephone wires to flash up on terminals in places beyond my imagining.'[13] No more was the body needed to communicate a self; it could be uploaded directly to the 'net' for others to interact with and experience. One reading of Haraway's *Cyborg Manifesto* might argue that the human/machine hybrid has been here for some time: certainly now with smartphones clasped into our hands at all times and smart devices strapped to our wrists.

Such a feeling is difficult to recreate on a phone line, where the volunteer routinely make assumptions about a caller's gender, age, race and class. Anonymity on the internet, unlike the lesbian lines, could go both ways. For some dykes this was particularly freeing, allowing for an out-of-body experience and experimentation. As one cyberdyke describes it: 'I think the net is something special for dykes: it's like life, but you can afford to play. The dislocation from my "fixed" identity, my body, is a comforting anonymity.'[14] For these early cyberdykes the internet was to be embraced for its potential for liberation, from the body, gender and even humanity itself: 'In my unity with my computer I am no longer woman as opposed to man. I am an-other. I am fluid, dynamic, a hybrid. I have no essential nature, not because I can act out any social role at will, but because I am no longer just human.'[15] Some even predicted that such anonymity could mean labels such as 'dyke' and 'lesbian' would no longer be needed and 'the idea of the lesbian confined to history'.[16] Far from something to worry about, for some cyberdykes it was seen as a goal to work towards as ideas about the self evolved and changed.

23.5.96 – log by Linda: ***wants to be a lesbian at the moment***

Now that I'm 99 per cent certain I'm a lesbian, okay maybe 90 per cent, maybe even 80 per cent. It's hard to be sure because I haven't actually done anything with a woman yet, but I think I would like to. So maybe there's 20 per cent of me that still likes men but it feels like that part of me is in the past.

Anyway, now that I'm up to 80 per cent I think it's only right that I call up the Lesbian Line to find more about it all. When I told Michelle at work I thought I might be a lesbian now she told me that I couldn't be because I've never even kissed a woman and that it was probably just a phase and that I'd just gone too long without a boyfriend. Which could be true I guess, but I do want to see how being a lesbian might pan out. I rang the line on a Thursday after I'd finished my shift. I'd asked to be put on an early so I would be back home in time to make my tea before phoning. I don't just want to take Michelle's word for it. I need to speak to a proper lesbian. And she was really nice. She didn't even say anything when I said that this was all new to me. Just reeled off a list of groups I could go to and a

> couple of pubs near me that had a 'women's night'. Sorted then, I thought to myself. Maybe after this I'll be 100 per cent sure.

It is surprisingly difficult to find out what the internet used to look like using only the internet. Perhaps I was foolish to think that the internet captures everything because why would we need to remember things now that the internet does that for us? But the reality is that the internet is a patchy, messy and forgetful archive at best. The internet is not like rings of a tree or layers of soil waiting for an archaeologist to carefully uncover it years later. No, a lot of what the internet once was is gone forever and was never saved – you can see the traces in broken URLs and 404 errors. And so of course finding a historical lesbian internet is even harder. A few times while trying to research this topic I've unthinkingly typed in some variation of 'lesbian websites '90s' and been presented with a list of porn sites or just straight-up naked pictures of women. It shouldn't be surprising by now – yet I am caught off guard every time. If I want find the actual websites lesbians in the '90s 'surfed' I need to try a different approach, or rather a better search.

Thankfully the internet does have an archive of sorts via the Wayback Machine, which is of course stored on the internet, like an ouroboros eating its own tail. For years it has trawled the Web, creating copies of every web page it came across. It now holds versions of hundreds of billions of old websites. There are other traces of the lesbian net also, as we've seen, in magazines and books from the time. In the March 1997 issue of US magazine *Curve*, from Charlie Kiss's collection at

Islington's Pride, between ads for queer bookstores, thumb rings, vibrators and letters about Ellen DeGeneres, and Linda Perry (of 4 Non Blondes fame) is an article on 'Taking Back the Net'. It offers to the uninitiated lesbian reader a guide to the best 'Web sites' online covering everything from art and literature, to sex, activism and starting a family.

The first URL they mention, lesbian.org, I of course immediately enter into my search bar. Up pops a text-only version with further links from the owner, Amy Goodloe, to her more recent work and published articles. But thanks to a link on her website and the power of the ever-useful Wayback Machine, I can see lesbian.org in all its original 1997 rainbow pixelated glory. The home page hosts a 'What's New' section and a series of links to local events such as the Chicago Lesbian Avengers and the San Francisco Dyke March, as well as various mailing lists, newsletters and book clubs to join. It describes itself as 'dedicated to promoting lesbian visibility on the internet, and to providing resources and information for cyberdykes everywhere. Started in February 1995, the site has grown to include the largest collection of annotated, lesbian-specific links on the internet, as well as a variety of resources to help lesbians find each other, find out more about themselves and find ways to promote lesbian visibility and rights in the culture at large.' Primarily focused on US issues and events it nevertheless had a wide reach and appeal.

In a TV interview from 1996 Amy, chin-length hair tied back in a scrunchie, explains that she wanted to create lesbian.org to cater to the specific needs of lesbians. At the time there were sites for women's issues and for gay men and lesbians, but not many just for lesbians. The website aimed to curate a selection of commonly asked questions and concerns so that lesbians could find each other and talk about their experiences. It also notably focused on activism work and providing information for groups such as the Lesbian Avengers and dyke marches happening around the US in pride and protest. The site offered information on topics like coming out, finding lesbians and support groups in your area, what it's like to go to the doctor as a lesbian or becoming a lesbian mum. But more than anything, Amy says in her interview, it is a place for 'people who don't have much visibility to come together and know they are not alone'.[17] At the very core of the website were message boards where users could post comments and discuss current topics.

Analogous UK sites to lesbian.org did exist, including ones like *Diva*'s 'Blue Room', an online offshoot of the print magazine with its own forums and message boards for UK lesbians to connect to one another. Topics ranged from posts on Mel and Sue to places to buy formal suits, local meet-ups and 'Dyke-fiction'.[18] And although the forum side of the website has since shut down, *Diva* continues to foster and encourage a community through its members-only Facebook pages and social media feeds.

Other UK forums and communities have since been and gone, including Gingerbeer in the early 2000s, a London-based site for lesbians and bi women to talk, date and plan social events or see listings for lesbian and female-focused nights out. It was staunchly not for profit and run by a group of volunteers. In 2007 their founder described her hopes for its future: 'I'd like Gingerbeer to be the definitive guide to Lesbian London and to be able to expand the current definition of the "lesbian scene"; it's not all about bars and clubs for the baby dykes. I'd like to think that I'm very approachable and hope that my positive and laid back attitude instils a highly sociable and accepting outlook for our website.'[19] Gingerbeer, like *Diva*, wanted to create space for women to speak to one another but also to be able to meet and gather in person and know where they would be welcomed.

When you compare the aims of such websites, then, to those of the lesbian lines they are not so different. They both saw the need for lesbian-only spaces separate to the services that catered to men or mixed groups and a place for women to explore their feelings in a safe and knowledgeable environment. As well as offering information on similar subjects or helping women from rural areas to find each other. Always at the heart of these lesbian-specific spaces, whether they are helplines, in-person groups or websites, is a focus on community building, increasing visibility and information sharing. They provided the beginning – it was up to you where you went from there.

If forced to think about my past selves since being a teen, I find the easiest way to organise my thoughts is by what social media I was using at that point in my life. Taken together they form a fracturing, overlapping, evolving picture of who I am, or thought I wanted to be at the time. Of course, social media is not 'real', but because they are projections and reflection of our selves in many ways they end up being unintentionally more real and more revealing than many of us might like to admit. I read a tweet once that said if you don't look back at yourself and cringe at who you were five years ago you're doing something wrong. I hope they were right.

The first social media that I properly used as a way to create an identity that felt separate to my real self was MySpace. Once signed up you were able to curate your profile page with a picture, edit the layouts and colours with some basic HTML knowledge and add a list of your favourite songs, which would play automatically when you clicked onto your profile. Crucially, and for maximum teenage drama, you could also choose your 'top eight friends' to display. Falling off someone's 'top eight' was a big deal. My MySpace was characterised at that time by an emo aesthetic that my friends and I shared. Imagine if you will a lot of pictures taken from above, long fringes swathing across one-half of our faces as we pouted upwards towards the camera, my friends with their bat-wing eyes (I didn't wear make-up – I never got the hang of it), and dyed black hair (which I again avoided). My greatest contribution was a homemade white T-shirt I drew over *trompe l'oeil* style with a fake collar, pocket (complete with pens) and pin badges. My MySpace self reflected a person who needed to fit in. I didn't like emo music – aside from Avril Lavigne – and I didn't quite fit the mould of emo girl, but I did like the baggy clothes and not having to wash my hair, which was to my shoulders at that point. On my mother's gentle encouragement I wore dresses when I needed to look 'nice'.

Typical for me all of my top eight friends were girls, but then I don't think that's so unusual for the age I was. And while the emo aesthetic really wasn't something I could convincingly pull off, my friendship group during my GCSE and college years had a much more casual approach to sexuality.

While no one particularly used any specific labels, there was a vague sense of fluidity in the air when it came to sexual partners, especially at parties and especially for the girls. In the late 2000s it was considered pretty cool to kiss a girl at a party when you were a little drunk, but it also came with a tinge of male voyeurism and no mention of it the next day. Perhaps this was why I never partook myself – I unfairly felt embarrassed for the girls who did, angry at the boys who encouraged it and annoyed at the girls when they went back to their boyfriends without really knowing why (now I know why). Bisexuality of course had yet to be invented[20] and no one at our school was out. So during what should have been a time for discovery and figuring out what and whom I liked, I only reinforced my own internalised homophobia. To me, kissing a girl was only for when you were drunk and you wanted a boy's attention. An attitude I think is unfair to the girls who were kissing other girls, exploring their own sexuality and having a grand time doing so. As if to prove a point I found a boyfriend around this time but it was Facebook that I turned to when it came to updating my newly boyfriend-ed 'status'.

I am old enough to remember when Facebook became public and no longer the domain of those with a university email address like my older brother. Facebook represents my peak 'straight phrase', when I really tried to give heterosexuality a chance. I went off to uni, the one boyfriend under my belt, thinking that made me 'normal' and that I'd proved my point. They would be plenty of others I was sure. I wasted a lot of time at uni believing myself to be in love with one boy or another.

A picture that I can recall clearly from my Facebook days is one snapped by a friend on her digital camera on a night out in Leeds. Because *back in my day* you used to go out dancing and one friend with a camera would take pictures, download them all the next day and upload every single one to Facebook with minimal editing, past Facebook's crap filters which made the whole image too dark and too saturated. In this picture I'm wearing a short shirt-style dress, white with a red and yellow pattern along the bottom. Very 2008. I bought it from Dorothy Perkins before I went to uni. My hair is long, just touching my shoulders and has been straightened within an inch of its life. The image is blurry, the lights burning together and creating a ghostly image of myself of where I was seconds ago. I'm dancing, hands flung out to the sides, my face half-obscured by my hair but happy. You can see my bra straps. It's not so much this image that is seared into my brain but a comment from an old school friend. She had written 'You look like a real girl!!!' underneath the picture. Reading it at the time was a mixture of acceptance and annoyance. I'd never striven to look like a girl, or be particularly girly, but this acknowledgement felt like (finally) some recognition of the hard work I was putting in trying to be more feminine. The type of person I thought I should be – girly, soft, wearing dresses, going out and having a good time. It's very easy to make grand statements about how society pressures women to look at certain way, and while this is of course true, the mechanisms of it are much harder to see. It happens on TV and in magazines and in schools, but it's upheld in the thousands of little comments like that one my friend innocently made. We do it to each other without even realising. It's being rewarded for looking and acting a certain way. Social media has just made it more visible – a literal like – a dopamine rush of attention for presenting yourself the 'right' way. But compliments can cut you as much as they can uplift you. I don't see myself as that person in that picture any more. And I'm very glad she found a way out.

During this time was when I also discovered Tumblr, which was like a foil to the person I was on Facebook. If Facebook was my public university persona – straight, Christian, surrounded by friends – then Tumblr was a space just for me. I had joined it during its heyday, long before it was sold to Yahoo and went downhill. It helped that on Tumblr I followed and was followed by very few people who knew me in real life and most of those that did were friends from home. Looking back, my gay awakening really found its home on Tumblr. I'm not saying that Tumblr made me gay, but it was certainly an enabler. Tumblr for me was less like social media where I talked to peers and more like a cultural identity curation platform. I shared a few pictures of myself but mostly I used to 'reblog' and post the things I was interested in: TV shows I was watching, books I was reading, fashion I liked and illustrations of fan fictions I might be reading. Tumblr stayed with me all through university and into my adult life as I moved to London and got my first proper office job. I didn't talk about it with anyone. Ideally no one in my real life would know it existed.

Tumblr felt like a place where I was unknown, and that anonymity allowed me to discover for the first time what I actually was into without the burden of social pressure. Ironically, it was by being antisocial on social media that

I was able to allow myself freedom to discover who I was. And slowly the content I was watching and liking and following became much more gay. There was one particular hashtag that started to pop up on a lot of the posts I was liking: #wlw – women loving women – the same hashtag I would see on TikTok years later. It's a wholesome description for much of the sapphic content I was finding on Tumblr. Whether that was GIF sets of women kissing from TV shows and Web series, or 'drabbles' – short fan fiction pieces where two women who may or may not be gay in a TV or book series shared a romantic moment or cute date. These were my gateway into allowing myself to consider that maybe I did like girls. While mainstream media offered me snippets of subplots featuring lesbians, it was on Tumblr that I found confident female-centred stories and imagery – often created *by* queer women *for* queer women. And so Tumblr for a long time became my secret self. The one that watched *Call the Midwife* not for the daily dramas of midwifery but the tiny snippets of romance between Patsy and Delia. The one who got obsessed with YouTube shows like *Carmilla* and *Brown Girls* but would make up something else when asked what I was watching. I keep this part of myself tucked away in a corner of the internet. My own digital closet.

And for a while this worked well. But I wanted more. As my sense of myself as a lesbian grew so did my public persona on social media. I had long been on Twitter – where I was perhaps the most 'professional' of the social media sites I frequented. There I attempted to project a social self who was literary but goofy, who understood the memes and references *du jour* but could also critically dissect whatever book I was reading at the time. It sounds exhausting now when I think of it and I'm sure was mostly a failed attempt. At least if you can judge things from follower count.

Yet despite this I've found many friends on Twitter and it was here that I first began to engage with other lesbian and queer people, some of whom I'd met in real life and some whom I've still never met. If Tumblr taught me the language and memes of being gay online then it was on Twitter where I put my skills to the test. I followed other queer content creators and IRL friends and made my first ever subtle forays into posting content which was queer coded as I had been doing more regularly on Tumblr. Maybe I was being a good ally, maybe I was gay – who could say? I kept it ambiguous on purpose. A large reason for this was that unlike Tumblr, on Twitter friends and work colleagues also followed me. And more recently my mum had joined Twitter in order to see what the fuss was about and I was certain she saw nearly everything I tweeted.

To my mind there is nothing more horrific than someone mentioning something to you in real life that you have written about or posted on social media. That is a different self and I would rather the two didn't overlap. It's one thing, say, to mention your holiday pictures on Instagram, versus bringing up some inane tweet you made at 2 a.m. about how you wish you could be like the frogs in *The Wind in the Willows* riding their bikes through country lanes and how you think they are probably 'boi-friends'. The thought that my mum would read everything I tweeted was like a panopticon of my own making and so I found the setting to stop my mum from seeing my tweets. I did this because I am a coward who can't have an adult conversation about how it makes me uncomfortable. As you may recall this plan terribly backfired and I ended up coming out to my mum because of it. Whether I wanted it to or not, Twitter had forced my new-to-me-queer social media self and secret-but-queer real self to finally merge.

Social media then, for me and I suspect many others of my generation who grew up with it, became the place to curate and shape an ever-changing persona. For me and other LGBTQ+ people, however, it also provided a safe space to present as queer before I was ready to in the 'real' world. It gave me a shared language with other queer people – it exposed me to tropes and stereotypes that I could play into or avoid if I wished. Tumblr was often the place I first encountered feminist and queer discourse, later verifying it with books and articles from my studies. It was where I first found the Lesbian Masterdoc, a modern day cult piece of online lesbian history that introduced me to the concept of compulsory heterosexuality.[21] The internet has influenced my fashion and found me real friends. It made me feel part of a community before I was ready to declare it for myself. I remember the first time I posted on National Coming Out Day, and all the times I read other people's posts and was too afraid to add my own.

The internet has become our generation's first port of call for much that the lesbian lines and London Friend once provided: information, connection and identity. #LesbianVisibilityDay hashtags and rainbow flag emojis serving to announce ourselves just as carabiners and intentionally bad haircuts do in the real world. In doing so we're part of a long history of lesbians and queer people online. So while social media has taken much from me (mostly time) I acknowledge that it has given me access to friends, community and, crucially, hot pictures of Cate Blanchett in suits when I needed them most.

12.11.95 – log by Bea: ***she hung up when I got a bit too challenging for her***

Bea knows she shouldn't roll her eyes but she can't help it. The woman on the phone is going off about the lesbian scene, how it's all the same and she's bored bored bored of it. She sounds older, keeps mentioning how she's been out on the scene for years, probably before you were even born, the woman says. You don't know what it was like for us back then. I was spat at just for holding hands with a girl. Now you lot have your fancy bars in Soho and pretend like you're normal. Bea asks her to explain what she means by that. She knows it's not a comment aimed at her personally but it's hard not to take offence. The woman sighs, that came out wrong, I just mean, lesbians nowadays, they all look the same, there's no style. When I was younger we wore turned up trousers and DMs and looked proper butch. We went on dyke marches and nearly got our heads kicked in. When we went out we had a pretty femme on our arm. It was all very clear and you knew what was what. The other day I walked into a so-called lesbian bar and I couldn't tell who was a dyke and who wasn't. Everyone was in jeans and T-shirts! Not to mention the gay men hanging on. In my day you looked different and that meant

> you had to be tough. It took real courage. I don't think you appreciate just how hard it was. Bea tries to be reasonable, she says she thinks that lesbians today still have a lot of the same issues, and as for the fashions . . . well, things change. That's the way of the world isn't it? Hello . . . ?

When I read about the future of the internet wanted by the cyberdykes – one of a liberated democratic space where people could meet and discuss freely, organise and express themselves to the point of total disembodiment – I fail to recognise it in my Instagram feed and online browsing history. The cyberdykes themselves foresaw the dangers they would be up against even in the infancy of the internet – chiefly that the internet left unchecked would only replicate the inequality they already saw around them in the real world. Dement explains: 'Unsurprisingly, since those with access to the most powerful equipment control the internet, much of the interplay becomes a direct microcosm of an unequal society, with cybernetic bodies reinstating negative stereotypes.'[22] The beginnings of the internet was dogged by such misogyny and assumptions that technology was the natural realm of men, despite many women being foundational to its creation.[23] When *Diva* asked Dement what could be done to prevent the 'mainframe [being] open to all kinds of sexist, racist exploitation?' she replies comically, 'The problem is in men's heads. If you give them a pencil, they'll do something stupid with it.'[24] While her answer is flippant there is some truth to it. As Dement is alluding to, it doesn't matter so much in this instance what the medium is, but rather who is making the message. And to her eyes men being in charge of that medium was only going to create more inequality.

She was not alone in this fear as Haskel notes in *Assaults on Convention*: 'The internet may have been transformed from its origins, but it is not ahistorical, and like any other cultural arena it carries within its very structure the values of the world that produced it.'[25] It's fascinating for me that at the very beginning of the internet lesbians were asking such prescient and insightful question about its use. For lesbians and dykes the internet presented an exciting new space that allowed for reinvented identities and connection, but which held the same trappings as all technologies before it, including letters, mail, in-person events and, of course, the telephone – that of reflecting back society and their own communities' inequalities and prejudices. The Web never was and never will be a purely democratic space. Already women were being marginalised from cyberspace, and lesbians doubly so, despite being some of its earliest adopters and forebears.[26]

Today we can see the impact the powerful have over the internet and why the cyberdykes' warnings regarding claiming space for ourselves were so prophetic. Sites with the most reach and internet traffic (through a network of hyperlinks) tend to be older and larger sites – so long as they stay relevant, so it's true that those who got online early and stayed online hold a lot of power and sway. Capitalism pushes for monopolisation to control the market and makes it so much harder for new websites to establish themselves. Today the same few large corporations through their many subsidiaries hold most of the online capital. Companies like Alphabet (who own Google and all its subsequent applications, YouTube,

Android), Amazon (Audible, Goodreads, Twitch) and Meta (Facebook, Messenger, Instagram, WhatsApp), to name just a few, control great swathes of the Web.[27] You can see this play out in microcosm through social media where sites like Twitter prioritise and push to larger audiences accounts which already have large followings or generate high engagement (often through controversial or divisive statements), facilitating further growth.[28] The content doesn't matter quite so much, rather connectivity, engagement and hypervisibility are key. The more extreme the better to generate further conversation and keep attention and users on their websites, in turn keeping advertisers and investors happy. The so-called 'attention-economy'. Sites which operate not for profit or who are volunteer led (like many of the lesbian websites and organisations) are by their very nature more precarious and difficult to maintain in the current Web climate. Some now live primarily on social media platforms, binding them to the rules of that platform and requiring them to 'compete' with other brands, influencers and organisations for attention and reach.

This extends too, of course, to the individual online. The rise of social media has remapped the way we present our digital selves and pushed to the forefront individual expression and 'branding' in ways the cyberdykes could not have expected. While some cyberdykes welcomed the idea that the body and personal identity might be deconstructed and erased online, it now seems like the very opposite is true. The body, and the individual, has once again become central to how we see ourselves online with both positive and terrifying consequences. At the time the cyberdykes were online the default form of communication was through writing on forums and blog posts; digital cameras were still in their infancy, were low resolution and for most unaffordable. When text was king you really could be anyone online and disappear. Now anonymity is more likely to be viewed with suspicion, a blank profile page and avatar usually the sign of spam accounts and trolls. Most popular apps like TikTok, Snapchat and Instagram prioritise image and video over text. The body is back in the frame, quite literally. While this may have increased our visibility and broader queer representation, we need to consider the other consequences of such 'visibility'.

If social media becomes the default way many young LGBTQ+ people come to find themselves and their peers online, what does this mean for the way that we construct the self and how we form community? How might this shape how we relate to 'authenticity' online? If such a thing is possible. Queer video essayist Lily Alexandre, describes how content created online is now made not for a real body but for an algorithm, for a particular aesthetic as something to aspire towards and be consumed. She describes how, as young people look to the internet as their primary social space without a grounding in community, the sense of self is filtered through an individualistic lens. She describes the internet not as this space for connection but one of profound loneliness:

> Browsing the internet doesn't give you a cross-section of human experience – it's one of the most solitary experiences possible, fine-tuned to each user's wants and

> needs ... As a result if the internet is where you start defining your identity, you're likely to define yourself not as a community member, but as an individual consumer, of posts, of media, of content ... What we consume has become shorthand for what we are, and the act of consuming, all by itself, has been held up as a reasonable foundation for a person's identity.[29]

As the cyberdykes in the early '90s feared, capitalism got its filthy claws into the internet and reproduced its neoliberal values of individualism and consumerism for a new generation. And queer people are not immune. I've certainly been influenced to buy a brand of clothes because I see other lesbians wearing it and want to make myself look and feel as good as they appear to. I follow queer social media influencers and envy their seemingly perfect, cooler-than-me lives and I've been guilty of trying to replicate such posts myself.

Daisy Jones, writing on lesbian and bi culture today, neatly sums up this dynamic when describing her experience following queer creators, friends, exes and writers on Instagram: 'They were all there; an echo chamber of my own design. A community of queers at my fingertips, very unlike that which could ever be experienced in real life.'[30] Consumer culture and influencer culture have profoundly complicated the line between expressing sexuality through shared identifiers and a slippery slope towards a didactic way of 'looking' like a lesbian through the clothes we choose to wear and the brands we associate ourselves with. What we see is governed by algorithms designed to turn our attention into profit, to feed us content it knows we already like because it has told us we should like it: our 'For You' page and our 'Suggested for You' posts.

Ironically this drive towards the individual does not necessarily mean greater individuality. The globalisation of lesbian identity online and increased visibility of (certain) lesbian bodies has had a hegemonizing effect on lesbian culture. In English-speaking spaces online, American lesbian culture often dominates, whether that's through fashion, language or politics. Once again such questions and anxiety were around right at the very beginning of online lesbian culture. Here's Haskel again: 'It's both nothing new and something entirely alien which allows for a "dystopia" of misunderstanding, misrecognition and impersonation, of complex technology and a worrying shift in our relationship to the real world . . . and the anxiety of all media, namely who is included and who is excluded? Who speaks for whom?'[31]

An accepted myth about the internet is that is has given everyone a voice. Who gets to speak and who gets heard online is irrevocably linked to capital, status, notions of authenticity, censorship and representation. On one hand we have LGBTQ+ influencers providing content and representation in a way that has never been possible before and to so many people. But when you look to the biggest queer stars who have made it into the mainstream they are largely cis white gay men who mostly cater to a straight, female audience. What does it say about queer culture online when some of the largest social media platforms like Instagram and TikTok censor words like 'dyke' and 'lesbian'? On TikTok 'lesbian' is often written as 'le$bian' to get around this so-called 'shadow-banning' of queer content and has created its own kind of language as a result.[32] Corporations are happy to profit from the views generated by lesbian content, yet will happily censor the same content when its suits them.

Visibility online is inherently political, both in terms of what people choose to share of themselves (or not share), and whose bodies and stories are boosted on social media. By far the majority of lesbians who reach a larger mainstream audience conform to stereotypes that we have deemed acceptable (thin, white, able-bodied, masculine but not *too* masculine). When I spoke to the anonymous founder of the Instagram British Asian Lesbians (@bal.br) she shared that being anonymous online was difficult because 'people want to see representation', but that she also needs to protect herself online – especially as she's not out to her family. Likewise, she warned against the danger of conforming online to a prescriptive version of lesbian identity: 'it's easy to fit into online categories that aren't real'. She went on to cite just one example of how masc/femme dynamics on TikTok are represented with little awareness of its working-class history and often perpetuate unhelpful stereotypes. It adds pressure to conform to one set label: that you have to wear certain clothes or act a certain way in a relationship as lesbians, which didn't feel true to her own experience as a British Asian lesbian, she added. 'I want people to be able to express themselves through their Asianess and connect to their own communities.'

Shon Faye notes a similar pressure for trans influencers who aim to make their appearance palatable to others: 'For trans women the standards are strikingly similar to the standard for cis women in the mainstream media: whiteness, thinness, conventional feminine aesthetics all dominate.'[33] As Faye goes on to discuss, the reasons for this are complex; adhering to these standards is a form of safety and assurance of acceptance, but if done right can also be profitable and ultimately the content created by these influencers benefits the platform's shareholders. We might joke that this is equality – that trans women get to be basic-bitch white-girl influencers just like everyone else – but I don't think we're at that point of equality yet when we're still playing by the rules of capitalism.

While the early articles on the internet talk about greater visibility and opportunities for lesbians to be seen, the reality is that such exposure comes at a cost. That visibility is also vulnerability. Once a post is public the poster has little control over how that content is distributed and commented on. There are little protections online for LGBTQ+ people on the receiving end of such abuse, and little support from platforms to report or prevent it. Unfortunately, being more authentically and open online can expose us to real harm. It shouldn't be this way. And when that harm is found in the same spaces where we also connect to our friends and community (such as social media) it can be difficult to find ways to protect ourselves that don't also close us off to others.[34]

We should be able to show off ourselves however we want, to whom we want, and under our own agency. I hope there is a net gain to be found in having queer bodies more visible than ever, but as we have seen there are inherent risks that can and do extend into the real world. Black and LGBTQ+ people of colour, genderqueer and trans people and disabled queers are disproportionately subject to abuse online, especially if their views reach a demographic outside of their control. A 2020 survey by Galop revealed that 80 per cent of people had experienced anti-LGBT+ hate crime and hate speech online in the last five years.[35] *Diva's* 2024 survey of LBQ+ women and trans people revealed that only 10 per cent of its respondents said they felt 'very safe' on social media – a lower percentage than the in-person physical spaces also surveyed such as bars, gyms and public transport (although not by much).[36] Taken together with data from the official government statistics, it's clear that hate crime towards LGBTQ+ people both online and offline has risen dramatically in the last five years.[37] More research is needed on how online and offline abuse impact one another for LGBTQ+ people.[38]

This is not to say we cannot create spaces online for ourselves on such platforms that resist the drive to turn us into consumers and that we cannot represent a 'real' self online. More that I think a greater awareness is needed and better protections put in place. There will always be a tension between an attempt at an 'authentic' self and the curated version you want others to see. This could be aimed at a mainstream audience or it could be crafted to appeal to a very niche subculture. Signifiers and self-branding have become part of the language of creating a personal identity online (just as it does offline) even if that 'brand' is an alternative, anarchic queer one. This is not necessarily a bad thing, as I found during my time on Tumblr. And still to this day I find a lot of joy in it. In much the same way that I find it joyful to dress myself with a butch lesbian audience in mind when going to a queer event. In making ourselves visible both in coded and uncoded ways we regain a sense of control over how we are seen. Being able to shape and play with the ways others read you both IRL and online, whether through your gender or sexuality, your fashion sense or your star sign, is part of the fun of being queer. In spite of attempts to censor our voice or our bodies, we must continue to carve out a space for ourselves. You know it when you see it: queer content that is made by the queer for the queers. It's a little rough and ready. It doesn't have a million views. It embraces mess. If you showed it to your straight friend they would be confused and underwhelmed. But to you it *means* something – it is a symbol of how you understand yourself and your relationship to being queer. I could write a whole book about how I feel as a lesbian or I could simply repost a meme from Maddy Court, also known as @xenaworrierprincess on Instagram, that says 'this fish is a lesbian icon' and the fish in question is a fortune-telling fish that you win in a cracker.[39] If you get it, you get it.

14.6.94 – log by Gabby: *Please refer callers to their office (number on the 'what goes on at LF' sheet over the phone)*

Sometimes you get a night on the phones when you feel like a switchboard, not *that* Switchboard, a regular one. Someone will call for information on another group, maybe what time they meet or if they're on tonight and Gabby will look up the information (if she can't reel it straight off) and send them on their way. It can make her feel like a robot, or the talking clock, yes LAFS is on tonight, you want the Duke of Wellington on Balls Pond Road, try

> Silver Moon or Gay's the Word, they usually have a copy . . . Other times it's groups ringing her and she has to hastily update her notes so the other women know where to send callers instead: Stonewall Housing aren't meeting here after all, here's their office number, and so on and so on. Gabby feels like a tiny node in a vast network that stretches out across London – that's more fun to think about than essentially being a speaking telephone directory. But at least she knows she's been helpful at the end of a busy shift like this. Everyone got an answer even if she had to ring round the houses to find it.

In 2023 I saw Travis Alabanza and Debbie Hannan's play *Sound of the Underground* at the Royal Court Theatre. Here all sorts of queer lives were celebrated and presented to an audience in a way which never would be possible on mainstream social media. Cis, trans, female, male and non-binary bodies were revealed, flaunted, clothed in incredible costumes and teased to the audience to cheers, gasps and on one occasion a powerful, confronting silence. *Sound of the Underground* is about pushing back against the assimilation and flattening of queer culture that has happened over the last ten years through popular media and online culture (*Drag Race* is a particular target) and asks those of us who have found easy acceptance either through our whiteness, our cis or able bodies, to question our complicity within that and our tokenism of those more marginalised.

The internet has accelerated this absorption of queer culture into the mainstream and along with it what queer bodies look and sound like and who are seen as acceptable.

Yet for queer people we are not all unaware of the bubble we have created. For as many silly TikTok videos I have seen there are just as many discussing political queer issues such as trans inclusion, ableism, racism and lesbian activism. I have watched videos of lesbians discussing their struggles with fertility and parenthood, of the fetishization of Black and masc lesbians and the erasure of femme lesbians. I've watched videos of older butch dykes giving advice to young lesbians and nuanced conversations around the inclusion of trans men in lesbian spaces. Thoughtful commentary on lesbian issues can be found here as it could be anywhere if you seek it out. Every generation can be guilty of believing we've invented debates around identity and the representation of the self within a community, but they've been around since the internet began (and long before that too). As always, lesbians, dykes and queers have been central in thinking through such questions: in who gets a voice and who is welcome in a space, in constructions of gender and in what it means to inhabit a body and how we relate to one other. Be that in a newsletter, on the telephone or through the internet. The danger comes from forgetting our shared histories.

Ellen Broidy, in her article 'Cyberdykes, or Lesbian Studies in the Information Age', hints at some of these concerns and trade-offs, that many of us, as users of the internet today, would recognise. For instance, she touches on the inherent challenges in this new technologically connected global network: 'Whether we like it or not, we now debate our differences and disagreements and celebrate our points of cohesion in a hitherto unimaginably public manner . . . Chaos can be liberating. However, as we have seen, not all resources are equal, even (or especially) in cyberspace. We run the risk of being trapped in a maze of too much information.'[40] Despite being almost thirty years old her words sound eerily familiar. With so many people talking online, who is there to listen? One of the common themes in lesbian discourse and community building is how much time should be spent debating with each other and how much should be dedicated to putting aside differences to tackle wider societal issues that affect not just the lesbian community but the LGBTQ+ community as a whole.

These are anxieties that were around long before the internet, but which the Web only helped to amplify. The singular nature of the lesbian lines kept conversation contained (for better or worse), but on an internet forum, grievances and concerns could reach a wider audience than ever. Such debates can be weaponised by those in bad faith to distract from more pressing issues and conversely, a contentious or ill-informed question can result in a stifling of any dissent in favour of the 'right' answer. I don't mean to talk about cancel culture here but rather the sense of correctness being the most important thing which can tamp down some of the messy complexities of being a lesbian before they've had a chance to be spoken about. I think we're still finding out the consequences of so many more lesbians being able to talk to each other than ever before.

There are possibilities too, of course, in the ability to communicate more globally. Especially when it comes to political action – the cyberdykes saw this as another key area of the internet they needed to take advantage of. Activism online is often accused of being performative, especially when it intersects with personal branding and influencer culture in its most ungenerous but not entirely invalid reading. Similar arguments were aimed at lesbians during the '90s with the mainstreaming of lesbians in popular culture, and the truth, as I hope we've seen by now, is always more complex. Just as there was then, today there are still many lesbians and other queer people doing this political work and activism both online and in person. Social media can be a useful tool for communicating information and representing to others what in-person and online action and organising looks like. And it cannot be denied that movements like Occupy, Black Lives Matter, MeToo and Ceasefire Now have significant followings online which has brought attention to these issues and galvanised in-person action. On a recent visit to the Whitworth art gallery I saw placards on display attesting to this. Theirs was an active, ongoing collection of protest banners showing support for a wide range of issues such as trans and Black queer visibility, access and funding for housing and healthcare and AIDS awareness. My wife and I created our own protest signs in June 2024 to join the first Dyke March in London since 2013, spurred in part by Instagram and WhatsApp messages with friends about attending. While marching I bumped into several people I only knew from online and celebrated the opportunity to meet in person for the first time as part of a larger community. The march was attended by over five thousand people who held aloft signs for various causes including visibility, trans rights, a free Palestine and access to IVF for queer people, to name just a few. For many, online and offline activism can, and does, go hand in hand.

*

There's no doubt that queer community is found and created online. For many LGBTQ+ people, online is their preferred or only way to connect either because of location, safety, lack of disabled access, caring responsibilities or, as in my case, a deep fear of going to in-person events alone. A UK nationwide survey in 2000 found that 57 per cent of lesbians and 51 per cent of gay men used the internet, one-third using it on a daily basis.[41] There seems to have been a tipping point at the turn of the twenty-first century, where over half of queer people were finding their way online – a number which has only grown since then. A 2016 National Statistics report from the Department for Culture, Media, and Sport found that LGB people were twice as likely to use Twitter and Instagram as heterosexuals, with almost 90 per cent of LGB respondents using social media of some kind in the past year.[42] The baseline in 2016 for all adult users of social media was 70 per cent. When the clubs close and the lesbian centres shut down, one of the only spaces left is online, and for many it's an important life-line as a way to not only experience lesbian culture but create it too. We are not just part of internet culture, we *are* internet culture.

The telephone continues to play an important role in this, despite the assumption that young people have abandoned phone calls in favour of texts or messaging. For many the two continue to coexist – often our phones *are* the internet. Likewise, voice to voice communication retains its appeal. During the Covid-19 pandemic it was reported that the number of telephone calls rose as people sought out connection when they couldn't physically meet in person.[43] As Cait McKinney, an academic who has studied lesbian helplines, points out, LGBTQ+ phone lines continue to receive many telephone calls, despite offering text and live-chat services because:

> [H]otline callers want the very intimacy with queer or trans community they are supposed to fear, according to digital 'phone-phobia' narratives. This persistent seeking out of supposedly outmoded opportunities to talk on the phone presents a problem for the stories we tell about telephone media history. Queer social movements used to rely on the telephone, but they also *continue to use the telephone.* Today's hotlines might be best understood within a longer genealogy that does not turn around digital networks as a fundamental transition in queer, community-based communication strategies.[44]

What McKinney points towards is the intimacy and immediacies of the telephone which queer and trans communities continue to seek out. The telephone offers direct access to a person who will understand, empathise or have some shared connection to their situation. I've seen it many times over in the logs: the sense of relief to be finally talking to someone who *gets it.* Now that phones are no longer tied to domestic spaces (a landline within a home) or public spaces (phone boxes) they have become an important tool, particularly for young people to be able to access help and community without the risk of 'outing' themselves before they are ready.

Similarly, in-person interactions still hold great importance. It's not unusual to come across videos from young lesbians online talking about how lonely and disconnected they feel from other lesbians. Some have even set up in-person meet-ups to counteract this, from queer picnics to craft clubs.[45] When I spoke to Alessia on her experiences as a trans lesbian, she told me that she had met most of her closest friends online. Living in an English coastal town, she explained that while the internet was instrumental to finding a community it couldn't totally replace meeting in person: 'What's a girl to do when there's nothing going on in her town and she can't afford to travel all the time? I say thank God for the internet but it still doesn't beat interacting face to face, skin to skin.' She described to me taking part in her local LGBT group's first Pride event, and how she helped some older ladies to hold their flag and met a young person who reminded her of herself at that age. These are the sort of casual intergenerational interactions that make us feel part of something bigger than ourselves, something that might never have happened online while consuming content carefully crafted to keep us scrolling.

When I think about lesbian community and the ways that such groups try to navigate both online and in-person spaces, I think about *Modern Queers*, an IRL newsletter that is promoted and its content sourced online before being printed out and posted to subscribers. I think of Butch Please's Instagram, which acts as an ongoing document of and advertising for its events – the excited comments when people spot their friends on the grid. I think about *Diva*'s Facebook message boards and the work of people I've only discovered because I follow them on Twitter. I think of the online/in-person group 'butch lineages', a butch discussion group that aims to straddle the generational and historical gap between butches through events in person, while holding space online to archive its conversations. I think about Black and Gay Back in the Day, who archive Black queer experience on their Instagram and in their podcast and who run in-person events and club nights. These are just a handful I know of – there are many more both online and around the country. All these groups navigate online spaces in a way that uses technology, but not for its own ends. They all seek to make connections and recognition across the digital and the analogue. They seek to be a place for conversation not for any single person's gain but to document and entertain – to bring people together.

Without a (hyper)link back to our history, much of which is within living memory, we end up recycling empty worn-out ideas of what a lesbian can be and without knowledge of the work it has taken to reach this point. As *Sound of the Underground* concludes, without spaces, real inclusive community spaces, whether online or in person (ideally both), we will never be able to share and validate the full spectrum of our experiences. The joy and sorrow that is to be found in lesbianism, dykeism, in queerness, in our rich history of gender presentation, of ways of loving and fighting for each other, the stereotypes we have created and the ones we continue to rail against. We won't find community within online spaces where ultimately the imperative is to keep us consuming, even if at times that consumption makes us feel less alone or seen. It can only sustain us so much. It's not that I think community can't be made and found only online, but that we have to be able to set the terms of engagement for ourselves and resist the impulses of capitalism that put the individual above all else. Not to mention such spaces are precarious and open us up to censorship and erasure. Many of the lesbian websites I found in magazines and articles no longer exist – not everything is captured by the Wayback Machine. Instagram and TikTok won't last forever – our lesbian hashtags are there for now but one day they could be banned at the push of a button, or whole accounts deleted in a moment.

If we allow the internet to turn us into consumers of empty content that we seek to reproduce, it will actively damage the queer community. If we do not find other ways to connect, or consciously use the tools of the internet for different kinds of communication, we will be trapped arguing among ourselves about labels or sharing silly memes to validate our own identity while ignoring the real cries of help from others. I know it's a lot and I know I sound preachy, and if you knew me in real life (or follow me on social media) you would know I am guilty of all the things I am describing here. But I want us to be more than that. I want the funny memes, but I also want more.

We can make spaces for ourselves, just as the cyberdykes urged, away from false promise of representation on social media. It's time for the queers to take back the internet and we are already doing so. Such spaces exist as part of a wider 'Web Revival' movement, which seeks to evolve the early premise of the internet as an open and exciting place you could control.[46] In this movement you might include Web hosting sites like Neocities (a reference to the early Web hosting site GeoCities) and web pages like Run your own social, who offer guides for creating your own social media platform. There are also collectives like Geeks for Social Change who want to empower communities and individuals through digital autonomy to facilitate activist work and engage in community making. All of this, however, requires work and access to the knowledge, tools and funds to keep such sites running. By their very nature, like the pop-up lesbian and dykes nights, they will likely shine bright before disappearing. When I pointed this out to Dr Kim Foale at Geeks for Social Change, they confirmed this was often the case but it's 'only pure capitalism that just grows forever' (or thinks it can). Good things don't always last. Much like the lesbian lines. They worked because they were based on human connection, because they were a network created by lesbians for lesbians. They served a purpose and a need within a community. And the people on the other end of the phone line gave more than they got out of it. The internet didn't destroy what the lesbian lines stood for, it just changed the way we sought information and found each other. For better and for worse.

What Are Lesbians Coming To?

12.3.98 – log by Ros: ***Are there people getting no calls at all? – This hasn't happened to me before?*** Although she'd never admit it Ros is fed up and frankly a little bored. They've been doing solo shifts for the last few weeks because the phone lines aren't ringing like they used to. Ros is not someone who is good at not being busy. She is always moving and always on her feet if she can help it. She plays centre in her local netball team and midfield in football whenever she gets the chance. When she writes in the logbook her notes bounce all over the page in a messy scrawl because invariably she is jiggling her leg as she writes or is carrying the logbook, pen in hand, as she paces up and down their tiny office while on the phone. She likes to be busy and so the absolute dearth of calls tonight and on other nights is really getting to her. A few weeks ago she had over a dozen calls and barely had time to breathe let alone write down all the logs. For two and a half hours it was non-stop answering the phone, and 'umms' and 'ahhs', and

> asking the right questions or frantically looking up the details for the best lesbian pub in Croydon. And tonight it's zilch. Two calls is all she's had and one lasted for barely a minute, they just wanted some info on GEMMA and the other she wished was only that long. It was the usual spiel with the bloke, you've never met a man like me yadayada, I can change your mind etc., what do you do in bed, all of that shite that drives Ros up the wall. She put the phone down on him after yelling this was a line for LESBIANS, but even that wasn't enough to liven up her evening. If she has many more shifts like this she's not sure she'll stick around much longer. She joined Lesbian Line cos she wanted to help and make a difference. Being a glorified Rolodex-cum-sex line isn't exactly what she signed up for.

The last but one entry in the logbook is written a few months later and unlike this one is full of joyous excitement. Ros, the same volunteer who earlier had bemoaned the lack of calls, recounts how a woman, Beryl, called again and spoke to another Beryl at the line. She's ringing back again to let them know she came out to her parents and 'everything's fine'. In the same log Ros notes she takes four 'really good' calls and writes that 'my faith is now restored – it's evenings like this make it all worthwhile!' It's evident that previous shifts, the late nights, the lack of calls, or prank calls have all been getting to her. Perhaps others felt this way too and needed to channel her optimism. An unknown volunteer has put a big blue biro tick next to Ros's excited sentence and scrawled

'Yeh' in agreement. This is in stark contrast to many of the other logs that precede this one which are full of difficult repeat callers, wank calls or hardly any calls at all. When I read this exclamatory entry of Ros's I can't help but see it as a last hurrah – the sense of someone desperately trying to find something hopeful to cling onto in the face of a slow decline. The logbook, at least this one, is coming to a close.

The very final entry is from July 1998, again from Ros. She's had another great night of phone calls. She writes, 'let's hope the phone keeps ringing . . . ' with a tone of wilful enthusiasm. Even she is surprised to be receiving so many calls on this particular night: 8 July was also the semi-final for the '98 World Cup. It's France vs Croatia and one of the significant play-offs of that tournament with the hosts, France, facing off against the relative newcomers. I had to look all that up because I was ten at the time and although I vaguely remember the World Cup that year I have little interest in football. Something I clearly had in common with the callers to the Lesbian Line that night, much to the surprise of Ros. She obviously expected more lesbians to be watching the match and jokes in that final log: 'What are lesbians coming to these days?' To be fair to her, it's a reasonable question to ask.

The ending of the logbook appears without fanfare, it simply ends. Yet this is not the ending of the London Friend Lesbian Line, although it didn't last much longer to my knowledge. As we've seen, not many lesbian lines made it far into the twenty-first century. Being women only and separate from other organisations, while granting them certain freedoms also put the lesbian lines in a more precarious position. They were reliant on a smaller pool of donations, especially from women: historically underpaid with less disposable income, alongside marginalisation from those dispensing funding. Many lines ran frequent donation and volunteer drives to drum up interest. In the archive at Bishopsgate Institute I find flyers from the London Lesbian Line and the Southwark Lesbian Line, with headings like 'Lesbian Line Needs You!' and adverts for tenth birthday celebrations featuring lesbian discos, vegan food options and poetry from Jackie Kay. The dissolution by Thatcher's government of the Greater London Council, which had supported many gay and lesbian organisations in London, played a significant part in their loss of funding. It wasn't just financial pressure, however. As we've seen, a loss of volunteers and a decrease in demand for calls as the internet age took over all contributed to the lesbian lines' demise. The London Lesbian Line closed around 1999, when their funding had been cut by 20 per cent. Although in an interview with one of the last volunteers on the line, she claimed it wasn't the funding that stopped them but rather the lack of willing volunteers: 'You can't go on with just one person, there was no one to be accountable to. I was writing in the logbook but no one was reading it.'[1]

London Friend's Lesbian Line was no exception and it's likely that the lesbian and mixed lines merged into one not long after this last entry. In December 1998 London Friend itself nearly closed due to lack of funds and went on an intense fundraising drive to raise six thousand pounds by March of 1999. Thankfully they made enough to keep going, but I can imagine with the threat of near closure and a lack of resources it felt prudent to focus on one phone line that they could run daily. It's also possible that by this time the passion and need for a separate Lesbian Line was simply waning and that London Friend wanted to become more inclusive and open to all LGBTQ+ people who used their services. An updated flyer in the archive from the early 2000s gives a single helpline number and their tag line has changed to 'Supporting the lesbian, gay, bisexual & transgender community'. The description of the helpline is free from gendered language and instead focuses on the needs of the callers: 'Our trained volunteers will happily talk with the callers about safer sex, same-sex relationships, coming out, and other issues.'

London Friend continues to this day to provide counselling services and in-person social support to the LGBTQ+ community in London. Perhaps then the Lesbian Line's time was simply up. Lesbian separatism was no longer seen as so positive or necessary and 'the gay and lesbian movement' (as it was known) opened up to be more inclusive of bisexual, trans and queer people. This is not to say that lesbian or bisexual female-only spaces disappeared at London Friend. It continues to run its long-standing Changes group for 'all women of all ages and backgrounds, coming to terms with their sexuality', as well as social groups for Black lesbians and bisexual women and other support groups. Alongside this they also continue to give space for mixed groups and groups for gay men.

Of course, I can't help but feel a sense of loss with the ending of the line and the unanswered questions I still have about exactly why it closed. Perhaps I would rather let this question hang there unanswered, a phone left ringing in an unattended room. This logbook is certainly not the last and the gaps in records would suggest for a time they had concurrent logbooks. There's a chunk of pages at the very end of the notebook that have been ripped out; it's tempting to suspect they contained hidden secrets, but more likely someone needed some extra paper and nabbed it from the back. The last few pages themselves are blank except for the same words written in a red biro scrawl across the top:

> *Please start new (green) log book from Aug 1 Ta!*
> *Please start new (green) log book from Aug 1 Ta!*
> *Please start new (green) log book from Aug 1 Ta!*
> *Please start new (green) log book from Aug 1 Ta!*

I have no idea where this other logbook might be and the other calls it holds, but it's proof that the Lesbian Line lived on and the phones continued to be answered, at least for a little while longer. But for me, this is the end. This is all I get and I feel lucky to have seen and heard so much from all these women.

I mean it when I say 'heard'. I feel like I've been on the end of some of those calls, it's like the volunteers have been speaking to me and of course I've had the privilege of listening to many different lesbians as I've written this book: both through interviews I've conducted and through reading their work or hearing their oral testimonies. When I spoke to ex-phone workers about their time on helplines many stressed to me the importance of listening. Of *really* listening when taking calls. Of attuning oneself to what is *not* being said to uncover what is trying to be expressed and therefore what a call might truly be about. There is a lesson here for a kind of radical queer listening which makes this space for others, for discussion and response. Sara Ahmed writes, 'To describe oneself as a lesbian is a way of reaching out to others who hear themselves in this *as*', and that naming yourself as a lesbian is an immediate act of community making. To speak 'as a lesbian' is also to hear 'as a lesbian' and hear others 'as lesbians'. To be spoken and to be truly heard is the groundwork of community making.

But what do we really mean when we talk about community? I have spoken about it over and over and yet we have seen the ways in which lesbians are not a monolith, and the different kinds of community that form under the umbrella of 'lesbian'. We have seen the failures of white lesbians and of cis lesbians to listen and include others. Our communities (because they are multiple) are stratified and intersected by class, race, gender expression, age, geography and disability. Looking at community only through the lens of identity reveals that it can only take us so far. It is useful but not universal. In an interview with Teresa Salazar Hope, an advice and information worker at Camden Lesbian Centre in 1993, she challenged the idea of a single community, let alone a single lesbian one:

> If you are talking about a group of people with common ideals and common resources, then no, we haven't got one. We don't have a close-knit community where we all share a vision for the future. On the other hand, there are groups where you find similarities and support, but then we're talking about isolated pockets within this larger existence of lesbians and gay men ... The most important thing is finding an ideological frame of reference for that group of

people to identify with and then we would be talking about a community.[2]

For Teresa, the purpose of community is both social and political in nature and works as an organising principle for enacting action and change. She resists community as a general sweeping statement about all lesbians and gay people based around their sexuality or proximity to one another. She urges us to align ourselves not based on identity but our values and hopes for the future.

I was naive when I first started thinking about the 'lesbian community' – that there was one to find in the first place. The reality for lesbians is no different to that of other groups in society, we find pockets of community and family as we go. Joining together with those who share our beliefs and interests can be powerful for enacting change and validating our own identities. It's vital (some would say life saving) for a group of people marginalised by the mainstream. But we must be wary too of cliques, bias, defensiveness and resistance to change within these communities. The idea of one lesbian community where everyone gets along and everyone is included is vastly appealing and vastly unrealistic, but that doesn't mean that community does not exist, overlap and coexist despite difference. There is still power in calling ourselves lesbians.

In part, to be a lesbian is to listen to the unsayable. To hear what is not being said or what has been silenced. I think of us deviating from the given path. I think of lesbians as the *ums* and *ahhs* of Cheryl Slack's recording at the British Library, I think of lesbians as the pause before the straight woman on the radio says the word 'lesbian'. I think of lesbians in the silences, the unspoken question of the man who stares at you in the street because he can't figure you out. I think of lesbians as the sighs in Lorraine Birch's telling of setting up the lesbian line in Bradford. I think of lesbians as the silence in the moment before the click of the phone being answered and the present stillness of hanging up. I think of the silence of when the phone didn't ring. In the quiet spaces when the call was over and the volunteers picked up their pen to write. Of the lesbians who never needed the Lesbian Line. Their voices lost because they were happy and knew who they were and where to go. In love or alone. I think of lesbians as the unspoken squeeze of a hand in public, the silent nod, the friendly dykish glance. I think of lesbian as the ellipsis in a question, the slow trailing off, *is she a . . .* If lesbians are in the *ums* and the not *ums*, in the spoken and the unspoken, in the loud and the silence – then we are everywhere.

I don't believe the rhetoric that lesbians are disappearing.[3] If anything we are rising up. We have always been rising up because we've always been here, so what is new about that? I think there is a joyful abundance of lesbians to be celebrated. What are lesbians coming to? Well, here they are, alive and online and in person, they are going out, they are finding each other, they are talking and wearing what they like and churning out endless conversations about what it means to be a lesbian. They are making mistakes and saying the wrong thing and learning from each other and finding space for one another, online and alone and with others. Wherever they can find it. Reinventing what has already been reinvented and reclaiming what has already been reclaimed but making it new each time. What are we coming to? Everything and anything.

At the end of Sara Ahmed's *Living a Feminist Life* she writes how lesbian feminism can bring 'feminism back to life' by questioning the status quo and the walls society puts in place to stop lesbians living freely. If we cannot destroy the walls, she writes, then they should speak instead and tell a lesbian feminist story. Because for Ahmed, 'A story too can shatter: a thousand tiny little pieces, strewn all over the place. Lesbian feminism: in making the ordinary out of the shattered pieces of a dwelling, we dwell.'[4]

When I first read those words they affected me deeply. Ahmed gets to the core here of something I hadn't even realised I had been searching for within the lesbian lines. That of a dwelling – a space for temporary being within which to work. I say 'temporary' to mean both the sense of ending but also in the sense of ongoing. I mean temporary in the sense of not perfect, but a place to start from. I think again of Jo Smith's description of London Friend as 'providing a starting point'.[5]

The lesbians in the logbook, both the phone workers and its callers, were trying to make the ordinary out of what they had around them. The everyday actions of the volunteers – turning up for their shifts, organising the rota and updating the logbook – may not be what we think of when we speak about political activism but through such work they contributed to furthering the rights and visibility of lesbians in the UK. Empowering others to come out, organise and think politically. To make an ordinary life for oneself when the world wants to see you as extraordinary is a radical act, as Ahmed says. The women working on the lesbian lines demonstrated that being a lesbian was an everyday achievable thing to those who thought it was impossible. As we've seen we must not mistake ordinariness as a desire to maintain the status quo, or accept what a heteropatriarchal capitalist world will tell us is 'good enough'. I want a future for lesbians where the radical is ordinary. Where we proudly stand in solidarity with our gay, bisexual, queer, intersex and trans families, an ordinary that is anti-racist and trans inclusive, that fights for disability and worker's rights. That seeks climate justice and a better future.

I hope too that this book can become a temporary dwelling space for lesbian lives, that for a time it can hold the stories of the many voices I have encountered while writing it. There are so many stories in the logbook I've not shared and there are so many lesbian lives not told. The story of the Lesbian Line is an unfinished and incomplete one. Deliberately so. The logbook is only one part of the story of what it means to be a lesbian. And in those other gaps are more stories and more people and more thoughts and more feelings. I hope you see, like me, that these are not silences or elisions but an opening, an invitation to you, to lesbians, to all queer people, to write and tell our stories.

I hope that in retelling and remaking the voices in the logbook I have created something that too might shatter and be strewn about the place. I want this book to splinter into a hundred pieces and become just one small part of the vast map of lesbian history. And it is a map, we are a map for ourselves and others. A way to find each other and a guide for those who come after us. There will always be more lesbians.

We are not going to become extinct and we do not go out of fashion. We continue proudly, joyfully, casually to call ourselves lesbians. We will always be here, have always been here, we will go on dwelling here. We will continue to find new names for ourselves and new ways of being. Because it is a map that is constantly being redrawn and made up of temporary dwellings. Our borders there to be defended but also expanded. I hope these stories lead you someplace new. I want us to take the thousand splinters of life we are given, because nothing is given to us whole and without work, and make a place for dwelling. A space to be. Whatever that might look like. A book can be a dwelling place, so can a telephone call. Just for a moment. The phone workers on the Lesbian Line provided space and time for those callers in which to speak their stories. In which to construct the fragmented pieces of their lives into something that could be shared with another person. I want that for us. A space to dwell in together.

21.3.23 – log by unknown volunteer: *a strange call but she obviously needed to talk*

It's a sunny Saturday morning in London when she finally picks up her mobile to dial the number she knows off by heart. It shouldn't even be working any more but there is that unmistakable ringing as the line connects. She calls not because she finally finds the courage, but because she knows this is her last chance to talk to the women at the Lesbian Line. She calls partly to apologise, she has been reading their logs and thinking about them for so long it's sometimes hard to remember they are real people with their own lives and feelings. She has made them into people they were not so she could tell as true a story as she could. She hopes they can forgive her for anything she got wrong. She has lost herself in their entries, all the calls and the lives of the volunteers. She knows she has tangled up her own life with theirs in a way which might be seen as a bit much. But isn't that actually quite lesbian of her? To make them all into one messy network of connections and conversations. She set out to find a history and here it is right in front of her. She's living it right now. Living proof that the Lesbian Line hasn't ended.

She wants them to know how much they mean to her. Even the bits that make her sigh in disappointment, perhaps especially those parts. She hopes they don't mind that she has been writing about them. The woman at the other end of the phone doesn't say much but she can hear the sound of pen on paper, another entry being written in a logbook she'll never see and that's just fine. She has so many questions she could ask and so many things she could tell them but can't think where to start. She's just glad they existed for her to find.

She waits a long time for the woman on the phone to hang up, but she knows she has to be the one to say goodbye. She says thank you one last time and puts down the phone and gets on with her life.

Notes

Where Are All the Lesbians?

1. House of Lords debate, 15 August 1921, Hansard Vol. 43, col. 573.
2. Huw Lemmey and Ben Miller, *Bad Gays: A Homosexual History* (Verso Books, 2022), p.8.
3. Michel Foucault, *The History of Sexuality* (Pantheon Books, 1978), p.43.
4. Foucault, p.47.
5. The novel *After Sappho* by Selby Wynn Schwartz (Galley Beggar Press, 2022) offers a playful imagining of early twentieth-century sapphic life across Europe.
6. Diana Souhami, *No Modernism Without Lesbians* (Head of Zeus, 2020), p.224.
7. Rebecca Jennings, *A History of Lesbian Britain: Love and Sex between Women since 1500* (Greenwood World Publishing, 2007), p.187.
8. Lorraine Birch, interviewed by Ray Larman on 19 September 2019, West Yorkshire Queer Stories <https://wyqs.co.uk/stories/bradfords-lesbian-scene/full-interview>.
9. Debbie Luxon, 'The 1970s lesbian phone line that was a lifeline to rural Cambridgeshire women', CambridgeshireLive, 26 April 2020 <https://www.cambridge-news.co.uk/news/cambridge-news/70s-lesbian-feminist-phone-line-18147065>.

The Other Half of the Conversation

1. 'How Britain's colonial legacy still affects LGBT politics around the world', University of Reading, 21 May 2018 <https://research.reading.ac.uk/research-blog/how-britains-colonial-legacy-still-affects-lgbt-politics-around-the-world/>.
2. For just one instance of the impact of British colonial administration on Ugandan law, see 'Gay Rights and the Politics of Anti-Homosexual Legislation in Africa: Insights from Uganda and Nigeria', by Lere Amusan et al., *Journal of African Union Studies*, Vol. 8, No. 2 (2019), pp.45–66 <https://www.jstor.org/stable/26890403>. For a more in-depth analysis, see 'Specters of Colonialism' in *Out of Time: The Queer Politics of Postcoloniality* by Rahul Rao (Oxford Academic Books, 2020).

3. Danielle Brathwaite-Shirley, Black Trans Archive <https://blacktransarchive.com>.
4. Alexis Aceves Garcia, 'Terms & Conditions: Danielle Brathwaite-Shirley on archiving the Black trans experience', *Deem* <https://www.deemjournal.com/stories/danielle-brathwaite-shirley>.
5. Ali Smith, *Artful* (Hamish Hamilton, 2012), p.25.
6. Saidiya Hartman, *Wayward Lives, Beautiful Experiments: Intimate Histories of Riotous Black Girls, Troublesome Women and Queer Radicals* (W.W. Norton & Company, 2019), pp.xiii–xiv.
7. Clare Hemmings, *Considering Emma Goldman: Feminist Political Ambivalence and the Imaginative Archive* (Duke University Press, 2018), pp.21–2.
8. The phrase 'intimate trace' takes its origin from *Radical History Review*'s issue 'Queering Archives: Intimate Tracings', ed. by Kevin P. Murphy, Daniel Marshall, Zeb Tortorici, Vol. 2015, No. 122, May 2015.

A Brief History of the Lesbian Lines

1. 'Only a phone call away – London's switchboards', GLC Women's Committee, No. 17, Special Lesbian Issue (1984), p.17.
2. Ibid.
3. Lisa Power, 'Voices in my ear' in *Radical Records: Thirty Years of Lesbian and Gay History, 1957–1987*, ed. by Bob Cant and Susan Hemmings (Routledge, 1988), p.144.
4. If you're interested to hear more about Switchboard, *The Log Books* podcast by Shivani Dave, Tash Walker and Adam Zmith details its history and the lives of its callers and volunteers.
5. Lois Stone, 'Manchester Women's Liberation Newsletter and the Lesbian Community', Queer Beyond London: Sexuality and Locality in Brighton, Leeds, Manchester and Plymouth <http://queerbeyondlondon.com/manchester/manchester-womens-liberation-newsletter-and-the-lesbian-community/>.
6. Debbie Luxon, 'The 1970s lesbian phone line that was a lifeline to rural Cambridgeshire women', CambridgeshireLive, 26 April 2020 <https://www.cambridge-news.co.uk/news/cambridge-news/70s-lesbian-feminist-phone-line-18147065>.
7. Patrick Hall, interviewed by Ray Larman on 5 May 2015, West Yorkshire Queer Stories <https://wyqs.co.uk/stories/discovering-the-gay-liberation-front/full-interview>.
8. Power, p.146.
9. 'Only a phone call away – London's switchboards', p.17.
10. Power, p.146.
11. 'Celebrate Lesbian Line set up in 1977–1996 to support lesbians', Lesbian History Group, 16 February 2021 <https://lesbianhistorygroup.wordpress.com/2021/02/16/celebrate-lesbian-line-set-up-in-1977-1996-to-support-lesbians/>.
12. Jo Smith, 'Lesbians at London Friend', GLC Women's Committee, No. 17, Special Lesbian Issue (1984), p.17.
13. 'Celebrate Lesbian Line set up in 1977–1996 to support lesbians'.
14. Anita Naik, 'Chat Back: On Homosexuality,' *Just Seventeen*, 18 January 1989, p.43.
15. Ibid.

16. Smith, p.17.
17. 'Celebrate Lesbian Line set up in 1977–1996 to support lesbians'.

Coming Out?

1. Sara Ahmed, *Living a Feminist Life* (Duke University Press, 2017), p.224.
2. Jenn Shapland, *My Autobiography of Carson McCullers* (Tin House, 2020), p.157.
3. Alys Fowler, *Hidden Nature: A Voyage of Discovery* (Hodder & Stoughton, 2017), p.178.
4. Adrienne Rich, *Compulsory Heterosexuality and Lesbian Existence* (Onlywomen Press, 1980), p.19.
5. Rich, p.4.
6. Ibid. p.29.
7. Jen Richards, *Disclosure: Trans Lives on Screen*, dir. by Sam Feder (Netflix, 2020)
8. Rebecca Jennings, *A Lesbian History of Britain*, (Greenwood World Publishing, 2007), p.184.
9. For example, see Asiel Adan Sanchez, 'The whiteness of "coming out": culture and identity in the disclosure narrative', *Archer Magazine*, 7 July 2017 <https://archermagazine.com.au/2017/07/culture-coming-out/>.
10. The full interview with Cheryl Slack is held in the British Library Sounds archive. All quotes are taken from this interview. <http://sounds.bl.uk/Oral-history/Observing-the-1980s/021M-C0456X0025XX-0001V0>. It is currently not available online due to a cyberattack on the British Library website in October 2023.
11. Zoe Williams, 'Sandi Toksvig: "I came out, and the tabloid press thought I was Cruella de Vil"', *Guardian*, 25 May 2020 <https://www.theguardian.com/culture/2020/may/25/sandi-toksvig-i-came-out-and-the-tabloid-press-thought-i-was-cruella-de-vil>.
12. 'Lesbians protest over charity ban', *Independent*, 4 October 1994 <https://www.independent.co.uk/life-style/lesbians-protest-over-charity-ban-1440911.html>.
13. 76 per cent of Gen Z identify as heterosexual compared to the national average of 86 per cent. Only 54 per cent of Gen Z say they are exclusively attracted to the opposite sex. 'Sexual orientation and attitudes to LGBTQ+ in Britain', Ipsos, 26 June 2020 <https://www.ipsos.com/ipsos-mori/en-uk/sexual-orientation-and-attitudes-lgbtq-britain>.
14. 'The majority of Britons (60 per cent) believe that people from LGBTQ+ communities face at least a fair amount of discrimination (16 per cent say they face a great deal) This differs by age, with three quarters of adult Gen Z (73 per cent) and Millennials (74 per cent) saying LGBTQ+ communities face a great deal or fair amount of discrimination, compared to just over half of Baby Boomers (54 per cent) and Gen X (55 per cent).' Ibid.
15. Eley Williams, *The Liar's Dictionary* (William Heinemann, 2020), p.173.
16. Ibid.
17. Ibid. p.73.
18. Ibid.
19. For more on the history of Polari, see Paul Baker, *Fabulosa! The Story of Polari, Britain's Secret Gay Language* (Reaktion Books, 2019).
20. I find this deeply irritating still.

Gay, Lesbian, Woman?

1. See Dr Julia Shaw, *Bi: The Hidden Culture, History and Science of Bisexuality* (Canongate Books, 2022) for a more in-depth analysis of bi history and erasure.
2. Liz Gibbs, 'Introduction' in *Daring to Dissent: Lesbian Culture from Margin to Mainstream*, ed. by Liz Gibbs (Cassell, 1994), p.2.
3. Del Martin and Phyllis Lyon, 'From 'Lesbians United' in *The Stonewall Reader*, ed. by The New York Public Library (Penguin, 1972:2019), p.25.
4. See *Women in Revolt!*, ed. by Linsey Young (Tate Publishing, 2023).
5. There's a rather bemused interview with some of the London Lesbian Avengers that in no way takes seriously them or their mission as to raise lesbian visibility. The journalist comments, 'The Avengers are a typical campaign group of the 1990s: a sexily-named, young, energetic, quick-response unit, campaigning on a single issue with a combination of naivety and media awareness.' 'Lesbian with a vengeance' by Alex Spillius, *Telegraph*, 1 July 1995 <https://www.independent.co.uk/life-style/lesbian-with-a-vengeance-1589490.html>.
6. Perhaps the greatest headline of all time: 'BEEB MAN SITS ON LESBIAN', *Daily Mirror*, 24 May 1988.
7. Inge Blackman and Kathryn Perry, 'Skirting the Issue: Lesbian Fashion for the 1990s', *Feminist Review*, No. 34, 1990, pp.67–78 <https://doi.org/10.2307/1395306>.
8. Ibid. p.76.
9. Lynn Sutcliffe, *There Must Be Fifty Ways to Tell Your Mother* (Mansell Publishing, 1995), p.128.
10. Gibbs, p.142.
11. While 'queer' has become a useful umbrella term for many (and one I sometimes use myself) it still holds the potential to erase lesbian identity if used when exclusively speaking about lesbians. The majority of the time 'queer women' is a useful term if needing to include lesbian, bisexual and pansexual identities so long as this is clear and accurate. As always, it's about ensuring the right context and acknowledging that no one word will suit all. For more on the usage of 'queer' by lesbians (both positive and negative) in the '90s, see Cherry Smyth, *Lesbians Talk: Queer Notions* (Scarlet Press, 1992).
12. As was the case for Melania Geymonat and her girlfriend, Christine Hannigan, who were subjected to a brutal homophobic attack in 2019 when they refused to kiss for a group of male teenagers. 'London bus attack: Teens admit threatening women who refused to kiss', BBC News, 28 November 2019 <https://www.bbc.co.uk/news/uk-england-london-50586498>.
13. Jill Gutowitz, 'Lesbian Culture Went Viral, Finally, in 2019', *Wired*, 22 December 2019 <https://www.wired.com/story/lesbian-culture-viral>.
14. Here I'm using the terms 'Black lesbians' and 'lesbians of colour' to include racialised identities from the global majority including Africa, Asia, the Pacific nations, Latin America and the original inhabitants of Australasia, North America and the islands of the Atlantic and Indian Ocean but acknowledge it's an imperfect definition and where possible I have aimed to be specific or reflect the language use within the context of the time.
15. Valerie Mason-John and Ann Khambatta, *Lesbians Talk: Making Black Waves* (Scarlet Press, 1993), p.40.

16. Ibid. p.39.
17. Khin Su, 'Queering the "Global Gay": How Transnational LGBT Language Disrupts the Global/Local Binary', LSE, 20 June 2019 <https://blogs.lse.ac.uk/gender/2019/06/20/queering-the-global-gay-how-transnational-lgbt-language-disrupts-the-global-local-binary/>.
18. Lucy Brownson, 'Camden Lesbian Centre and Black Lesbian Group: Collectives and communities', Glasgow Women's Library, 15 October 2021 <https://womenslibrary.org.uk/2021/10/15/camden-lesbian-centre-and-black-lesbian-group-collectives-and-communities/>.
19. Mason-John and Khambatta, p.39.
20. Rani Kawale, 'Inequalities of the heart: The performance of emotion work by lesbian and bisexual women in London, England', *Social & Cultural Geography*, Vol. 5, No. 4 (2004), p.576.
21. Mason-John and Khambatta, p.40.
22. Terri-Jane Dow, 'Why popular culture is returning to the riot grrrl aesthetic and values', *Dazed*, 18 March 2019 <https://www.dazeddigital.com/life-culture/article/43714/1/why-popular-culture-is-returning-to-the-riot-grrrl-aesthetic-and-values>.
23. In popular culture such spellings have been satirised in film and literature: *Transparent*, 'Man on the Land' [S2E9], 11 December 2015; Andrea Lawlor, *Paul Takes the Form of a Mortal Girl* (Rescue Press, 2017); Alison Bechdel, *Dykes to Watch Out For* (comic; 1983–2008).
24. Sara Ahmed, *Living a Feminist Life* (Duke University Press, 2017), p.224.
25. Lola Olufemi, *Feminism, Interrupted: Disrupting Power* (Pluto Press, 2020), p.65.
26. Monique Wittig, 'The Straight Mind' in *Out There: Marginalization and Contemporary Cultures*, ed. by Russell Ferguson, Martha Gever, Trinh T. Minh-ha and Cornel West (The MIT Press, 1992), p.57.
27. Leslie Feinberg, *Transgender Warriors: Making History from Joan of Arc to Dennis Rodman* (Beacon Press, 1996), p.109.
28. Ahmed, p.224.
29. Joelle Taylor, 'ROUND FIVE *the body as backroom*' in *C+nto & Othered Poems* (The Westbourne Press, 2021), p.43.
30. Daniel M. Lavery (writing as Daniel Mallory Ortberg), 'Product Review: When Every Bra Size is Wrong', Shondaland, 18 September 2017 <https://www.shondaland.com/live/style/a12256604/product-review-g2cb-binder/>.
31. Darcy Leigh, *boi tits* (Easter Road Press, 2020), p.5.
32. Ibid. p.7.
33. Ibid. p.9.
34. Jack Halberstam, *Female Masculinity* (Duke University Press, 1998), p.xxi.
35. See 27 May 2022 *Times* article: 'Teachers "should not pander to trans pupils"' – a quote from (at the time) Attorney General Suella Braverman. 'Pandering' in the article refers to using a child's preferred pronouns and allowing them to dress in the school uniform that is allowed for their gender.
36. Brighton & Hove City Council, 'Trans Inclusion Schools Toolkit (2021)', Mermaids <https://mermaidsuk.org.uk/wp-content/uploads/2019/12/BHCC_Trans-Inclusion-Schools-Toolkit-_Version4_Sept21.pdf>.
37. Sophie Lewis, 'How British Feminism Became Anti-Trans', *New York Times*, 7 February 2019 <https://www.nytimes.com/2019/02/07/opinion/terf-trans-women-britain.html.
38. For a short overview of how transgender theory has influenced lesbian

and gender identity as well as the history of some lesbians exclusion of trans women, see Juliet Jacques, *Trans: A Memoir* (Verso Books, 2015), pp.103–12.

39. Travis Alabanza, *None of the Above: Reflections on Life Beyond the Binary* (Canongate Books, 2022), pp.48–9.

Becky Rang

1. Ann Cvetkovich, *An Archive of Feelings: Trauma, Sexuality and Lesbian Public Cultures* (Duke University Press, 2003), p.179.
2. See @h_e_r_s_t_o_r_y, Instagram <https://www.instagram.com/h_e_r_s_t_o_r_y/>. However, it looks as though the post has since been deleted as I can no longer find it. Likely due to containing the words 'pussy' and 'dykes', which Instagram has a habit of removing as it is deemed offensive or misunderstood to be pornographic.
3. Alison Kafer, *Feminist, Queer, Crip* (Indiana University Press, 2013), p.122.
4. See interview with Elsa Beckett one of the founders of GEMMA in *Inventing Ourselves: Lesbian Life Stories* (Routledge, 1989), pp.59–75.
5. Lucy Brownson, 'Camden Lesbian Centre and Black Lesbian Group: Collectives and communities', Glasgow Women's Library, 15 October 2021 <https://womenslibrary.org.uk/2021/10/15/camden-lesbian-centre-and-black-lesbian-group-collectives-and-communities/>.
6. Aspen, 'Don't Expect Me to Put Up With Your Shit: Lesbians and Disability', *Bad Attitude*, Issue 6, June–August 1994, p.23
7. Ibid.
8. Sara Westrop, '"How Disabled are You?" Queer, Disabled and Looking for a Date', The Unwritten, 19 January 2021 <https://www.theunwritten.co.uk/2021/01/19/how-disabled-are-you-queer-disabled-and-looking-for-a-date>.
9. Hannah Shewan Stevens, 'Disabled and Sexual: Disabled LGBTQ+ People Deserve to Feel Welcome in Queer spaces', The Unwritten, 29 June 2021 <https://www.theunwritten.co.uk/2021/06/29/disabled-and-sexual-disabled-lgbtq-people-deserve-to-feel-welcome-in-queer-spaces>.

You Can't Choose Your Family (Except You Can)

1. David Batty, 'Lockdown having "pernicious impact" on LGBT community's mental health', *Guardian*, 5 August 2020 <https://www.theguardian.com/society/2020/aug/05/lockdown-having-pernicious-impact-on-lgbt-communitys-mental-health>.
2. Ibid.
3. 'All young people should be safe to be who they are', akt <https://www.akt.org.uk/mission-vision/>.
4. Jo Bhandal and Matt Horwood, 'The LGBTQ+ youth homelessness report 2021', akt, pp.10–12 <https://www.akt.org.uk/wp-content/uploads/2023/07/akt-thelgbtqyouthhomelessnessreport2021.pdf>.
5. Ibid. p.12.
6. Batty, 'Lockdown having "pernicious impact" on LGBT community's mental health'.

7. Michel Foucault, *The History of Sexuality* (Pantheon Books, 1978), p.47.
8. Deepa Lalwani, 'The hidden costs facing potential LGBTQ+ parents', Stonewall, 18 April 2023 <https://www.stonewall.org.uk/about-us/news/hidden-costs-facing-potential-lgbtq-parents>.
9. Richard Littlejohn, '"Please don't pretend two dads is the new normal": Richard Littlejohn says children benefit most from being raised by a man and woman', *Daily Mail*, 15 February 2018 <https://www.dailymail.co.uk/debate/article-5397713/Please-dont-pretend-two-dads-new-normal.html>.
10. 'Gays Can Work With Kids', *Islington Gazette*, 31 March 1983, Islington's Pride archive: S/IP/1/7/21.
11. Patrick Kelleher, 'The anti-trans brigade is attacking children's charity Mermaids for helping its users protect their identity. Yes, really', PinkNews, 26 March 2020 <https://www.pinknews.co.uk/2020/03/26/mermaids-transgender-charity-exit-button-website-twitter-janice-turner-shon-Fae>.
12. Glen Owen, 'An increasing portrayal of transgender characters on TV is "fuelling rise" in the number of young people seeking medical help to change sex, says a leading expert', *Daily Mail*, 9 August 2020 <https://www.dailymail.co.uk/news/article-8608307/Expert-transgender-characters-TV-fuelling-rise-young-people-seeking-help.html>.
13. Joe Ali, 'Drag Queen Story Hour host blames Tories for "queer hate" in UK ahead of Tate Britain appearance', PinkNews, 13 January 2023 <https://www.thepinknews.com/2023/01/13/drag-queen-story-hour-tories-queer-hate-tate-britain/>.
14. Myeshia Price-Feeney, Amy E. Green and Samuel Dorison, 'Understanding the Mental Health of Transgender and Nonbinary Youth', *Journal of Adolescent Health*, Vol. 66, No. 6 (2020), pp.684–90.
15. 'Birmingham LGBT teaching row: How did it unfold?', BBC News, 22 May 2019 <https://www.bbc.co.uk/news/uk-england-48351401>.
16. Matt Bagwell, 'How Protests Over Diversity Lessons In Birmingham Ended In A Win For LGBTQ+ People Everywhere', HuffPost, 28 June 2020 <https://www.huffingtonpost.co.uk/entry/andrew-moffat-interview-parkfield-school-no-outsiders-protests-one-year-on_uk_5ef5ecadc5b612083c4c57bf>.
17. 'Milestone for equality in schools', Scottish Government, 23 September 2021 <https://www.gov.scot/news/milestone-for-equality-in-schools/>.
18. Sheelagh Stewart, 'Experience: I was pregnant at the same time as my partner', *Guardian*, 2 July 2021 <https://www.theguardian.com/lifeandstyle/2021/jul/02/experience-i-was-pregnant-at-the-same-time-as-my-partner>.
19. Jules Cassidy and Angela Stewart-Park, *We're Here: Conversations with Lesbian Women* (Quartet Books, 1977), pp.13–14.
20. Debbie Luxon, 'The 1970s lesbian phone line that was a lifeline to rural Cambridgeshire women', CambridgeshireLive, 26 April 2020 <https://www.cambridge-news.co.uk/news/cambridge-news/70s-lesbian-feminist-phone-line-18147065>.

Lesbian Lifelines

1. Peter Edelberg, 'Archive Discipline: An Interview on the Danish Gay and Lesbian Archive with Karl Peder Pedersen', *Radical History Review*, Vol.

2015, No. 122 (2015), pp.201–10 <https://doi.org/10.1215/01636545-2849621> (p.208).

2. Jack Jen Gieseking, 'Useful In/stability: The Dialectical Production of the Social and Spatial Lesbian Herstory Archives', *Radical History Review*, Vol. 2015, No. 122 (2015), pp.25–37 <https://doi.org/10.1215/01636545-2849504> (p.30).
3. Joan Nestle, 'The Will to Remember: The Lesbian Herstory Archives of New York', *Feminist Review: Perverse Politics: Lesbian Issues*, Vol. 34, No. 1 (1990), pp.86–94 (p.93).
4. *The Archivettes*, dir. by Megan Rossman (Women Make Movies, 2018).
5. Andrea Lawlor, *Paul Takes the Form of a Mortal Girl* (Rescue Press, 2017), p.321.
6. Tracy Chapman, 'For My Lover', *Tracy Chapman* (Elektra Records, EW 835, 1988).
7. *The Watermelon Woman*, dir. by Cheryl Dunye (First Run Features, 1996).
8. Audre Lorde, 'Learning from the 1960s' in *Your Silence Will Not Protect You* (Silver Press, 1982), p.123.
9. Colleen Kelsey, 'Cheryl Dunye's Alternative Histories', *Interview*, 11 November 2016 <https://www.interviewmagazine.com/film/cheryl-dunye>.
10. Kevin Brazil, 'The Uses of Queer Art', *The White Review*, October 2018 <https://www.thewhitereview.org/feature/uses-queer-art>.
11. Nestle, p.93.
12. Brazil, 'The Uses of Queer Art'.
13. Adrienne Rich, 'Compulsory Heterosexuality and Lesbian Existence', (Onlywomen Press, 1980), p.21.
14. Rebecca Jennings, *A History of Lesbian Britain: Love and Sex Between Women Since 1500* (Greenwood World Publishing, 2007), pp.187–89.
15. Rich, p.20.
16. Michelle Tea, 'The City to a Young Girl' in *Against Memoir* (And Other Stories, 2019), p.239.

No More Lesbian Sheroes

1. 'Celebrate Lesbian Line set up in 1977–1996 to support lesbians', Lesbian History Group, 16 February 2021 <https://lesbianhistorygroup.wordpress.com/2021/02/16/celebrate-lesbian-line-set-up-in-1977-1996-to-support-lesbians/>.
2. Martin F. Manalansan IV, 'The "Stuff" of Archives: Mess, Migration, and Queer Lives', *Radical History Review*, Vol. 2014, No. 120 (2014), p.105.
3. Jose Esteban Muñoz, 'Ephemera as Evidence: Introductory Notes to Queer Acts', *Women and Performance: A Journal of Feminist Theory*, Vol. 8, No. 1 (1996), p.10.
4. For more on the concept of Thing Theory and the relationship between humans and objects, see Bill Brown, 'Thing Theory', *Critical Inquiry*, Vol. 28, No. 1 (2001), pp.1–22 <http://www.jstor.org/stable/1344258>.
5. Jack Jen Gieseking, 'Useful In/stability: The Dialectical Production of the Social and Spatial Lesbian Herstory Archives', *Radical History Review*, Vol. 2015, No. 122 (2015) <https://doi.org/10.1215/01636545-2849504> (p.27).
6. My computer actually did irrevocably break in the middle of writing this book. Let that be a lesson to you to always back up your files.

7. Carmen Maria Machado, *In the Dream House* (Graywolf Press, 2019), p.48.
8. Manalansan, p.97.
9. Sara Ahmed, *Living a Feminist Life* (Duke University Press, 2017), p.217.

White Fragility and the Failure to Listen

1. Reni Eddo-Lodge, *Why I'm No Longer Talking to White People About Race* (Bloomsbury Publishing, 2018), p.49.
2. Rani Kawale, 'Inequalities of the heart: the performance of emotion work by lesbian and bisexual women in London, England', *Social & Cultural Geography*, Vol. 5, No. 4 (2004), p.575.
3. 'Episode 2 – Femi Otitoju with Fopé Ajanaku', Black and Gay, Back in the Day, 11 October 2022 <https://auntnell.com/episode-2-femi-otitoju-with-fope-ajanaku>.
4. Kawale, p.575.
5. Dolores, 'Black Lesbians finding ourselves in each other', GLC Women's Committee, No. 17, Special Lesbian Issue (1984), p.19.
6. 'Ethnic minority' is now generally considered to be an inaccurate term, both for its lack of specificity and in establishing racialised identities as a 'minority' when such ethnicities are part of the global majority.
7. London Friend Information Update, 16 October 1989, Islington's Pride archive.
8. Lucy Brownson, 'Camden Lesbian Centre and Black Lesbian Group: Collectives and communities', Glasgow Women's Library, 15 October 2021 <https://womenslibrary.org.uk/2021/10/15/camden-lesbian-centre-and-black-lesbian-group-collectives-and-communities>.
9. Lola Olufemi, *Feminism, Interrupted* (Pluto Press, 2020), p.18.
10. Valerie Mason-John and Ann Khambatta, *Lesbians Talk: Making Black Waves* (Scarlet Press, 1993), p.11.
11. Yvonne Taylor, 'Oral Histories', Haringey Vanguard, 27 November 2024, <https://www.hqbh.co.uk/campaigning/yvonne-taylor/>.
12. Rachel Datey, 'Archiving oral histories of black queer collectives in London', *Gal-Dem*, 10 February 2021 <https://gal-dem.com/archiving-oral-histories-of-black-queer-collectives-in-london/>.
13. Jason Okundaye, '"It was a proper shebeen, man!": How Sistermatic blazed a trail for Black queer sound systems', *Guardian*, 15 February 2023 <https://www.theguardian.com/music/2023/feb/15/it-was-a-proper-shebeen-man-how-sistermatic-blazed-a-trail-for-black-queer-sound-systems>.
14. Indeed, the website where it was reposted has since been taken down.
15. Robin DiAngelo, *White Fragility: Why It's So Hard for White People to Talk About Racism* (Beacon Press, 2018).
16. 'Lesbians Hit Prime Time', *Spare Rib*, Issue 213, June 1990, p.41.
17. Ibid. p.42.
18. Mrittika Datta, 'Avenging "Talking Black"', Mrittika Datta, *Bad Attitude*, Issue 8, Autumn 1995, p.17.
19. Ibid.
20. Deborah Ogunnoiki, '"I'm a Black lesbian feminist woman, who is absolutely in support and stands in solidarity with my trans siblings": In conversation with founder of Black Pride and activist, Lady Phyll', *Cherwell*, 20 June 2023 <https://cherwell.org/2023/06/30/

im-a-black-lesbian-feminist-woman-who-is-absolutely-in-support-and-stands-in-solidarity-with-my-trans-siblings-in-conversation-with-founder-of-black-pride-and-activist-lady-phy/>.
21. Datta, p.17.
22. Paula Akpan, 'Gal Wine: The Secret History of Sistermatic', *Crack*, 20 March 2023 <https://crackmagazine.net/article/profiles/sistermatic/>.

What Happens When a Lesbian Makes a Move

1. The documentary, *Rebel Dykes*, dir. Harri Shanahan and Siân A. Williams (Riot Productions, 2021), offers a history of the '80s radical SM dykes and is one example of how subcultures operate, resist and complicate within lesbian and queer communities.
2. Clare Summerskill, *Gateway to Heaven: Fifty Years of Lesbian and Gay Oral History* (Tollington Press, 2012), p.60.
3. Ibid. p.75.
4. Joelle Taylor, 'A Lesbian Walks into a Bar', in *C+nto & Othered Poems* (Westbourne Press, 2021), p.58.
5. Ibid. p.16.
6. Paula Akpan, 'Gal Wine: The Secret History of Sistermatic', *Crack*, 20 March 2023 <https://crackmagazine.net/article/profiles/sistermatic/>.
7. Jeremy Atherton Lin, *Gay Bar: Why We Went Out* (Granta, 2021), loc. 1173.
8. Emily Crooked, 'La Camionera: What went down at the opening of London's new lesbian night', *Dazed*, 16 February 2024 <https://www.dazeddigital.com/life-culture/article/61973/1/what-went-down-at-the-opening-of-la-camionera-lesbian-bar-broadway-market>.
9. El Hunt, 'Inside London's lesbian renaissance, from La Camionera to Strapped', *Standard*, 10 April 2024 <https://www.standard.co.uk/going-out/bars/london-lesbian-renaissance-bars-clubs-popups-b1150557.html>.
10. Anezka Turek, 'Settling the stereotype: The last lesbian bar in London', *Artefact*, 21 January 2020 <https://www.artefactmagazine.com/2020/01/21/settling-the-stereotype-the-last-lesbian-bar-in-london/>.
11. Beverley Skeggs, 'Matter out of place: visibility and sexualities in leisure spaces', *Leisure Studies*, Vol. 18, No. 3 (1999), p.216.
12. Trish Bendix, 'Instagram Is Censoring Lesbian Content For Violating "Community Guidelines"', *Into*, 28 May 2018 <https://www.intomore.com/culture/instagram-is-censoring-lesbian-content-for-violating-community-guidelines/>.
13. NB this is a joke, I am thirty-six.
14. Eleanor Margolis, 'Lesbians mourn as Soho's Candy Bar announces it will close,' *Guardian*, 27 October 2013 <https://www.theguardian.com/lifeandstyle/shortcuts/2013/oct/27/lesbians-soho-candy-bar-close-london>.
15. Lin, loc. 434.
16. Lesbian bed death is a stereotype within long-term lesbian relationships that sexual intimacy decreases over time.
17. The quantities studies on this tend to focus on orgasms and the statistics show lesbians do orgasm more than heterosexual women during sex and that heterosexual women report a lower sense of 'satisfaction' during sex. See Hannah Jane Parkinson, 'Do lesbians have better sex than straight women?', *Guardian*, 9 July 2018 <https://www.theguardian.com/lifeandstyle/2018/jul/09/do-lesbians-have-better-sex-than-straight-women>.

18. *Rebel Dykes.*
19. bell hooks, *Feminism is for Everybody: Passionate Politcs* (Pluto Press, 2000), p.98.
20. Emma Healey, *Lesbian Sex Wars* (Virago, 1996), p.9.
21. Ibid. p.181.
22. Ibid. p.12.
23. Sue O'Sullivan and Pratibha Parmar, *Lesbians Talk: (Safer) Sex* (Scarlet Press, 1992), p.36.
24. Anna Silman, 'A Brief History of All the Drama Surrounding *Blue Is the Warmest Color*', Vulture, 24 October 2013 <https://www.vulture.com/2013/10/timeline-blue-is-the-warmest-color-controversy.html>.
25. Verity Ritchie, 'The Lesbian Gaze', YouTube, 25 November 2022 <https://youtu.be/3LcV2HmZUfY?t=1095>.
26. 'The 2022 Year in Review', Pornhub Insights, 8 December 2022 <https://www.pornhub.com/insights/2022-year-in-review#categories>.
27. Cindy Patton and Sue O'Sullivan, 'Mapping: Lesbians, AIDS and Sexuality', *Feminist Review*, No. 34 (1990), pp.120–33 (p.121).
28. O'Sullivan and Parmar, pp.34–36.
29. Ibid. p.37.
30. Ibid. p.20.
31. Katherine Angel, *Tomorrow Sex Will Be Good Again: Women and Desire in the Age of Consent* (Verso, 2021), p.67.

I Don't Want To Talk About Wanking in That Way

1. Lorraine Birch, interviewed by Ray Larman on 19 September 2019, West Yorkshire Queer Stories <https://wyqs.co.uk/stories/bradfords-lesbian-scene/full-interview>.
2. Debbie Luxon, 'The 1970s lesbian phone line that was a lifeline to rural Cambridgeshire women', CambridgeshireLive, 26 April 2020 <https://www.cambridge-news.co.uk/news/cambridge-news/70s-lesbian-feminist-phone-line-18147065>.

Stop Making Us Look Bad: Lesbian Break-Ups and Abuse

1. Julie, 'Make or Break: Love in the '90s', *Spare Rib*, Issue 233, April 1992, p.30.
2. Ibid.
3. Ibid. p.31.
4. Joelle Taylor and Tracey Chandler, *Lesbians Talk: Violent Relationships* (Scarlet Press, 1995), p.52.
5. Carmen Maria Machado, *In the Dream House* (Graywolf Press, 2019), p.126.
6. Taylor and Chandler, p.47.
7. Ibid. p.56.
8. Ibid.
9. Ibid. p.58.
10. Rebecca Jennings, *A Lesbian History of Britain: Love and Sex Between Women Since 1500* (Greenwood World Publishing, 2007), p.178.
11. 'LGBT+ People & Sexual Violence', Galop, 2022 <https://galop.org.uk/

wp-content/uploads/2022/04/Galop-LGBT-People-Sexual-Violence-April-2022.pdf> (p.28).

Trans Lesbians Exist: Get Over It

1. Travis Alabanza, *None of the Above: Reflections on Life Beyond the Binary* (Canongate Books, 2022), p.29.
2. See Kit Hayem, '"A feminine soul confined by a masculine body": The entangled history of gay and trans experience' in *Before We Were Trans: A New History of Gender* (Basic Books, 2022). For an exploration on the specific intersection of butch identity and transsexuality, see Jack Halberstam, 'Transgender Butch' in *Female Masculinity* (Duke University Press, 1998), pp.141–74.
3. Zachary I. Nataf, *Lesbians Talk: Transgender* (Scarlet Press, 1995), p.63.
4. Shon Faye, *The Transgender Issue* (Allen Lane, 2021), loc. 5.
5. Hayem, loc. 48.
6. Ibid. loc. 286.
7. Ibid. loc. 291.
8. See Stephanie Dutchen, 'The Sound of One's Own Voice', *Harvard Medicine*, Autumn 2015 <https://hms.harvard.edu/magazine/voices/sound-ones-own-voice>.
9. Serena Daniari, 'What does a woman sound like? Vocal training helps trans women find their voices', *Guardian*, 20 May 2019 <https://www.theguardian.com/society/2019/may/20/what-does-a-woman-sound-like-vocal-training-helps-trans-women-find-their-voices>.
10. Until 2013 vocal training for people choosing to transition was usually not available through the NHS. See Ruth Pearce, *Understanding Trans Health: Discourse, Power and Possibility* (Policy Press, 2018), p.67.
11. Angela Chen, 'How Transgender Women Are Training Their Voices to Sound More Feminine', *Smithsonian*, 15 December 2015 <https://www.smithsonianmag.com/innovation/how-transgender-women-are-training-their-voices-sound-more-feminine-180957537/>.
12. Diana James, interviewed 25 September 2019.
13. Central Station letter from Transgender London, 16 June 1997.
14. Nataf, pp.20–22.
15. See Alabanza, p.44, on the notion of 'proper trans' and Hayem, loc. 152, on why medical testimonies tend to edit lived experience for a more believable narrative.
16. *Trans Britain: Our Journey from the Shadows*, ed. by Christine Burns (Unbound, 2018), p.252.
17. Ibid. p.129.
18. Ibid. p.177.
19. Ibid. p.134.
20. Ibid. p.209.
21. *The Crying Game*, dir. by Neil Jordan (Miramax, 1992) and *Ace Ventura: Pet Detective*, dir. by Tom Shadyac (Warner Bros., 1994), being notable examples. For more on this topic, the documentary *Disclosure*, dir. by Sam Feder (Netflix, 2020), is a valuable resource.
22. Burns, p.198.
23. Lee Konemann, *The Appendix: Transmasculine Joy in a Transphobic Culture* (404 Ink, 2021), p.10.
24. Faye, loc. 210.

25. Sophie Lewis, 'How British Feminism Became Anti-Trans', *New York Times*, 7 February 2019 <https://www.nytimes.com/2019/02/07/opinion/terf-trans-women-britain.html>.
26. Faye, loc. 4.
27. Ibid. loc. 25.
28. See Lola Olufemi, *Feminism, Interrupted* (Pluto Press, 2020), p.60.
29. Léonie Chao-Fong, 'Recorded homophobic hate crimes soared in pandemic, figures show', *Guardian*, 3 December 2021 <https://www.theguardian.com/world/2021/dec/03/recorded-homophobic-hate-crimes-soared-in-pandemic-figures-show>.
30. 'UK: Keep calm and respect diversity says UN expert', United Nations, 11 May 2023 <https://www.ohchr.org/en/press-releases/2023/05/uk-keep-calm-and-respect-diversity-says-un-expert>.
31. Patrick Kelleher, 'Major legal action launched against NHS over spiralling trans healthcare wait times', PinkNews, 30 September 2021 <https://www.pinknews.co.uk/2021/09/30/trans-healthcare-good-law-project/>.
32. Bex Wade, '"It's Hell" – 3 Trans People on the NHS Crisis in Gender-Affirming Surgery', *Vice*, 2 December 2021 <https://www.vice.com/en/article/5dggj5/nhs-transgender-bottom-surgery-waiting-list>.
33. Olufemi, p.66.
34. Caroline Lowbridge, 'The lesbians who feel pressured to have sex and relationships with trans women', BBC News, 26 October 2021 <https://www.bbc.co.uk/news/uk-england-57853385>.
35. Julie Bindel, 'Lesbians are being erased by transgender activists', *Spectator*, 29 June 2021 <www.spectator.co.uk/article/lesbians-are-being-erased-by-transgender-activists>.
36. Konemann, p.10.
37. Ibid. p.30.
38. It's actually quite tricky to get a clear picture of the number of trans people in the UK. 2022 was the first year a question about gender identity was included in the UK census and even then many trans people may not have declared their gender identity. As seen elsewhere LGBTQ+ people have a long history and legacy of distrust when it comes to the ways that governments monitor and record its population. Regardless, the 2022 census showed in England and Wales around 0.1 per cent of the population identifies as a trans woman and likewise 0.1 per cent as a trans man. See Robert Booth and Michael Goodier, 'England and Wales census counts trans and non-binary people for first time', *Guardian*, 6 January 2023 <https://www.theguardian.com/uk-news/2023/jan/06/england-and-wales-census-counts-trans-and-non-binary-people-for-first-time>.
39. Leslie Feinberg, *Transgender Liberation* (World View Forum, 1992) <https://www.workers.org/books2016/Feinberg_Transgender_Liberation.pdf> (p.22).
40. Faye, p.315.
41. Rachelle Foster, 'Why I Co-Founded a Movement for Lesbians to Stand with Trans People', *Vice*, 9 October 2018 <https://www.vice.com/en/article/xw9537/why-i-cofounded-lwiththet>.
42. Nancy Kelley, 'The data is clear: Most people are supportive of trans rights', Stonewall, 14 June 2020 <https://www.stonewall.org.uk/about-us/news/data-clear-most-people-are-supportive-trans-rights>.
43. Alabanza, p.59.
44. Nataf, p.59.
45. In fact research suggests that lesbians are more likely than other groups to be supportive of trans rights. See Amy Shenden, 'Lesbians being anti-trans

is a lesbophobic trope', *Gay Times*, 31 March 2023 <https://www.gaytimes.co.uk/originals/lesbians-are-not-anti-trans/>.

Gobs of Lesbians Online

1. I hope you can hear my body crumbling into dust from here.
2. Lena Wilson, 'For Lesbians, TikTok Is "the Next Tinder"', *New York Times*, 29 June 2020 <https://www.nytimes.com/2020/06/29/style/lesbian-tiktok-dating.html>.
3. Debbie Luxon, 'The 1970s lesbian phone line that was a lifeline to rural Cambridgeshire women', CambridgeshireLive, 26 April 2020 <https://www.cambridge-news.co.uk/news/cambridge-news/70s-lesbian-feminist-phone-line-18147065>.
4. Patrick Hall, interviewed by Ray Larman on 5 May 2011, West Yorkshire Queer Stories <https://wyqs.co.uk/stories/discovering-the-gay-liberation-front/full-interview>.
5. They wouldn't have been alone. A 1995 article in *Newsweek* thought it was just a fad, full of too much data and too many voices – no replacement for newspapers or in-person shopping. See Clifford Stoll, 'Why the Web Won't Be Nirvana', *Newsweek*, 26 February 1995 < https://www.newsweek.com/clifford-stoll-why-web-wont-be-nirvana-185306>.
6. Kevin Pratt, 'UK Website Statistics 2024', *Forbes*, 3 October 2024 <https://www.forbes.com/uk/advisor/business/software/website-statistics>.
7. Lisa Haskel, 'Cyberdykes: Tales from the internet' in *Assaults on Convention: Essays on Lesbian Transgressors*, ed. by, Nicola Godwin, Belinda Hollows and Sheridan Nye (Cassell, 1996), pp.50–61 (p.50).
8. Cherry Smyth, 'Alien bodies: The emergent cyberdyke', *Diva*, Issue 2, June 1994, p.30.
9. Haskel, p.52.
10. Suzanne Cody, 'Taking Back the Net', *Curve*, Vol. 7, No. 1 (March 1997), p.33.
11. Smyth, p.31.
12. Haskel, p.53.
13. Ibid.
14. Ibid. p.55.
15. Ibid. p.54.
16. Ibid.
17. Jane Wither, Andrew deVries and Stewart Cheifet, 'Women on the Web' (1996) <https://archive.org/details/nc105_women>.
18. The Diva Blue Room forum capture from 23 Feb 2002 <https://web.archive.org/web/20020223153821/http://br.millivres.co.uk/binn/ultimatebb.cgi?ubb=forum&f=2>.
19. 'Gingerbeer – a womans perspective', DimSum, 27 September 2007 <https://web.archive.org/web/20070927185636/http://www.dimsum.co.uk/culture/gingerbeer---a-womans-perspective.html>.
20. As we know this is very much not true.
21. Ione Gildroy, 'How the Lesbian Masterdoc helped a generation of lesbians like me to come out', PinkNews, 26 April 2024 <https://www.thepinknews.com/2024/04/26/lesbians-lesbian-masterdoc-just-like-us/>.
22. Smyth, p.30.
23. See Claire L. Evans, *Broad Band: The Untold Story of the Women Who Made the Internet* (Portfolio, 2018).

24. Smyth, p.30.
25. Haskel, p.51.
26. See Cait McKinney, 'The Internet That Lesbians Built: Newsletter Networks', *Information Activism* (July 2020) on the ways that lesbian feminist newsletters acted as a precursor to the kinds of distribution networks that would be found online as well as how such newsletters moved and interacted online.
27. See José van Dijck, Thomas Poell and Martijn de Waal, *The Platform Society: Public Values in a Connective World* (Oxford University Press, 2018), pp.12–14, on the hierarchy of the platform ecosystem of the North American and European online infrastructures operated by Alphabet-Google, Facebook, Apple, Amazon and Microsoft.
28. See José van Dijck, *The Culture of Connectivity: A Critical History of Social Media* (Oxford University Press, 2013), p.69.
29. Lily Alexandre, 'Millions of Dead Vibes: How Aesthetics Hurt Art', YouTube, 25 February 2023 <https://www.youtube.com/watch?v=CMjxxzq88R0>.
30. Daisy Jones, *All the Things She Said* (Coronet Books, 2021), p.165.
31. Haskel, p.51.
32. Brit Dawson, 'TikTok admits to censoring LGBTQ+ hashtags', *Dazed*, 14 September 2020 <https://www.dazeddigital.com/science-tech/article/50444/1/tiktok-admits-to-censoring-lgbtq-hashtags-gay-lesbian-transgender>.
33. Shon Faye, 'Trans Influencers' in *We Can Do Better Than This: 35 Voices on the Future of LGBTQ+ Rights*, ed. by Amelia Abraham (Vintage, 2021), p.114.
34. Switchboard has a guide on digital self-harm and notes the ways in which users can sometimes seek out harmful comments either aimed at themselves or homophobic or transphobic content on other websites. They provide a useful list of ways to keep yourself safe online while still being able to access social media apps that are part of day-to-day life for many queer people. 'Digital Self-Harm: A Guide for LGBT+ People', LGBT Foundation <https://lgbt.foundation/wp-content/uploads/2024/01/Digital20Harm20Resource_print.pdf>.
35. Luke Hubbard, 'Online Hate Crime Report 2020', Galop, 2020 <https://galop.org.uk/wp-content/uploads/2021/06/Online-Crime-2020_0.pdf>.
36. 20 per cent of LGBTQ+ and trans people feel 'very safe' in gyms, 13 per cent using public transport and 11 per cent in bars and nightclubs. 'Diva Survey 2024: Still not safe to be me?', Kantar, 22 April 2024 <https://www.kantar.com/company-news/diva-survey-2024-still-not-safe-to-be-me>.
37. For data on hate crime as reported to the police see 'Hate crime, England and Wales, 2022 to 2023 second edition', gov.uk, 2 November 2023 <https://www.gov.uk/government/statistics/hate-crime-england-and-wales-2022-to-2023/hate-crime-england-and-wales-2022-to-2023>.
38. Rachel Keighly, 'Hate Hurts: Exploring the Impact of Online Hate on LGBTQ+Young People', *Women & Criminal Justice*, Vol. 32, No. 1–2 (2022), pp.29–48 <https://doi.org/10.1080/08974454.2021.1988034>.
39. @xenaworrierprincess, 'this fish is a lesbian icon', Instagram, 14 December 2021 <https://www.instagram.com/p/CXcpJCJIZGS/>.
40. Ellen Broidy, 'Cyberdykes, or lesbian studies in the Information Age' in *The New Lesbian Studies: Into the Twenty-First Century*, ed. by Bonnie Zimmerman and Toni A. H. McNaron (Feminist Press at The City University of New York, 1996), p.207.

41. Nina Wakeford, 'New Technologies and "Cyber-queer" Research' in *Handbook of Lesbian and Gay Studies*, ed. by Diane Richardson and Steven Seidman (Sage, 2002), p.117.
42. 'Taking Part focus on: Social media', Department for Culture, Media & Sport, April 2016 <https://assets.publishing.service.gov.uk/government/uploads/system/uploads/attachment_data/file/519678/Social_media_-_FINAL.pdf> (p.10).
43. Cecilia Kang, 'The Humble Phone Call Has Made a Comeback' *New York Times*, 9 April 2020 <https://www.nytimes.com/2020/04/09/technology/phone-calls-voice-virus.html>.
44. McKinney, p.96.
45. Chantelle Billson, 'A lesbian reached out online for friendship – around 400 queer people showed up', PinkNews, 7 April 2024 <https://www.thepinknews.com/2024/04/07/lesbian-friendship-big-queer-picnic-tik-tok/>.
46. 'Intro to the Web Revival #1: What is the Web Revival?', Melon's Thoughts, 20 September 2023 <https://thoughts.melonking.net/guides/introduction-to-the-web-revival-1-what-is-the-web-revival>.

What Are Lesbians Coming To?

1. 'Celebrate Lesbian Line set up in 1977–1996 to support lesbians', Lesbian History Group, 16 February 2021 <https://lesbianhistorygroup.wordpress.com/2021/02/16/celebrate-lesbian-line-set-up-in-1977-1996-to-support-lesbians/>.
2. Clare Ramsaran, 'From a ghetto to a community', *Bad Attitude*, Issue 4, June–July 1993, p.19.
3. Lesbians love to talk about whether we're disappearing while simultaneously proving we're not. See the documentary 'Where Have All the Lesbians Gone?', dir. by Brigid McFall (Channel 4, 2022) <https://www.channel4.com/programmes/where-have-all-the-lesbians-gone>.
4. Sara Ahmed, *Living a Feminist Life* (Duke University Press, 2017), p.222.
5. Jo Smith, 'Lesbians at London Friend', GLC Women's Committee, Issue 17, Special Lesbian Issue (1984), p.17.

Acknowledgements

This book would not exist without the support of many people, without the luxury of time and a safe space to write and think. This book was written on weekends and time off from work, revised on buses and tubes and finished on a laptop near breaking point. But we did it.

While writing this book I needed champions and I couldn't find a better two in Abi Fellows, my agent and Hannah Chukwu, my editor. Thank you for seeing the worth in this book even when (especially when) I couldn't see it myself. Enormous thanks to the Dialogue Books team for making this book a reality, for your hard work across every aspect of its design and production and getting it into the hands of readers.

I would be lost without support from fellow writers. Thank you to everyone I've workshopped this book with, in its many incarnations: my cohort at Birkbeck, the writing groups Future is Queer and the Creative Non-Fiction group, but especially Equal Writes – the best writing gang anyone could ask for, here's to many more years.

I'm grateful for mentors and teachers that have encouraged me to keep writing. Thank you to Kerry Ryan from Write Like A Grrrl for starting me off on this journey in the first place, Katherine Angel for her support during my studies and Olumide Popoola and Spread the Word for giving me the opportunity to be a writer-in-residence in the archives.

Thank you Sara, for being at the end of every WhatsApp spiral ready to pick me up again. Thank you Charlotte, for believing in this book and making me get on with it. Thank you to the Game Pube Discord server for the #work-in-progress chat and turning my online friends into IRL friends.

I'm so grateful to my family for their love and support and checking in on how that 'book thing' was getting on. Thank you Mum, for sharing your love of reading with me.

Thank you to my wife, Jaqueline, for not only providing me with her Candy Bar story but for being the most understanding and patient person while I hid away in the spare room to write. I never thought this life was possible but here we are. I'm so lucky to have found you.

My profound gratitude to everyone I interviewed and spoke to writing this book. Thank you for trusting me with your stories. Likewise, every archivist who works tirelessly to preserve our stories. But especially those working at Islington's Pride, for sharing their expertise with me and introducing me to the London Friend archive. London Friend continue to deliver a vital service supporting the LGBTQ+ community, please consider supporting the work that they do.

Finally, thank you to those who worked and called the lesbian lines and lived their brilliant ordinary lives. Thank you for writing them down. I hope you don't mind I wrote a book about you. To every lesbian who came before me and showed me the way, I cannot thank you enough.

Lesbians are everywhere.

Bringing a book from manuscript to what you are reading is a team effort.

Dialogue Books would like to thank everyone who helped to publish *Thank You for Calling the Lesbian Line* in the UK.

Editorial
Hannah Chukwu
Adriano Noble
Eleanor Gaffney
Meera Ghanshamdas

Contracts
Anniina Vuori
Imogen Plouviez
Amy Patrick
Jemima Coley

Sales
Caitriona Row
Dominic Smith
Frances Doyle
Ginny Mašinović
Rachael Jones
Georgina Cutler-Ross
Bukola Ladega

Design
Sophie Ellis

Production
Narges Nojoumi

Publicity
Hope Ndaba

Marketing
Emily Moran

Operations
Kellie Barnfield
Millie Gibson
Sameera Patel
Sanjeev Braich

Finance
Andrew Smith
Ellie Barry

Audio
Carrie Hutchison

Copy-Editor
Karyn Burnham

Proofreader
MaryAnn Johanson